W9-AAW-070

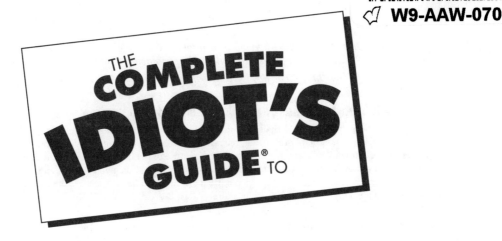

THE
COMPLETE IDIOT'S GUIDE® TO

National Security

*by Michael Benson, Danny O. Coulson, and
Allan Swenson*

ALPHA

A member of Penguin Group (USA) Inc.

ALEXANDRIA LIBRARY
ALEXANDRIA, VA 22304

To Meade, Boyd, Drew, and Peter—four good men who have made me very proud of all of you and your own worthwhile accomplishments.—Dad
To Philip Semrau, for a lifetime of friendship.—MB

Copyright © 2003 by Michael Benson, Danny O. Coulson, and Allan Swenson

All rights reserved. No part of this book shall be reproduced, stored in a retrieval system, or transmitted by any means, electronic, mechanical, photocopying, recording, or otherwise, without written permission from the publisher. No patent liability is assumed with respect to the use of the information contained herein. Although every precaution has been taken in the preparation of this book, the publisher and authors assume no responsibility for errors or omissions. Neither is any liability assumed for damages resulting from the use of information contained herein. For information, address Alpha Books, 201 West 103rd Street, Indianapolis, IN 46290.

THE COMPLETE IDIOT'S GUIDE TO and Design are registered trademarks of Penguin Group (USA) Inc.

International Standard Book Number: 1-59257-139-5
Library of Congress Catalog Card Number: 2003108345

05   04   03   8   7   6   5   4   3   2   1

Interpretation of the printing code: The rightmost number of the first series of numbers is the year of the book's printing; the rightmost number of the second series of numbers is the number of the book's printing. For example, a printing code of 03-1 shows that the first printing occurred in 2003.

Printed in the United States of America

Note: This publication contains the opinions and ideas of its authors. It is intended to provide helpful and informative material on the subject matter covered. It is sold with the understanding that the author and publisher are not engaged in rendering professional services in the book. If the reader requires personal assistance or advice, a competent professional should be consulted.

The authors and publisher specifically disclaim any responsibility for any liability, loss, or risk, personal or otherwise, which is incurred as a consequence, directly or indirectly, of the use and application of any of the contents of this book.

Most Alpha books are available at special quantity discounts for bulk purchases for sales promotions, premiums, fund-raising, or educational use. Special books, or book excerpts, can also be created to fit specific needs.

For details, write: Special Markets, Alpha Books, 375 Hudson Street, New York, NY 10014.

Publisher: *Marie Butler-Knight*
Product Manager: *Phil Kitchel*
Senior Managing Editor: *Jennifer Chisholm*
Acquisitions Editor: *Gary Goldstein*
Development Editor: *Nancy D. Lewis*
Production Editor: *Billy Fields*
Copy Editor: *Cari Luna*
Illustrator: *Chris Eliopoulous*
Cover/Book Designer: *Trina Wurst*
Indexer: *Heather McNeill*
Layout/Proofreading: *Ayanna Lacey, Donna Martin*

Contents at a Glance

Contents

Foreword

Since the tragic and horrifying events of September 11, 2001, the United States—and indeed, the world—is a different place.

We are bombarded daily on TV, radio, and in the newspapers of the terrorist threats that can occur at any time—dirty bombs, weapons of mass destruction, and chemical weapons. Sadly, all of these expressions have become part of our daily vocabulary. A few years ago it was inconceivable that we'd have a Department of Homeland Security—today it's a reality. For most of us, terrorism was something that happened in faraway places like Israel or Africa. Not anymore. We greet each new day with elevated terror warnings and with colors to match. Many of us in the United States, especially those of us who reside in big cities like New York, Chicago, Los Angeles, Boston, Dallas, or Washington, D.C., even wonder if we'll make it home alive when we leave for work in the morning.

Today, it's more vital than ever before for Americans to understand all there is to know about national security. What are our government and our elected officials doing to make our lives safer and to spare us from another major terrorist event like 9/11? What are the CIA, the FBI, the State Department, our military, and the NSA doing—or not doing—to ensure that our lives and the lives of our loved ones are protected from the scourge of terrorism? Are these endless lines at the airport and heightened security enough to really protect us from a maniacal martyr with a desire to wipe out a city? And perhaps most importantly, what can we do to *protect ourselves and our families* from the likes of Osama Bin Laden and other terrorists bent on our destruction?

The Complete Idiot's Guide to National Security answers all of these questions and more. We're fortunate to have people like Michael Benson, Danny O. Coulson, and Allan Swenson on our side. They have written a comprehensive and essential book, one that explains in meticulous detail the many complex aspects of national security. What, for instance, does the government mean when they advise us to "stay vigilant"? What can we learn from natural disasters that may prepare us for yet another terrorist attack? Do we really need to start growing victory gardens again, as we did during World War II?

You may think you know all there is to know about national security. Maybe you do. But if you're reading these words now, odds are there is much you have yet to learn. And to that end, *The Complete Idiot's Guide to National Security* may just prove invaluable.

—E. R. Thompson, Maj. Gen. (Ret.), former Assistant Chief of Staff for Intelligence, U.S. Army

Introduction

National security, by definition, is the condition of the nation, in terms of threats, especially threats from outside. One of the major jobs of the federal government is to ensure the security of the nation.

Since 9/11, the main thrust of national security has turned inward. Once thought of as an "away game," a battle for security most often fought thousands of miles from home, the new and deadly threat to our homeland has changed our priorities.

Today the list of security priorities show just how much of an effect 9/11 has had on how we view the world and the threats it may present to our nation. Here are some of the tasks that our military and intelligence community currently face:

◆ Routing out and destroying terrorist cells both at home and abroad

◆ Improving security at airports and on commercial airliners

◆ Linking the databases of various law enforcement and intelligence-gathering agencies

◆ Stockpiling antibiotics and vaccines and improving the public health infrastructure to limit the effects of a potential biological attack

◆ Training and equipping those responsible for responding to various types of terrorist attack (biological, radiological, chemical, etc.)

◆ Diminishing the underlying conditions that terrorists seek to exploit

◆ Improving security at our borders

◆ Protecting potential sites of terrorist attacks

How This Book Is Organized

This book is divided into four sections:

In **Part 1, "The History of National Security,"** we will look at national security from the birth of our nation during the American Revolution right up to the end of the Cold War.

In **Part 2, "National Security Today,"** we will look at the agencies and organizations that are responsible for our national security today, including our local law enforcement agencies, the members of the U.S. intelligence community, and our military services.

In **Part 3, "Types of Threats and How to Combat Them,"** we will examine, one by one, the various types of threats we must combat, whether they be from the military might of foreign powers, such as North Korea or Iraq, or from terrorists who know no government or borders, such as the Al Qaeda terrorist network of Osama bin Laden. We will look at what is (and isn't) being done to protect us against biological, chemical, radiological, nuclear, and cyber terrorism—as well as new security systems involving air travel. If some of those terms are unfamiliar to you, don't worry. All will be explained as we go along.

In **Part 4, "Feeling Safe vs. Feeling Free,"** we will look at the sacrifices Americans must endure if we are going to be successful in this relatively new and frightening War on Terrorism. Unfortunately, some of these sacrifices will come in the form of personal freedoms that we have long taken for granted. Many governmental leaders worry about striking the appropriate balance between needed new security procedures and still preserving America's traditional liberty and civil rights.

What's in the Box?

Throughout the text, you will find boxes that will help you understand the various aspects of national security. The sidebars will fall into several repeating categories. These are:

Security Speak

Definitions of vocabulary words that you might not otherwise be familiar with.

Ounce of Prevention

Ways that the government (or you) can make America safer.

Security Factoid

Interesting tidbits regarding the shadowy world inhabited by those who seek to keep America safe and secure.

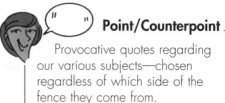

Point/Counterpoint

Provocative quotes regarding our various subjects—chosen regardless of which side of the fence they come from.

Author's Corner
These reports are based on reports from our intelligence sources—who have been composited into the fictional intelligence officer Wilson McLean. Many of these people have served with distinction around the world and want to share their experiences but for personal and security reasons must remain anonymous.

Acknowledgments

Our special thanks go out to the following individuals, without whom this book would not have been possible: the Association of Former Intelligence Officers, Jake Elwell, Gary Goldstein, and Nancy Lewis.

Trademarks

All terms mentioned in this book that are known to be or are suspected of being trademarks or service marks have been appropriately capitalized. Alpha Books and Penguin Group (USA) Inc. cannot attest to the accuracy of this information. Use of a term in this book should not be regarded as affecting the validity of any trademark or service mark.

Part 1

The History of National Security

Before we get to the matter of national security today, we're going to go on a rapid journey through time, from our country's birth during the American Revolution to the tragic events of 9/11 and their aftermath. Our journey will emphasize the recent past. We'll fly by the eighteenth and nineteenth centuries, when matters of national security were greatly simplified by the comparatively primitive methods of war-making available to the military forces of the day. Once we get to the Industrial Revolution and the twentieth century, we'll slow down, examining the ways in which technology has made protecting our nation more difficult.

National Security Before Pearl Harbor

In This Chapter

- ◆ What intelligence is
- ◆ Guarding the waterways
- ◆ Learning to keep secrets
- ◆ The first foreign war
- ◆ Battling radicals

The United States' national security force, through the gathering and processing of intelligence, is designed to provide our nation with an envelope of protection—a security blanket, if you will.

Intelligence is information needed by our nation's leaders, also known as policy makers, to keep our country safe. Some of that intelligence is overt, or publicly available. The rest is covert intelligence, secret information, info that other countries will not share with the United States but that we want anyway.

Categories of Intelligence

There are many different categories of intelligence, but these are the major categories:

♦ **Current intelligence,** which follows day-to-day events

♦ **Estimative intelligence,** which looks at what might be or what might happen

♦ **Warning intelligence,** which gives notice to our policy makers that something urgent might happen that may require their immediate attention

♦ **Research intelligence,** which is an in-depth study of an issue

♦ **Scientific and technical intelligence,** which is information on foreign technologies

 **Point/Counterpoint**

The gathering and processing of intelligence has been around as long as human civilization. It existed in the time of Julius Caesar, and it certainly existed in the time of William Shakespeare. References in Shakespeare's play *Henry V* include these two references to message interceptions: "The King hath note of all that they intend" and "By interception which they dream not of …."

Intelligence can be gathered by human beings (human intelligence is also called HUMINT), or through electronic listening and seeing devices. This is called electronic intelligence. Of course, electronic intelligence is a rather modern form. Intelligence existed long before electricity was harnessed by mankind.

Counterintelligence is the science of preventing your enemies from learning your secrets. This can be accomplished in two ways: Either you can make sure that your secrets are very difficult to discover, or you can impede the efforts of those who want to learn those secrets.

Protected by Oceans

Until Pearl Harbor to some extent, and 9/11 absolutely, the best feature of the United States' national security was geographical. We were simply far away from the other powerful nations in the world. Asian countries had to cross the Pacific to get to us and European countries had to cross the Atlantic.

To fight a war with us on our own turf, these countries would have to cross great expanses of ocean just to get their troops here. And, once here, they would have to cross that same ocean again and again to keep their war effort in supplies. That would require extensive logistical support to sustain.

In this chapter we will look at our national security effort during the eighteenth, nineteenth, and early twentieth centuries—as the geographical security we enjoyed was slowly whittled away by technology.

Forts on the Harbors

In the early days of America, before airplanes and before the onset of the Industrial Revolution, the only way for foreign powers to attack us was by slow-moving ships. They could attack along a coastline, which was difficult because troops would have to move from larger ships onto shore in smaller boats. Or they could attack at the harbors and at the mouths of rivers.

For this reason, many of the first fortresses built to protect our national security were placed at the mouths of America's major waterways. Those that were not built along the coasts were usually designed to protect U.S. military forces from attacks by Native Americans.

Fort Monroe and Fort Wool protected Hampton Roads Harbor in Virginia. Fort Hamilton in Brooklyn and Fort Wadsworth on Staten Island sat on either side of New York Harbor. Fort McHenry in Maryland protected Chesapeake Bay.

Early Intelligence Systems

Even in the early days of our nation, intelligence still went through a process known as the intelligence cycle. This is the development of raw information into intelligence-for-use. There are five steps:

1. Planning and direction
2. Collection
3. Processing
4. All-source analysis and production
5. Dissemination

Behind Enemy Lines in the American Revolution

As long as there has been a United States, there has been a U.S. intelligence system. Army intelligence is every bit as old as our nation and dates back to 1776 when

Point/Counterpoint

During the Revolution, Washington said in a letter to one of his officers, "The necessity of procuring good intelligence is apparent and need not be further urged. All that remains for me to add is that you keep the whole matter as secret as possible."

Nathan Hale spied on the British under the command of Gen. George Washington.

During the campaign for New York, Washington needed information about the opposing British forces. Hale, an officer from Connecticut, was sent behind enemy lines. The first time he successfully completed his mission and Washington received the intelligence he needed. On a subsequent trip, however, Hale was captured by the British and hanged. His last words became famous: "I only regret that I have but one life to give for my country."

Lessons Learned in the War of 1812

In the War of 1812, the British attempted to get their colonies back—the colonies they had lost in the American Revolution 35 years before. Because the troops were arriving by ship, and all of their supplies were arriving by ship, they never got far from the nearest river or coastline.

The largest battles were fought in Washington, D.C., along the Potomac, in Baltimore, at the previously mentioned Fort McHenry on Chesapeake Bay, and in New Orleans, at the mouth of the Mississippi River. Philadelphia was protected from British ships by mines placed in the Delaware River.

On the intelligence front, the United States still had a lot to learn. It was unnecessary in some cases for the British to spy on us to find out what we were planning. We were giving the information away.

In the first two years of the war, American newspapers regularly published accounts of troop movements, official military correspondence, and letters from officers describing operations and actions. Naturally, British generals read these papers, which became a prime source of intelligence.

By 1814 the problem was so severe that the U.S. Army had to publish an order forbidding the publication of military information in newspapers. Ever since, the U.S. military and the press have worked hand in hand during times of conflict. Our free press remains free, but not at the cost of American lives to enemy attack.

Intelligence that can be used by the enemy that is already publicly available is called *overt intelligence*. If a spy has to snoop around to find out the information, this is called *covert intelligence*. The three keys to national security ever since have been to …

- ◆ Maintain a strong military defense.

- ◆ Acquire the capability to learn the secrets of enemies and potential enemies.

- ◆ Keep our own secrets secret.

There were other national security lessons learned during the War of 1812 as well. These were as follows:

- ◆ The citizen militia would not always respond to the government's call to arms. The more localized a defense force was, the less secure our nation became.

- ◆ Farmers who were part-time soldiers were often ill-equipped. Supplying a national army needed to be done on a grand scale and in a consistent manner. Large industrial complexes and not individual farms were necessary to ensure defense.

Security Speak

Overt intelligence is strategically valuable information that is publicly known, such as that which has been published in newspapers. **Covert intelligence** is information a spy has to find out through contacts developed within enemy government agencies and essentially by snooping around.

In other words, our national security had to be organized on a national level. A real U.S. Army was necessary, federally funded, with standards for training and equipment. The days of the local farmer picking up his shotgun or rifle and going off to "defend his land" from foreign attack had grown obsolete.

Information Sources in the Civil War

The Civil War—the brutal conflict between our northern and southern states between 1861 and 1865—featured some of the bloodiest battles in our nation's history. Yet the subtle art of intelligence gathering and sophisticated methods of deceiving the enemy often determined the outcome of key battles.

Knowing where the enemy was going to be, when they were going to be there, and how many of them would be there, while keeping your own location and numbers secret, often made the difference.

In some cases, because the raw intelligence that led to victory was never publicly stated, historians tend to interpret the behavior of the confronting armies without taking intelligence into consideration. But there are cases where we know who knew what, and how that knowledge affected the action.

For example, while most history books discuss the cavalry solely in terms of their reconnaissance missions, they also employed spies, or "scouts," as they were often referred to at the time. The signal corps used codes and ciphers to send secret messages.

Other seemingly modern methods of gathering intelligence were used back then, as well, for example …

Security Speak

Disinformation is false information purposefully disseminated to mislead.

◆ Escaped slaves were interrogated for the information they may have had.

◆ *Disinformation* artists, those (usually fake deserters) who spread false information. That was done to mislead the enemy commanders into making the wrong moves so they could be more easily defeated.

◆ Aerial surveillance during the Civil War, with hot air balloons being used to observe the enemy from above.

Signals Intelligence was probably born in Kentucky in 1862 (as we'll discuss further in Chapter 2). The Confederacy had in their command a Canadian telegrapher who used a portable system that could tap into federal telegraph lines. Not only were messages intercepted, but false messages could be inserted in their place.

Confederate president Jefferson Davis created an economic intelligence operation that involved the opening of a land route between Maryland and Virginia for the secret movement of people, cotton, and money to finance the Southern war effort.

Pinkerton and the Secret Service

One of the most famous "scouts" of the Civil War was Allan Pinkerton, who became one of the world's most famous detectives. Born in Glasgow, Scotland, in 1819, he was the founder of the federal secret service—an organization that evolved into our modern Secret Service, the force in charge of protecting U.S. presidents.

Security Factoid

As famous as Pinkerton might have become, his performance during the Civil War was not without its flaws. It was Pinkerton, for example, who inaccurately advised Maj. Gen. George B. McClellan concerning the strength of the Confederate army.

Pinkerton first gained notoriety in 1842, 20 years before the Civil War, when he busted up a counterfeiting ring in Illinois. He formed the Pinkerton National Detective Agency in 1850. Pinkerton was known as "The Eye," which is why all detectives today are referred to as "private eyes."

He was assigned to guard President Abraham Lincoln in 1861. Pinkerton, in fact, foiled an assassination plot against Lincoln while he was en route to his inauguration in Washington, D.C. He died in 1884.

Formation of the Department of Justice (1870)

During the reformation that followed the Civil War, the U.S. government formed its own law enforcement force. Today we take federal law enforcement—in the form of the Federal Bureau of Investigation and other organizations—for granted, but no such force existed until after the conclusion of the war between the States.

The Department of Justice, to be headed by the attorney general, was created in 1870. The new department was in charge of …

◆ Detecting and prosecuting violations of federal law.

◆ Representing the federal government in civil suits.

◆ Helping the president and other federal officials fulfill their lawful duties.

At first the Justice Department did not have its own police force and borrowed agents from the Secret Service or from private detective agencies; the use of "private eyes" by the Feds was outlawed in 1892.

Spanish-American War

In 1898, when Cuba decided it wanted to be independent of Spanish rule, the U.S. Army came to help kick out the Spanish. This was quickly done. The most famous Army officer in this war was Col. Theodore Roosevelt, leader of the "Rough Riders" who became a hero in what was known as the Spanish-American War. Roosevelt later became U.S. president.

Superior U.S. intelligence was a key to the swiftness of victory in Cuba. Contact was made with Cuban Gen. Calixto García who supplied the U.S. with maps, intelligence, and a core of rebel officers to coordinate U.S. efforts on the island.

Security Factoid

Simultaneous to the fighting in Cuba was the liberation of the Philippine Islands from the Spanish, which was accomplished by the U.S. Marine Corps.

Early Twentieth Century and the First World War

In the first decade of the twentieth century, the Justice Department did get its own staff. Authorized by President Theodore Roosevelt in 1908, the force became known as the Bureau of Investigation (or BI).

Security Factoid

Protestant, native-born Americans, who often lived in cities, grew to hate the predominantly Catholic immigrants who usually settled in big cities. The immigrants further enraged the forces of big business in the United States by forming labor unions.

The First World War had a great effect on national security, both on the domestic and the foreign front. Many years of immigration had pumped millions of Europeans into the U.S. population, the presence of whom had enflamed the resentment of native-born citizens.

In the meantime, war was brewing in Europe. Hostilities commenced when Archduke Ferdinand was assassinated in August 1914, starting the third Balkan war in three years. This war, however, grew to consume the continent.

Germany and the Austro-Hungarian empire were pitted against the rest of Europe, including U.S. allies, England and France. The United States entered the war in 1917 and by November of the following year it was over, with America and her allies coming out on top.

Because the enemy during World War I was Germany, and Germany was trying very hard to get its friend Mexico to declare war on the United States, the patrolling of our southern border became of the utmost importance during these war years. Despite America's commitment to victory in Europe, some regiments remained behind in Texas, New Mexico, and Arizona, to make sure we were not invaded from the south.

Security Factoid

On January 18, 1918, Lothar Witzke, also known as Pablo Waberski, was taken into custody as a suspected German spy and saboteur in the Central Hotel in Nogales, Mexico. In his pocket was a coded message that was later decoded in Washington by the Military Intelligence Division to read: "The bearer of this is a subject of the Empire who travels as a Russian under the name of Pablo Waberski. He is a German secret agent. Please furnish him on request protection and assistance; also advance him on demand up to 1,000 pesos of Mexican gold and send his code telegrams to this embassy as official consular dispatches." He was convicted of spying and originally sentenced to death. His sentence was later commuted to life in prison by President Woodrow Wilson, and he was eventually released in 1923.

From the birth of our nation until World War I, all of the United States' wars had been fought on its own turf, or nearby. World War I was a new kind of war for the United States, a foreign war. All of the wars that the United States has participated in since have been fought predominantly on foreign turf. From the First World War on, intelligence gathering to protect our national security became more complicated. It became an international affair—replete with all of the geographical, cultural, and lingual complications that implies.

Victory in Europe in World War I came at a great price; the number of American troops killed in action was 116,700.

Espionage and Alien Acts

The introduction into American history of the foreign war helped give rise to the feeling that there was a foreign threat to national security right here inside the continental United States. Because of that rise, the first restrictions on immigration and the behavior of foreigners in the United States came about at this time.

Because of World War I, the U.S. Congress passed in 1917 the Espionage Act, which made *seditious* utterances (that is, statements against the U.S. government) "during the course of hostilities" a criminal act.

Other legislation that year limited immigration. Those who couldn't read and those who advocated the violent overthrow of the U.S. government were to be kept out. In 1918, Congress further toughened the laws with the Alien Act, which banned alien *anarchists* from the United States.

During World War I, 4,000 "enemy aliens" were rounded up. These included everyone from German spies to immigrants who had spoken unkindly of the U.S. government.

Security Speak

Anarchists are people who believe in no government. These people believe that all government represents oppression and must be destroyed. **Sedition** is the incitement of discontent against the government.

Earliest Roots of the Cold War

The Cold War, between the members of the free world and communism, dominated U.S. foreign policy (as we shall see in Chapter 4) from the end of World War II until the early 1990s, when the Soviet Union dissolved. The roots of that largely bloodless conflict affected our national security as far back as 1910, starting even before the

Communists were victorious in their Russian revolution in 1919. That revolution activated leftists in the U.S. labor unions and the labor movement, now thought of by a large segment of the U.S. population as necessary to prevent exploitation of workers by management but were thought of as radical and Communist back then.

And, lest there be a misunderstanding, the labor movement—infiltrated as it was by anarchists—was a dangerous force. In January of 1919, labor activists hit Seattle, Washington, with a general strike.

Law enforcement was called in and the strike was crushed in less than a week. During the days that followed, 36 mail bombs were delivered to antilabor figures around the country. It became the job of the Bureau of Investigation to take on the anarchists, something that it did with gusto.

In Communist Russia, Lenin's manifesto called for radicals to overthrow governments around the world by any means necessary. It was therefore extremely disquieting that there were 100,000 members of the American Socialist Party in 1919, many of whom took Lenin's words very seriously.

Security Factoid

Heading a mass roundup and deportation of alien radicals in 1919 was a young BI agent who would become a legend. His name: J. Edgar Hoover.

The radical division of the BI later became known as the less confusing Anti-Radical Division, and still later as the General Intelligence Division, with general intelligence being the gathering of background information on a particular subject rather than information gathered in the course of a specific criminal investigation.

Birth of the FBI

By 1924, J. Edgar Hoover was the head of the BI. Along with battling radicals, the start of Prohibition in 1920 spawned a new form of organized crime that had to be confronted: bootlegging.

His men also took on the famous bankrobbers of the day: John Dillinger, Bonnie and Clyde, Baby Face Nelson, Pretty Boy Floyd, and others. Hoover's method was simple: These criminals were wanted dead or alive. None were taken alive.

In 1934, the same year that Dillinger was killed outside the Biograph Theater in Chicago, America's number-one cop, J. Edgar Hoover, asked that his bureau be given a new name, a catchy name. It was Special Agent Edward Tamm, the third-highest bureau official at the time, who came up with the name FBI, for Federal Bureau of Investigation. Tamm added that the initials also stood for Fidelity, Bravery, and Integrity.

The Significance of the Airplane

There was one more significant development during the early years of the twentieth century that would affect the future of national security more than all of the others combined: the invention of the airplane.

The Wright Brothers successfully flew the first airplane at Kitty Hawk on December 17, 1903—120 feet in 12 seconds with Orville at the controls. It wasn't long before plans were under development to use the airplane as a weapon. After that, the usage of motorized aircraft from oceangoing vessels began almost immediately. In fact, naval interest in using aircraft off of ships increased dramatically the instant the Wright Brothers announced their success.

Thirty-eight years after the invention of the airplane, America would suffer what was, up till then, the deadliest attack on U.S. soil from a foreign enemy—and the weapons used would be aircraft-carrier-based warplanes.

The Least You Need to Know

- Early national security focused on harbors and waterways because foreign powers (except for Mexico and Canada) had no choice but to attack us by ship.

- The War of 1812 taught us that the system of defending the nation with a loosely organized group of local and state militia was obsolete.

- During the Civil War, the subtle art of intelligence gathering and sophisticated methods of deceiving the enemy often determined the outcome of key battles.

- The introduction into American history of the foreign war helped give rise to the feeling that there was a foreign threat to national security right here inside the continental United States.

- In the earliest days of what would become the FBI, J. Edgar Hoover and his men battled violent radicals, bank robbers, and organized crime brought about by the Eleventh Amendment prohibiting the manufacture, distribution, or consumption of alcoholic beverages.

Chapter 2

Global Warfare Demands Global Protection

In This Chapter

- ◆ Strategic Services
- ◆ "Father of American Intelligence"
- ◆ Intelligence = Victory
- ◆ Death of the OSS

The need for a single organization to determine the United States' intelligence objectives and to coordinate the nation's global intelligence gathering and processing occurred to President Franklin Delano Roosevelt even before the United States entered World War II.

But such an organization did not come into being until after the United States was drawn into the war by the Japanese attack on Pearl Harbor, Hawaii, on December 7, 1941. Years later, President Harry S Truman said that, if such an organization had existed before America entered the war, chances are the Japanese attack on Pearl Harbor would have been thwarted.

Pearl Harbor Changes Everything

Security Speak

SIGINT is short for **Signals Intelligence,** the art of sending coded messages that cannot be understood by the enemy while intercepting the enemy's coded messages and successfully translating them.

The United States' ability to break the codes of its enemies helped it win World War II both in Europe and in the Pacific. The difference made by our superior *Signals Intelligence (SIGINT)* was most dramatic in the war versus the Japanese. For example, because we knew ahead of time that the Japanese planned to attack the island of Midway, we were ready, won the battle, and that turned the tide.

Need for the OSS

By the time the United States entered World War II, global warfare had grown so complicated, fast, and modern, that the United States needed an organization to oversee the gathering, processing, and disseminating of wartime intelligence.

After all, at the start of WWII, the U.S. Army had only 70 intelligence officers to cover the entire world. The resulting organization, the father of today's Central Intelligence Agency, was known as the Office of Strategic Services, or the OSS.

Security Factoid

Some of the personal experiences you'll find in this book come from World War II OSS operatives who shared their experiences with us.

The OSS was mandated to collect and analyze strategic information required by the Joint Chiefs of Staff and to conduct special operations not assigned to other agencies. For the remainder of the war, intelligence supplied by the OSS played an important role in guiding various military campaigns.

Notables who served with the OSS included Arthur M. Schlesinger Jr. and future Supreme Court Justice Arthur Goldberg. TV chef Julia Child served with the OSS in what is present-day Sri Lanka (then known as Ceylon). She helped develop shark repellent, a critical ingredient in protecting explosives used to sink German U-boats.

Complaints of the OSS

The idea for the Office of Strategic Services came even before the Japanese attack on Pearl Harbor in 1941, when President Franklin D. Roosevelt became concerned with deficiencies in the United States' ability to gather intelligence.

But it wasn't until the Japanese attack on U.S. turf that the organization was actually formed. Because of in-fighting among the Pacific War Command, the FBI, and the White House, the OSS did not become the global intelligence organization that FDR had envisioned. The U.S. military services (the Army, Navy, etc.) and other agencies such as the FBI frequently had "turf wars" to protect what they saw as their own service's territory.

For example, Gen. Douglas MacArthur saw the OSS as an unwanted intrusion on his authority. MacArthur ordered that the OSS not be allowed in the Pacific. And, at FBI Director J. Edgar Hoover's insistence, the OSS was never allowed to work south of the U.S. border. The FBI instead broadened its scope and was in charge of foreign intelligence in Latin America during the OSS's existence.

Another opponent of the OSS was Gen. George Veazey Strong, the chief of Army Intelligence. He considered the OSS to be a "bunch of socially connected amateurs." General Strong did not trust Gen. William J. Donovan's information security (you'll meet General Donovan in the next section) and denied him access to the crown jewels of American intelligence, the decrypts of German and Japanese messages obtained through intercept operations known as *Magic* and *Ultra*. When General Donovan protested, President Roosevelt sided with the military.

Wild Bill Donovan

FDR asked a talented lawyer from New York, William J. Donovan, to write up a proposal for a foreign intelligence service. Donovan's report became the basis of the OSS, which was established in June 1942, with Donovan in charge.

Born New Year's Day 1883 in Buffalo, New York, Gen. William "Wild Bill" Donovan became known as the "Father of American Intelligence." His Office of Strategic Services offered the United States its first centralized agency to collect foreign intelligence and conduct covert action in Europe, the Middle East, and Asia.

Donovan went to Columbia University, where he earned his Bachelor's degree in 1905 and graduated from Columbia Law School in 1907. After school he returned to Buffalo to start up a law practice—but he soon became restless.

Donovan once wrote, "I wanted more excitement and the chance to serve my country. In 1912 I formed my own cavalry troop and fought in Mexican border skirmishes. When World War I came, I was there with the U.S. Army's 165th Infantry in France. I was wounded three times during that war and was awarded many medals, including the Medal of Honor, for my service. I was a colonel when discharged .... What with being a lawyer, a diplomat, public official, and army officer, I'd say that I've had a pretty full life ...." Donovan died in 1959.

Going to War with the OSS

For one of the OSS's most famous missions, Donovan's spies worked alongside British and Free French intelligence. In the days after D-Day and the Allied invasion at Normandy, France, teams of three, called Jedburgh teams—or sometimes Donovan's Private Army—were dropped behind enemy lines in France to help Allied troops who were advancing in that direction.

These teams were not only known for their ability to get useful intelligence to the people who needed to know, but they were known as soldiers as well, frequently being forced to battle German troops as they went about their tasks.

OSS in Europe

Following the Allied invasion of Western Europe, OSS bases sprang up in Bern, Switzerland; Istanbul, Turkey; Madrid, Spain; Stockholm, Sweden; and Lisbon, Portugal. Allen Dulles, the future Director of Central Intelligence, headed the OSS's Switzerland base.

From that location Dulles not only recruited the agents needed to arrange the Nazi surrender during the summer of 1945, he also foresaw the upcoming Cold War against the Soviet Union and formed Operation Paper Clip.

This program recruited many German agents from the German intelligence agency Abwehr to come to the United States and continue their anticommunist programs. Also recruited were space scientists whose research, formerly used to build rockets that could bomb England, would now be used to launch American astronauts into space.

Security Factoid _____

Recently discovered letters written by physicist Albert Einstein suggest he had a romance during and after World War II with a woman thought to have been a Soviet spy. Apparently, the woman's "mission" was to introduce Einstein to the Soviet Consul in New York, which she did. Actually, Einstein's theoretical work at the time had little to do with the practical details of the U.S. Manhattan Project. The goal was probably to influence the prominent physicist to think and speak favorably about the USSR.

OSS in the Pacific

The OSS was also busy in Burma, where it was helping the Allied effort to kick the Japanese off the Asian continent. Donovan himself went deep into Burma, 150 miles behind enemy lines, during the OSS campaign in that region.

For the most part, however, the OSS did not participate in the war against the Japanese. Gen. Douglas MacArthur didn't believe in the OSS, so they weren't allowed. When the OSS was dissolved following the war, two powerful men were not exactly heartbroken. One was General MacArthur and the other was J. Edgar Hoover, who believed that the OSS unnecessarily stepped on the FBI's jurisdiction.

> **Security Factoid**
>
> Gen. Claire Lee Chennault's Flying Tigers—an American Volunteer Group of pilots and planes that flew over China against the Japanese air force—were a covert entity of the OSS.

In some of the toughest battles of the South Pacific, Navajo code talkers transmitted thousands of radio messages in a code based on their intricate and unwritten language, in which fighter planes became "hummingbirds," dive bombers "chicken hawks," and submarines "iron fish."

Though the Japanese repeatedly broke other American military codes, they never came close to cracking the Navajos', which remains one of the handful of codes in military history that were never deciphered. In fact, the Navajos' secret was considered so valuable that it was kept classified until 1968.

> **Security Factoid**
>
> The use of the Navajo language as a code during World War II became the subject of the 2002 movie *Wind Talkers*. It was also the subject of a recent documentary on television's History Channel. It is celebrated in *The Code Book* (Doubleday, 1999), Simon Singh's history of cryptography. The Smithsonian Institution is putting together a display about the code talkers in its new museum of Indian history on the Mall in Washington.

Tales of the Cryptographer

In 1942, U.S. cryptographers had cracked a code used by the Japanese navy and had learned of an impending attack. They knew that "AF" was to be the target of a major

Author's Corner

According to McLean, the "AF is short of water" story is very relevant today. Remember: Whenever a member of the administration issues a terrorism warning based upon intelligence gathered from the enemy, we are giving them information. They will watch our reaction to intelligence to see whether they can figure out our sources, our methods, and our plans.

assault. Though the code-breakers knew that AF was an island in the Pacific, probably Midway, they didn't know for certain.

So Comdr. Joseph Rochefort, head of the Navy's cryptography center at Pearl Harbor, instructed the Midway installation to signal that their water distillery had been damaged and that they needed a shipment of fresh water.

Soon the code-breakers intercepted a Japanese transmission that "AF is short of water." AF was Midway, and the U.S. fleet gathered to defend the island. By watching the Japanese reaction to intelligence that he had planted, Rochefort was able to change the course of the war in the Pacific.

Intelligence at Normandy

One of the reasons that the D-Day invasion at Normandy was successful was the quality of the intelligence the United States and her allies were receiving. A study of documents in the National Archives has revealed how detailed and timely the intelligence was that the Allies had on the German defenses along the Atlantic coast in the critical months leading up to the Normandy landings.

Hiroshi Oshima, Japan's ambassador to Berlin and a confidant of Nazi leaders with access to German war plans, dutifully telegraphed his reports to the Foreign Office in Tokyo. These reports were intercepted, decoded, translated, and delivered to U.S. military leaders within hours.

Americans were known to read the messages before the Japanese did, as transmission problems between Germany and Japan could hold up the cables for hours. Without leaks, the messages were distributed to the president and ten other officials, all in the military except for the secretary of state.

Spies for Science

A British atomic scientist who spied for the Soviet Union was Alan Nunn May. He worked on the Manhattan Project. The fact that he was a double agent, sharing nuclear secrets with the Soviets, was revealed and his treason put to an end when a Soviet defector to Canada—Igor Gouzenko, a lieutenant in the Soviet military intelligence agency and cipher clerk at the Soviet Embassy in Ottawa—ratted him out.

May was born in Birmingham, England, and won a scholarship to study physics at Cambridge University. While lecturing at King's College in London, Dr. Nunn May joined the Communist Party. By World War II, he was working on a secret British project to develop radar and had allowed his party membership to lapse.

In 1942, he joined a team of Cambridge scientists who, as part of the Manhattan Project, were studying the feasibility of German plans to use heavy water to build an atomic reactor. A year later, he was transferred to Montreal, where he was recruited by Soviet military intelligence.

On July 9, 1945 of that year, a week before the Americans tested an atomic bomb, he passed small amounts of enriched uranium to his Soviet handler, later providing details of the bomb dropped on Hiroshima. In return, he received $200 and a bottle of whiskey.

"The whole affair was extremely painful to me, and I only embarked on it because I felt this was a contribution I could make to the safety of mankind," Alan Nunn May once said. "I certainly did not do it for gain."

May later served six years in a British prison for his treason. He claimed that he was simply sharing vital scientific knowledge.

Casualties of World War II

When the war was over and the casualties were added up, the numbers were sobering. Here is a list, by nation, of the number of people killed and wounded in World War II.

Casualties in World War II

Country	Men in War	Battle Deaths	Wounded
Australia	1,000,000	26,976	180,864
Austria	800,000	280,000	350,117
Belgium	625,000	8,460	55,513
Brazil	40,334	943	4,222
Bulgaria	339,760	6,671	21,878
Canada	1,086,343	42,042	53,145
China	17,250,521	1,324,516	1,762,006
Czechoslovakia	—	6,683	8,017
Denmark	—	4,339	—

continues

Casualties in World War II (continued)

Country	Men in War	Battle Deaths	Wounded
Finland	500,000	79,047	50,000
France	—	201,568	400,000
Germany	20,000,000	3,250,004	7,250,000
Greece	—	17,024	47,290
Hungary	—	147,435	89,313
India	2,393,891	32,121	64,354
Italy	3,100,000	149,964	66,716
Japan	9,700,000	1,270,000	140,000
Netherlands	280,000	6,500	2,860
New Zealand	194,000	11,625	17,000
Norway	75,000	2,000	—
Poland	—	664,000	530,000
Romania	650,005	350,006	—
South Africa	410,056	2,473	—
U.S.S.R.	—	6,115,004	14,012,000
United Kingdom	5,896,000	3,571,164	369,267
United States	16,112,566	291,557	670,846
Yugoslavia	3,741,000	305,000	425,000

The United States had lost more than a quarter of a million men, and that was a modest number compared to the millions lost by China, Germany, Japan, and the Soviet Union.

And these numbers do not include civilian casualties, which also numbered in the tens of millions worldwide.

October 1945: OSS Abolished

By the end of the war there were 9,028 employees in the OSS. But because the Office of Strategic Services had been formed specifically to aid the United States' war effort, there was no reason for it to exist once the war was over. So, in October 1945, the organization was abolished.

However, the need to determine national intelligence objectives and correlate all government intelligence did not go away just because the war had ended. As we'll learn in the next chapter, the void left by the death of the OSS did not last long. Within days of the OSS's demise, President Truman began making plans to replace it.

The Least You Need to Know

- ◆ The United States' ability to break the codes of its enemies helped them win World War II both in Europe and in the Pacific.

- ◆ The idea for the Office of Strategic Services came even before the Japanese attack on Pearl Harbor in 1941, when President Franklin D. Roosevelt became concerned with deficiencies in the United States' ability to gather intelligence.

- ◆ The biggest battle of World War II, the D-Day invasion, was a major success for the Allies because of superior intelligence.

- ◆ The OSS was abolished at the end of World War II but quickly evolved into today's CIA in the first few post-war years.

Chapter 3

The Nuclear Age

In This Chapter

- ◆ Replacing the OSS
- ◆ Truman signs
- ◆ Soviets bomb
- ◆ The formidable KGB

In this chapter, we'll talk about how that conflict of ideologies that led to the Cold War came about. American distrust of the Communist system plus Soviet distrust of the United States' nuclear monopoly got the hostilities started. When the Soviets joined the nuke club in 1949, it fanned the flame.

In our last chapter we talked about how the OSS was disbanded at the end of World War II. As we begin here, it is only several months later, and the detonation of the first atom bombs by the United States has opened a Pandora's Box, which, like the original, could never again be closed ….

The Central Intelligence Group (1946)

On January 22, 1946, President Harry S Truman founded the Central Intelligence Group (CIG) to take the place of the OSS. The CIG operated under the aegis of the National Security Agency during its short existence.

The CIG lasted only a year and a half, when a new act signed by the president replaced it with a new organization: the Central Intelligence Agency (CIA). As you will see in the next chapter, the first three men to hold the position of the Director of Central Intelligence (DCI) actually held the reins for the CIG rather than the CIA.

The First DCIs

Now let's take a look at the first two men to direct central intelligence in the United States: Rear Adm. William H. Souers and Gen. Hoyt S. Vandenberg.

Admiral Souers

Souers was appointed by President Harry S Truman as the first Director of Central Intelligence (DCI) on January 23, 1946, one day after Truman signed the presidential directive that gave birth to the Central Intelligence Group (CIG).

Souers, born in 1892, was a 1914 graduate of the University of Miami of Ohio. He was a businessman who had great success with his investments. Souers was appointed a lieutenant commander, an intelligence officer, in the Naval Reserve, in April 1929 and, as far as we know, was not called into active duty until 1940.

We do know that after getting the CIG up and running, Souers retired briefly to private life before returning to government work at the request of the Atomic Energy Commission, for whom he conducted a study to determine the security requirements of preserving the secret of *The Bomb*.

During the first years of World War II, Souers worked in district intelligence offices in Great Lakes, Illinois; Charleston, South Carolina; and San Juan, Puerto Rico. In July 1944, he received a major promotion when he was named assistant chief of naval intelligence in charge of plans and the deputy chief of naval intelligence in Washington, D.C. We can bet that he did some really good things, considering that significant jump in rank and duties.

He was promoted to rear admiral in 1945 and served on a committee representing the secretary of the navy, determining the feasibility of forming a central intelligence organization. President Truman liked Souers's proposal so much that he put him in charge of the Central Intelligence Group's formation and named him its first director. President Truman was said to have had an almost sixth sense for picking good people for important jobs, so we can assume that Souers had the credentials to achieve what the president wanted done and the perseverance to get it done.

In September 1947, Truman appointed Souers the first executive secretary of the National Security Council, and Souers remained in that position until 1950. He retired from the Naval Reserve in 1953 and spent much of the 1950s speaking out against McCarthyism and its indiscriminate anticommunism, a symptom of paranoia, he felt, more destructive than communism itself. He died in 1973.

General Vandenberg

Gen. Hoyt S. Vandenberg was born in 1899 and graduated from the U.S. Military Academy in 1923. At the start of the Second World War, he was the assistant chief of staff of the U.S. Army Air Forces. From 1943–1946 he was deputy chief of the air staff. In that capacity he became the senior air member of the U.S. military mission to Moscow in 1946. President Truman named him DCI that year. Vandenberg was the nephew of Sen. Arthur Vandenberg, the Republican president pro tem of the Senate during the late 1940s. It was under Vandenberg's leadership that the Central Intelligence Group was given the power to collect and analyze intelligence.

It was also during Vandenberg's tenure as DCI that Central Intelligence was given the responsibility of gathering intelligence in Latin America, which before that had been the responsibility of the FBI. When the U.S. Air Force was formed as its own branch of the service in October 1947, Vandenberg was named vice chief of staff with a rank of full general. From May 1948 until June 1953, Vandenberg served as chief of staff of the Air Force. He died in 1954.

The National Security Act (1947)

The CIA—as well as the National Security Council and other intelligence-oriented organizations—was born on July 26, 1947, with the signing by President Truman of the National Security Act.

The Act enabled a coordinated definition of intelligence needs and allowed the president, as the chair of the National Security Council, to oversee the entire intelligence-gathering process and sort out any difficulties between members of the U.S. intelligence community.

Intelligence Advisory Committee

On January 19, 1950, an Intelligence Advisory Committee was born to lend further organization and control over the multifaceted U.S. intelligence community.

According to the act that created it, the committee was to consist of "the Director of Central Intelligence, who shall be Chairman thereof, the Director, Federal Bureau of Investigation, and the respective intelligence chiefs from the Departments of State, Army, Navy, and Air Force, and from the Joint Staff (JCS), and the Atomic Energy Commission, or their representatives, shall be established to advise the Director of Central Intelligence."

The legislation continues: "The Director of Central Intelligence will invite the chief, or his representative, of any other intelligence Agency having functions related to the national security to sit with the Intelligence Advisory Committee whenever matters within the purview of his Agency are to be discussed."

> **Security Speak**
>
> **Consumer,** in this context, means recipient—for example, the president or other key leaders who need and use the intelligence.

The Directorate of Intelligence

During the first years of the CIA, the Office of Research and Reports managed the production of finished intelligence. But, in 1952, the Director of Central Intelligence, Gen. Walter Bedell Smith, who served as DCI from 1950–1953, created the Directorate of Intelligence, which further streamlined the process of creating intelligence ready for the *consumer*.

Loftus Becker, an attorney who had served as military adviser at the Nuremberg War Trials, became the first deputy director of intelligence.

> **Security Factoid**
>
> In 1952, President Truman ordered that all presidential candidates be given intelligence briefings. The reason was to prevent candidates from inadvertently exposing clandestine programs while criticizing an incumbent. In other words, the candidates needed to be briefed so that they would know what *not* to say.

The Soviet Union Explodes the Big One

The United States and the Soviet Union got along during World War II for one reason only: They needed each other as allies to fight their common enemy, Nazi Germany. Once the war was over, they no longer needed each other and tensions mounted.

The Soviet Union worried greatly that the United States—because it was the only country with atomic weapons—would use them to take over the world. They began their own nuclear weapons program, helped by spies in the United States who gave them our nuclear secrets. The director of the Soviet nuclear weapons program was Igor Kurchatov. He remained the director until his death in 1960.

It is fairly amazing that the Soviet Union developed their own bomb as quickly as they did. World War II had left their economy a mess. Hundreds of thousands of prisoners were used as slave labor in the uranium mines, many of whom got sick and died. Great damage was done both to the health of the workers and the environment.

The first Soviet atom bomb was exploded at Semipalatinsk, Kazakhstan, on August 29, 1949. Many would say that this was the date that the Cold War actually started. Russian fears that the United States would use the Bomb to dominate the world were replaced by global fears that a nuclear war between the United States and the Soviet Union would cause the extinction of the human race.

Security Factoid

The very first atom bomb explosion was on July 16, 1945 at Los Alamos, New Mexico. The second and third bombs were dropped on the Japanese cities of Hiroshima (on August 6) and Nagasaki (on August 9), ending World War II.

Sizing Up the KGB

KGB is the Russian abbreviation for the Committee of State Security, the *Komitet Gosudarstvennoy Bezopasnosti*. It was the Soviet intelligence organization equivalent to our FBI, CIA, NSA, and counterintelligence organizations all rolled into one.

It was a formidable organization and now-prime minister Putin was one of its leaders. Today it may have been reorganized and renamed in part, but there is no doubt that modern Russia still has a formidable and powerful intelligence and counterintelligence organization, whatever name it carries in whatever year.

Top Hat Was Top Cat

According to a retired Russian military intelligence officer, Dmitry Polyakov—code name Top Hat, recruited by the United States in 1961—was the leader in damage done to Soviet intelligence during the Cold War—military intelligence in particular. The source claimed that Polyakov betrayed two dozen Soviet agents working in the United States along with more than a hundred others recruited in the United States.

Security Factoid _____

At the start of the twenty-first century, with the Cold War over for almost a decade, the Russian strategic weapons system (laboratories, early warning systems, submarines, and silos) has greatly deteriorated. Thousands of workers and servicemen are not being paid. Serious incidents point up the dangers. The armed forces are experiencing extreme human stress. In 1998, a sailor in a nuclear-driven submarine went berserk and killed eight shipmates. If he had also blown up the ammunition in the sub, the country would have had a nuclear catastrophe, another Chernobyl.

Polyakov later passed information to his U.S. handlers from assignments in Moscow, Burma, and India. The double agent operated successfully for over 25 years before being snared, tried, and executed in 1986.

The Least You Need to Know

♦ The Central Intelligence Group (CIG) took the place of the OSS in 1946.

♦ The first two Directors of Central Intelligence were Rear Adm. William H. Souers and Gen. Hoyt S. Vandenberg.

♦ The first Soviet atom bomb was exploded at Semipalatinsk, Kazakhstan, on August 29, 1949.

♦ The Cold War was fought amid fears that a nuclear war between the United States and the Soviet Union would cause the extinction of the human race.

Chapter 4

The Cold War Years

In This Chapter

- ◆ Figures larger than life
- ◆ Another brick in the wall
- ◆ Missiles, pigs, and a nightmare on Elm Street
- ◆ Blackbirds over North Vietnam

The largely bloodless conflict of ideology between the United States and her allies (known as the Free World) and the forces of communism (the Soviet Union and its satellite states, plus Red China and hers) was known as the Cold War. The war began at the end of World War II, when the United States, Great Britain, and the Soviet Union—the victors—divided up the conquered nations.

The Soviet Union and the United States were allies in World War II in that they had a common enemy in fascism, but once the war was over, hostilities between the two superpowers commenced, and didn't stop until the 1990s when the Soviet Union collapsed due to extreme economic difficulties.

Photographing Korea

It was during the Korean War (1950–1953) that aerial reconnaissance photography came into its own. At 4:00 A.M., on June 25, 1950, North Korean troops invaded South Korea, crossing the 38th Parallel (the political dividing line between North and South Korea established after World War II). The Soviet Union supplied North Korea with modern military equipment—tanks, artillery, trucks, guns, ammunition, uniforms, and all other items needed to fight a modern war. The United States came to the aid of South Korea, both in the air and on the ground.

Intelligence collection was crucial during the Korean War. During World War II, photographic reconnaissance aircraft (RB-29s) had been fitted with six photographic cameras each, mounted in the forward bomb-bay with an auxiliary fuel tank in the aft bomb-bay. During the Korean War, six RB-29s performed bomb damage assessment and strategic target identification of North Korean troops and equipment.

Security Factoid

The RB-29 had no defensive guns and only limited armor protection for the crew. This aircraft provided pre-strike and post-strike reconnaissance photographs. That way we could determine where the bombs should be dropped and which targets needed to be bombed a second time.

The aircraft carried three cameras for wide-area coverage. The first was adjustable to photograph 20 to 30 miles, depending on the altitude. The other two were positioned in a split vertical mounting, for detailed interpretation, designed to photograph an area two miles wide. If necessary, a camera could be carried for night photography.

The night photographic missions required the plane to carry photo flash bombs, mounted in a rack, behind the cameras in the forward bomb-bay. These were dropped, ignited at specific altitudes to illuminate the target below, and timed to work with the camera's exposure meters, producing clear aerial reconnaissance photographs. Aerial surveillance became even more sophisticated during the Vietnam War, which we'll discuss more in the next chapter.

Legends of the Cold War

In the following section we will take a look at three American Cold Warriors whose efforts to defeat communism made them larger than life.

James J. Angleton

James Jesus Angleton was a *Cold Warrior* if there ever was one. During his time as the CIA counterintelligence chief, some thought Angleton to be somewhat overzealous.

He was obsessed with finding the Soviet *moles* he was certain had infiltrated the CIA. True, he never caught a spy in the United States. True, his suspicions cut down on CIA efficiency—or did it?

Security Speak _____

A **Cold Warrior** was an anti-Communist soldier during the Cold War. **Mole** is a term for a penetration agent who has infiltrated into an opposition intelligence service or government agency. In some cases it is used to describe a defector in place or sleeper agent. On occasion "moles" surface as captured spies. At times, as in the case of Kim Philby in Great Britain, they escape and flee to their chosen country, in his case the Soviet Union.

Later, when it was learned that there really were Soviet *moles* in the agency, people stopped laughing so much at Angleton. He was the prototype of spook paranoia, though, and he used every advantage in his efforts to win the Cold War.

After the assassination of President Kennedy, it was Angleton who strongly pushed the Oswald-as-part-of-a-Communist-conspiracy during the days following the assassination, using CIA memos out of Mexico City that Oswald had visited an assassination expert in the Soviet Embassy there as his evidence. This push greatly helped Angleton's friend, Warren Commissioner Allen Dulles, to sell the lone-gunman theory.

According to assassination researcher and theorist Peter Dale Scott, Angleton took charge of the CIA's investigation into the assassination and immediately pointed attention toward the Soviets.

Angleton said he had received a cable from Winston Scott, station chief of the CIA's Mexico City headquarters, that warned of an association between KGB killer Kostikov—the same Kostikov who supposedly met with Oswald in Mexico City—and Rolando Cubela, the very agent who had been recruited by the CIA's Desmond FitzGerald to kill Castro.

According to former Nixon aide H. R. Haldeman, in his book *The Ends of Power*, "The CIA literally erased any connection between Kennedy's assassination and the CIA … in fact … Angleton … called Bill Sullivan of the FBI [number-three man under J. Edgar Hoover, who later died of a gunshot wound] and rehearsed the questions and answers they would give to the Warren Commission investigators."

There were times when Angleton's techniques seemed counterproductive to gathering intelligence. When both soldiers from the Soviet army and those from the Chinese army reported to CIA sources that those two countries were not getting along, Angleton refused to believe it, preferring to think it was a massive conspiracy to deceive the United States Of course, China and the Soviet Union were not getting along at all, during that period.

When KGB agent Yuri Nosenko defected to the United States on January 20, 1964, and told the CIA that he had handled the Oswald case during Oswald's stay in the Soviet Union, the CIA interrogated Nosenko for 1,277 days.

By the time the interrogation was complete, Nosenko had lost all of his teeth. During that period Nosenko, though failing several lie-detector tests, maintained that the KGB had given Oswald two mental examinations. The tests showed that Oswald was not terribly intelligent and mentally unstable. Nosenko said Oswald was never used as an agent and had not been debriefed concerning his military background. While J. Edgar Hoover and Richard Helms, the respective heads of the FBI and the CIA, believed Nosenko, Angleton did not.

Along with the rest of the CIA's counterintelligence faction, Angleton believed Nosenko had been sent to the United States by the KGB, his assignment to stifle suspicions that the USSR had President Kennedy killed. Angleton believed that Nosenko had also been assigned to help maintain the cover of Soviet agents working within U.S. intelligence.

Edward Lansdale

Maj. Gen. Edward Lansdale (1908–1987) was the CIA's top Cold Warrior in Southeast Asia during the Vietnam era. Before World War II, Lansdale had been a family man in the advertising business. After Pearl Harbor he was recruited by the OSS, where he developed into an expert at *covert action*.

Security Speak

Covert action is clandestine activity designed to influence events in foreign countries without the role of U.S. intelligence or government being known. Such actions can range from placement of propaganda in media to attempts to overthrow a government that is deemed unfriendly to this country.

After the war, Lansdale continued in covert action, going to the Philippines where he took on left-wing insurgents. During the 1950s, Lansdale's focus shifted to Indochina, the area that would eventually split up into Vietnam, Laos, and Cambodia. By the time the French gave up on that war, Lansdale was DCI Allen Dulles's top man in Saigon. He remained in that position until his retirement in the mid-1960s. Lansdale remained in South Vietnam after his retirement, not returning stateside until 1968.

At least twice Lansdale was used as the basis for a fictional character in a novel. He is said to be the inspiration behind Graham Greene's *The Quiet American* (1955) and William J. Lederer's *The Ugly American* (1958).

William King Harvey

Another legendary Cold Warrior was William King Harvey (1915–1976), who earned a law degree at Indiana University before joining the FBI in 1940. Harvey was assigned to counterintelligence. Against FBI Director J. Edgar Hoover's wishes, Harvey left the FBI and joined the CIA in 1947, again specializing in counterintelligence.

Harvey was the first to order investigations of members of the Cambridge Spy Ring, and, while in Germany, was responsible for the building of Harvey's Hole, a.k.a. the Berlin Tunnel, in 1952. The Tunnel enabled the CIA to listen in on Soviet communications in East Berlin.

Allen Dulles

Born in 1893, Allen W. Dulles was the nephew of a secretary of state and the grandson of another. It was hoped by the family that Allen would become the family's third secretary of state, but, despite his many accomplishments, this was never to be. There was a third secretary of state in the family, but it turned out to be Allen's brother, John Foster Dulles.

Dulles's first government job was at the U.S. Embassy to the Austro-Hungarian Empire, but after the United States entered World War I he was moved to Bern, Switzerland. During World War II, Dulles was a master spy with the OSS. And in November 1942, future Director of Central Intelligence Allen W. Dulles opened the OSS office in Bern, Switzerland. He was designated Agent 110 and referred to in OSS communications as Mr. Bull. Dulles supervised the penetration of the Abwehr (Hitler's military intelligence agency) and the subsequent incorporation of many of its undercover agents into the CIA.

 Point/Counterpoint

According to the head of Gen. Dwight D. Eisenhower's chief of intelligence during World War II, Gen. Kenneth Strong, "Allen Dulles was undoubtedly the greatest United States professional intelligence officer of his time."

Some of those talented and well-connected intelligence people made major contributions to the United States. They had far-reaching contacts of their own that were important for us to have. Today, some critics of the CIA believe that we overlooked the bad side of Nazi intelligence personnel because we needed what they could deliver to us. That may be so. Intelligence, it must be remembered, is not the realm of saints. As Wilson McLean says, "The Spook business isn't a nice guys game. We often must deal with the slime at the bottom of the bucket."

After World War II, Dulles practiced law and then went to work for the CIA in January 1951. Eight months later he was named the agency's deputy director. As DCI, Dulles ordered his agents to carry out clandestine operations throughout South America and the Middle East. It was during his tenure that the U-2 spy plane was developed and he was responsible for the digging of the Berlin Tunnel. He also plotted to kill Fidel Castro, the revolutionary leader of Cuba who had declared his allegiance to the Communists. According to Dulles's deputy director of central intelligence, Richard Bissell, the CIA-sponsored attempts on the life of Castro were so secret that only Dulles received reports about them. Dulles was fired by JFK after the Bay of Pigs fiasco and later became a member of the Warren Commission.

The Berlin Wall

As mentioned earlier, the divvying up of Europe following World War II formed the front line for the Cold War, with Western Europe remaining free and Eastern Europe becoming Communist. This line was called the Iron Curtain and it went directly through Germany.

Germany split into two countries, East Germany, which was a Communist state and West Germany, which was free. There was even a line drawn through the center of the city of Berlin, with East Berlin being under Soviet rule and West Berlin being free.

To keep the people of East Berlin from simply moving to the western side of the city to live, as many of them wanted to, the Soviets built a wall through the city, the Berlin Wall, which became, more than anything else, a symbol of the Cold War.

Later in the book (Chapter 10) you'll learn about the super-secret U.S. intelligence agency known as the National Security Agency (NSA). For the entire time the Berlin Wall was in place, many NSA (as well as CIA) officers were totally occupied with finding out what was happening on the other side of the wall.

They would dig under it and visit the other side (sometimes merely buying an East Berlin newspaper before returning), and use electronic equipment to listen in to East

Berlin communications. They learned that people on the west side of the wall were much happier than those on the east—which, of course, was the reason the wall had to be built in the first place.

Duck and Cover

Today's Orange Alert frights due to the threat of terrorism remind older Americans of the 1950s when the threat of full-out nuclear war between the United States and the Soviet Union seemed all but inevitable.

The United States was the only nation to possess the knowledge of how to build nuclear weapons for a few blissful years. But, on August 29, 1949, the Soviet Union exploded their bomb, and the fright was on. Air raid drills became commonplace in America's schools and workplaces, and the phrase "Duck and Cover" became common, because that was what you were supposed to do when the Bomb hit.

"This is a test of the Emergency Broadcast System …" For the next 20 years, regular radio and television broadcasting was interrupted for tests of the Emergency Broadcasting System. Following a high-pitched "boop" sound, an announcer would tell us "This is only a test. If this had been an actual emergency, you would have been instructed to tune into the Emergency Broadcast System."

The system, thank heavens, never had to be used, but the regular repetition of the tests became a sort of mantra for the Cold War.

Another popular activity of the Cold War was the installation of the personal shelter, where one could, in theory, live for years following a nuclear attack, waiting for the radioactivity to cool off. In cities, people were expected to know where their local shelter was, which was usually located beneath a nearby school or civic center.

Author's Corner
Allan: I once bought a house in Basking Ridge, New Jersey, that came with a complete bomb shelter in the basement, fully stocked with cots, medicines, food, water, etc. My kids had a great time playing in it.

Allied Intelligence

The U.S. intelligence community wasn't alone in the Cold War. Intelligence officers from many countries helped out, most notably those from Great Britain.

Great Britain's MI5 and MI6

As in the United States, the gathering of domestic and foreign intelligence is handled separately in Great Britain. Just as the United States has the CIA and the FBI, Great Britain had MI5 and MI6.

The Security Service—better known as MI5—is the United Kingdom's security intelligence agency. Its purpose is, and I quote, "to protect national security from threats such as terrorism, espionage and the proliferation of weapons of mass destruction, to safeguard the economic well-being of the UK against foreign threats, and to support the law enforcement agencies in preventing and detecting serious crime."

Security Factoid

Intrepid is an interesting word of profound historic significance. It was the U.S. cable address and name for the late Sir William Stephenson, a Canadian who became Britain's most famous spymaster during World War II. The book by the same name is one of the most fascinating stories of modern spies and spying at the highest levels and worthwhile reading by all interested in national security. It involves secret early links between Prime Minister Winston Churchill of Great Britain and President Franklin Roosevelt.

MI5 was born in March 1909 when the Prime Minister instructed the Committee of Imperial Defense to consider the dangers from German espionage to British naval ports. On October 1, following the committee's recommendation, Capt. Vernon Kell of the South Staffordshire Regiment and Capt. Mansfield Cumming of the Royal Navy jointly established the Secret Service Bureau.

To fulfill the Admiralty's requirement for information about Germany's new navy, Kell and Cumming decided to divide their work. Thereafter, "K" was responsible for counterespionage within the British Isles (MI5) while "C," as Cumming came to be known, was responsible for gathering intelligence overseas (MI6). MI6 is known as the Secret Intelligence Service.

Point/Counterpoint

As Richard Deacon noted in his history of British Intelligence: "A great power without an efficient intelligence service is doomed. That has been the lesson from the heyday of Troy to the present."

MI5 has five divisions: Administration, Counterespionage, Security, Military Liaison, Aliens, and Overseas Control. These days MI5 is preoccupied with counterterrorism, with the bombing campaign of the Irish Republican Army being their primary foe. MI6 (the organization that James Bond would have worked for, had he been real) is active today in the war against Al Qaeda and global terrorism.

At MI6, headquarters is referred to as "Y." Overseas stations are called "YP." Y is divided into 10 divisions, each given a Roman numeral: (I) Political, (II) Military, (III) Naval, (IV) Air, (V) Counterespionage, (VI) Industrial, (VII) Financial, (VIII) Communications, (IX) Cipher, and (X) Press.

Israel's Mossad

Following World War II, and the attempted genocide of the Jewish people by the Nazis, the United Nations divided the land known as Palestine into a Jewish state and an Arab state. The idea of creating a Jewish state began with the Zionist movement in Europe in the late 1800s.

By 1914, 85,000 Jews lived in Palestine, then under Ottoman control. The vast majority of the population of 700,000 was Arab. Following the defeat of the Ottoman Empire in World War I, the League of Nations assigned England the Palestine Mandate.

Under the terms of the mandate, the British were to help Palestinian Jews establish a Jewish homeland. During the 1930s, immigration to Palestine grew as Jews fled Nazi persecution in Europe.

Security Factoid

Israel remains the United States' true ally in the volatile Middle East, and this fact is a contributing factor to the United States being a target of fundamentalist Islamic terrorism.

In 1939, however, Great Britain imposed strict limits on Jewish immigration, fearing increased Arab hostility. The state of Israel officially came into existence in 1948, three years after the end of World War II, but its history has been a violent one, as it is surrounded by unfriendly Arab states.

As such, it should come as no surprise that Israel's intelligence agency, Mossad, is considered the most secret of the secret agencies today. Mossad has no listed telephone number, no website, no spokesman, produces no press releases, and does not brief journalists. We would like to tell you more about Mossad, but frankly, we can't.

U-2 Incident: Spying From Above

The Cold War heated up in 1960 with what has come to be known as "The U-2 Incident." Since the mid-1950s, the United States had been spying on the Soviet Union from above, using a high-flying jet called the U-2 to take aerial photographs. The U-2 became obsolete rather suddenly—at least for use over the Soviet Union, on May 1, 1960, when a U-2, with 30-year-old pilot Francis Gary Powers aboard, was shot down over the Soviet Union. There was rejoicing in Moscow and consternation

Security Factoid

Although it is no longer state-of-the-art, the U-2 is still in use today, and has been used over Kosovo and Iraq during recent conflicts in those regions.

in Washington. Both the pilot and the aircraft were taken by the enemy. The United States at first tried to deny that it was a spy plane, saying that it was merely a plane that had wandered off course. After the Soviets found the complex photographic equipment aboard, the United States was forced to admit that Powers had been on a spy mission.

Powers was held in a Soviet prison for two years. He was released in 1962 when President Kennedy agreed to a spy swap. We got Powers back and we returned the captured spy, Col. Rudolf Abel, to the Soviets. Abel had set up a Communist spy ring in New York City during the late 1950s.

To those involved in the swap, the trade seemed a fair deal. To make sure that neither side got burned during the spy swap, the exchange took place on Berlin, Germany's Glienicke Bridge, which spans the River Havel. Powers stood on the east side of the bridge and Abel stood on the west side. At a signal, both prisoners were allowed to walk across the bridge simultaneously. They passed each other at the center of the bridge silently, offering only a barely perceptible nod as they passed.

Powers was not received warmly by his CIA comrades when he arrived back in the United States. His assignment had been to make sure the plane was destroyed in case it was shot down so that the Soviets would not be able to learn anything from it. He had also been trained to take a poison pill and commit suicide if he were captured, so that he would not be able to talk. Powers went into TV journalism and died in 1977 when the television news helicopter he was piloting crashed in Los Angeles, California. Powers is buried in Arlington Cemetery outside Washington, D.C. Coincidently, his grave is within a few rows of the grave of Allan Swenson's mentor, Lt. Col. John Paul Vann.

On May 1, 2000, U.S. officials presented Powers's family with the Prisoner-of-War Medal, the Distinguished Flying Cross, and the National Defense Service Medal during a 30-minute ceremony held at Beale Air Force Base, north of Sacramento and home to the modern U.S. U-2 force. It marked the fortieth anniversary of the incident.

Bay of Pigs

In 1961, President John F. Kennedy wanted to eliminate Castro and free the Cuban people. They had lived under oppression before and Kennedy seemed to express his strong feelings that Castro was as bad or worse. That set the scene and stage for the effort by the CIA to achieve what President Kennedy indicated he wanted, a free

Cuba without Castro. On April 17, 1961, the CIA sponsored an attack by *paramilitary forces* on Castro's Cuba—an invasion which came to be known as the Bay of Pigs. It was an attempt to get rid of Fidel Castro, the revolutionary leader of the island who had declared himself a communist and aligned himself with Communist Russia, then known as the Soviet Union.

Security Speak

Paramilitary forces is a term that is often misunderstood. These are forces or operations distinct from the regular armed forces of a national. They may resemble regular forces in organization and training, but they operate beyond the scope or authority of regular armed forces.

The key mass media (from the *New York Times* to the *Washington Post*) viewed Castro during and after he took over Cuba as a Liberator of the Cuban People. Few members of the major media ever identified him for what he had been and was, a devoted communist. Even after he began methodically eliminating those who had helped his revolution as he came to power, he was still seen as a *freedom fighter*. Few among the media cared or dared to report the obvious. Castro had been, was, and remained a dedicated communist.

President Kennedy had a good sense of history and political perspective. He disliked what he saw happening in Cuba and said so. His observations most likely were taken as directives and plans set in motion. It was thought intolerable to have a communist regime only 90 miles away from the United States. Something had to be done. But Cuba had the backing of the world's other superpower: the Soviet Union.

If the U.S. Army invaded Cuba and threw Castro out, they were risking the start of a nuclear war, the casualties of such would guarantee that there would be no winners. That probably was the assay of top leadership advisors to the president. Plans began under President Eisenhower for a covert action—a CIA invasion of the island, an invasion that perhaps we could do without it looking like we had done it. Before the plan could come to fruition, Eisenhower left office and was replaced by President John F. Kennedy.

Since this didn't involve the U.S. Army, the attack needed soldiers. The CIA used Cuban exiles, those who had fled the communist government and very much wanted to get their homeland back. The exiles were trained by the CIA in Guatemala—and some, very quietly, in Florida—and were supplied weapons and other supplies of war by the American military. The Cuban exiles also believed that they had been promised the support of the U.S. Air Force. The new soldiers—1,200 of them—who had been trained rather quickly to fight, went to Cuba by boat. They hit the beach at the Playa Giron, the Bay of Pigs. The plan assumed that, once the Cuban people heard of the attack, they would rise up in revolt. Soon Castro would be out of power, they thought. It didn't work out that way.

The invasion was a miserable failure. When the exiles landed they were given no air support. As it turned out, U.S. president John F. Kennedy had never promised U.S. military support, and he wasn't about to order in the Air Force at the last second because things were going poorly on the ground. Such a move, President Kennedy feared, might start World War III. During the short battle at the Bay of Pigs many died. The freedom fighters who were not killed by Cuba's army were captured on the beach. No Cubans rose up in revolt in response to the invasion. The invasion was poorly planned and carried out on every level.

At first the embarrassed CIA said that it had nothing to do with the invasion, that it had been entirely planned and carried out by the Cuban exiles. But the truth quickly came out. President Kennedy quickly went on TV and took full responsibility for the invasion. Many of the Cuban freedom fighters blamed President Kennedy for the failure of the invasion, feeling that the president had gone back on his word. The Cubans were not released from their prisoner-of-war cells until a few days before Christmas 1962, when President Kennedy made a deal with Castro. The United States gave Cuba food and medicine and, in exchange, the Cuban exiles were allowed to return to the United States.

Point/Counterpoint

Following the Bay of Pigs fiasco, JFK said, "There's an old saying that victory has a hundred fathers and defeat is an orphan. If someone comes to tell me this or that about the minimum wage bill, I have no hesitation in overruling them. But you also assume that the military and the intelligence people have some secret skill not available to ordinary mortals." The President never made that assumption again.

One of the many reasons that the Bay of Pigs operation was a failure was that, within the company, the left hand did not know what the right hand was doing. Obviously, the Directorate of Intelligence had not been consulted. If the DI had been informed of the plans, they would have told the Directorate of Operations not to attempt such an invasion. The notion—that the people of Cuba would turn on Castro once the battle started—was a foolish one.

There was ample evidence to prove that point then. Fact is, Castro has retained power for so long because he has continued to have substantial support among the Cuban people. Improved health, education, and other social programs the poor had never had actually made Castro a folk hero to many there. Even during the past decade and today, despite the poverty of many, Castro has remained in place. His position and power were secure at the time of the Bay of Pigs and the planners should have checked on their "spontaneous uprising" view then. That was one of the key failures of the invasion. According to Wilson McLean, this was "a monumental misjudgment by some overly enthusiastic Intel people."

Another problem with the plan is that the CIA wanted to make sure that, in case things did not go well, the invasion would look like it was purely a group of self-trained exiles invading in a patriotic attempt to get their island back.

Of course, with all the media stories about activities of Cuban exiles organizing and training in the swamps of Florida, it was rather obvious something was up. To have such "exercises" continuing meant the United States was involved, or at the least that the exiles had the blessing of the United States.

At the time, Castro had his own spies operating in Florida among the refugee and exile groups. He wasn't and isn't a stupid person. He kept his long distance eyes and ears open. That's especially easy to do in an open free society with free mass media. In other words, it was supposed to look like the United States didn't have anything to do with it. Turned out, a successful invasion cannot come with deniability. Deniability by definition is defeatist thinking, and that leads to defeat.

Security Factoid _____

Apparently, the Bay of Pigs invasion went forward despite the fact that the Soviets knew the date the invasion was to take place. In fact, the Soviets openly announced the event before it happened. David More, of Kampala, Hawaii, wrote that he was listening to Radio Moscow's English news via short-wave from Summit, New Jersey, in April 1962 when it was announced that "a plot hatched by the CIA," an invasion of Cuba, was to occur within a week. More recorded the report but considered it a propaganda fantasy. He was shocked when the Bay of Pigs took place the following morning.

Cuban Missile Crisis

In October 1962 the world came closer than it ever had before or since to nuclear war—and the CIA played a key role in the crisis. The same agency that had looked less than on-the-ball during the planning and execution of the Bay of Pigs invasion now showed the world that it was the eyes and ears of the Free World. Indeed, it was proven conclusively by the events of October 1962 that it is extremely difficult to keep a secret from the CIA.

The world stood at the brink of World War III after photos taken from the CIA's U-2 spy plane—the same plane that had taken photos over the Soviet Union until one piloted by Francis Gary Powers was shot down—showed that Soviet nuclear missiles were being installed.

Point/Counterpoint

Soviet General and Army Chief of Operations Anatoly Gribkov later said, "Nuclear catastrophe was hanging by a thread ... and we weren't counting days or hours, but minutes."

During the crisis, the U.S. armed forces were at their highest state of readiness ever and Soviet field commanders in Cuba were prepared to use battle-field nuclear weapons to defend the island if it was invaded.

In 1962, the Soviet Union trailed the United States in the arms race. Soviet missiles could only be launched against Europe. U.S. missiles, on the other hand, could strike anywhere in the Soviet Union.

In late April 1962, Soviet Premier Nikita Khrushchev decided to even things up by placing intermediate-range missiles in Cuba. This deployment in Cuba would double the Soviet strategic arsenal and provide a real deterrent to a potential U.S. attack against the Soviet Union. Installation of the missiles was well underway by the summer of 1962. Castro thought that the installation of the missiles on his island was a good idea also. He had been looking for a way to defend Cuba from a U.S. attack. Ever since the Bay of Pigs, he had felt that a second strike from the north was inevitable.

The crisis began on October 15, when CIA photos of Soviet missile sites under construction reached President John F. Kennedy. JFK huddled among a dozen of his most trusted advisers, a group he called Ex-Comm. The twelve men debated for a solid week concerning what to do about the missiles in Cuba. Kennedy decided to impose a naval quarantine around Cuba. This would immediately stop new weapons from coming onto the island.

On October 22, JFK announced to the world that he knew about the missiles and that the missiles had to go. Reconnaissance flights over Cuba were run every two hours, so that movements on the ground could be carefully watched. This obviously was risky, but it also provided real-time intelligence for the decision makers. Tensions finally began to ease on October 28 when Khrushchev announced that he would dismantle the installations and return the missiles to the Soviet Union, expressing his trust that the United States would not invade Cuba—and we haven't.

Point/Counterpoint

In a letter to President John F. Kennedy written during the Cuban missile crisis by Soviet Premier Nikita Khrushchev, "I understand your concern for the security of the United States, Mr. President, because this is the primary duty of a President. But we, too, are disturbed about these same questions; I bear these same obligations as Chairman of the Council of Ministers of the USSR. You have been alarmed by the fact that we have aided Cuba with weapons, in order to strengthen its defense capability—precisely defense capability—because whatever weapons it may possess, Cuba cannot be equated with you since the difference in magnitude is so great, particularly in view of modern means of destruction. Our aim has been and is to help Cuba, and no one can dispute the humanity of our motives, which are oriented toward enabling Cuba to live peacefully and develop in the way its people desire."

Assassination of JFK

United States president John F. Kennedy was killed by rifle fire at approximately 12:30 P.M., on November 22, 1963, as he rode westward in a motorcade. At the time of the shooting the presidential limousine was heading down a slight slope on Elm Street, on the north side of a symmetrically landscaped area called Dealey Plaza at the western edge of the downtown section of Dallas, Texas. Just ahead an underpass could be seen, Dallas's triple underpass. Then loud explosions were heard.

Kennedy had come to Dallas to mend political fences in the Texas Democratic Party and to campaign for re-election in 1964. He came at the invitation of the Dallas Citizen's Council, the Dallas Assembly, and the Science Research Center. At the time of the shooting, President Kennedy's motorcade had just completed a slow journey through downtown Dallas, heading from the Love Field airport to the Trade Mart, where the president was scheduled to deliver a luncheon speech.

Although there were indications that the accused assassin, Lee Harvey Oswald—who was himself shot and killed two days after the assassination—had ties to the Soviet Union and Castro's Cuba, the new president, Lyndon B. Johnson, and J. Edgar Hoover, Director of the FBI, quickly determined that Oswald, a former marine who had defected to the Soviet Union, had acted alone. Although evidence that this was not true went unrefuted, the official version of the assassination remained one least apt to cause international conflict.

DCI Richard Helms

With Richard Helms's appointment as DCI in June 1966, the top man at the CIA was himself a spymaster. This was the first time this was true since Allen Dulles was DCI. And some of the biggest abuses in the CIA charter occurred during Helms's watch.

Delving into what should have been the FBI's territory, in 1967, Helms established the Special Operations Group, which was put in charge of an internal security function—that is, keeping track of Americans who were against U.S. participation in the war in Vietnam. There were 7,200 U.S. citizens with files. Of course, there were good reasons for checking the records of some of these people, according to some inside and others outside the CIA.

For example, it was known during that period that the KGB had already set up a fair number of "sleepers," which were women who had been carefully trained, indoctrinated, and motivated to marry U.S. officers at the end of World War II, move to the United States, and "go to sleep"; not just with their husbands, but for the KGB. They would then be contacted periodically and "activated" as needed.

How many of these Soviet sleepers were involved in the Anti-Vietnam War we may never know. Best guess among veteran Intel people ranges from about 100 to several hundred. More important, they were the manipulators behind the scenes. Sleepers seldom did dirty work in the streets. Therefore, there was reasonable and sufficient motivation behind the thinking of CIA officials as they watched the anti-war protests spread, escalate and, in some ways, get far out of hand (see the following chapter).

Sadly, President Nixon fired Helms as DCI during the aftermath of the Watergate scandal. Nixon wanted Helms to say that the investigation into the Watergate burglary should be called off because it might accidentally expose CIA methods. Helms refused to lie and lost his job.

Helms had a history of not caving in to pressures from the White House. Early in his tenure as DCI, Helms had said no to President Johnson when LBJ asked that the CIA confirm the "Domino Theory," which stated that communism needed to be nipped in the bud in southeast Asia or else many other countries would, one by one, fall to communism. CIA studies, on the other hand, indicated that this probably would not be the case and that the Domino Theory was not a good reason to maintain a U.S. presence in Vietnam.

The Least You Need to Know

◆ It was during the Korean War that aerial reconnaissance photography came into its own.

◆ The Cold War was a war of ideologies between the Free World and the forces of communism.

◆ James J. Angleton, Edward Lansdale, Allen Dulles, and William King Harvey were legendary battlers of communism.

◆ During the Cold War, Americans were fearful of an all-out nuclear war between the United States and the Soviet Union.

◆ The Cold War did heat up on occasion, with the Cuban Missile Crisis, the Bay of Pigs, and the Vietnam War.

Chapter 5

The Vietnam Era

In This Chapter

- ◆ Another Civil War
- ◆ Blackbirds
- ◆ Pushing the envelope
- ◆ A no-win situation

The most frustrating war the U.S. Army ever fought was in Southeast Asia, where troops were used to support the efforts of democratic South Vietnam in their civil war against Communist-controlled North Vietnam.

Unfortunately for our cause, South Vietnam's government, though anti-Communist, was corrupt and weak. As it turned out, it didn't make any difference how many troops or equipment we poured into the tiny southeast Asian country, because it is impossible to help a country fight that doesn't want to fight for itself.

Just as was the case earlier in the Cold War with the Soviet Union, one of the key methods of gathering intelligence during the Vietnam War was from above. Nonetheless, ground intelligence also played a key role.

Aerial Reconnaissance over North Vietnam

In May 1967, President Lyndon Johnson was told by the National Security Council that the North Vietnamese government had purchased sophisticated surface-to-air missiles from the Soviet Union. The new SA-2 missiles represented a serious threat to the United States' aerial bombing campaign against Hanoi. In order to protect the American pilots, Johnson ordered an increase in aerial reconnaissance over North Vietnam.

The problem faced by American military planners was how to get the pictures. An SA-2 missile had shot down a U-2 reconnaissance aircraft being flown by Taiwan in 1965. The new Soviet missile had rendered our number-one spy plane obsolete.

Security Factoid

As you'll learn in Chapters 6 and 8, unmanned drones have improved greatly since the Vietnam days, and have been used successfully in the War Against Terrorism in Afghanistan. Today's drones not only locate the enemy, but they can fire upon the enemy as well.

Using unmanned reconnaissance drones was suggested, but they were of limited value and many were falling prey to the enemy's increasingly sophisticated anti-aircraft system.

It seemed an insurmountable problem until Richard Helms, then the Director of Central Intelligence (remember from the last section of Chapter 4), suggested using the new A-12 strategic reconnaissance aircraft.

The A-12, or SR-71 as the later improved version was designated, was an ideal choice. It had been developed during the Cold War when the Americans needed a high-flying, high-speed aircraft to gather intelligence about what was going on behind the Iron Curtain.

Photos from the Lockheed SR-71A

The Lockheed SR-71A (strategic reconnaissance) made its first flight on December 22, 1964. The new aircraft—with its long, narrow, delta-shaped fuselage—was 107 feet, five inches long.

The thin delta wings, mounted well back on the fuselage, had a span of 55 feet, seven inches. Two inward-canted tail assemblies located on the wings gave the aircraft a height of 18 feet, six inches.

The aircraft was powered by two Pratt & Whitney J58-1 turbo ramjet engines with afterburners. Each engine delivered 32,500 pounds of thrust. Those engines could propel the aircraft at an astounding 2,193 miles per hour. The craft had an operational ceiling of 81,000 feet. At top speed the aircraft covered 33 miles a minute.

The SR-71 weighed 65,000 pounds when empty. Fully load with fuel, surveillance equipment, and a two-man crew it weighed 170,000 pounds.

The aircraft carried its photographic equipment in a bay located behind the cockpit. It could carry either the Type H or KA-102A camera, which produced high-resolution, high-quality pictures. The Type H camera had a 60-inch focal length and used Kodak 3414 film with an ASA of eight. The film provided image resolution of two inches from 80,000 feet.

The KA-102 had a focal length of 48 inches and took pictures on a 700-foot roll of film. In addition to the cameras, a wide array of other sensors were carried, including ground-mapping radar and a D-21 drone that was carried on the back of the aircraft and could be launched into high-threat environments.

The first Lockheed SR-71A was delivered to the 4200th Strategic Reconnaissance Wing stationed at Beale Air Force Base in California. The aircraft arrived wearing a coat of black paint, specially developed for high-altitude flight. The sleek, black aircraft was immediately nicknamed "Blackbird" by the men of the *Wing*.

Security Speak

A **Wing** is the designation of an Air Force organization having a selected number of aircraft.

Since there were so few of the aircraft and the maintenance and crew selection was so specialized, the Air Force consolidated all the aircraft into one Wing. When missions required, small one- and two-plane detachments were deployed to various bases throughout the world.

President Johnson authorized sending the first two SR-71s to Okinawa, Japan, on May 22, 1967. When the aircraft landed they were immediately escorted into a hangar. The doors were closed and no information was forthcoming to explain the arrival. Naturally, the arrival of the two aircraft caused a great deal of interest among both locals and military personnel.

The new secret plane was called the "Habu," named after an aggressive, all-black snake that was native to the island of Okinawa—which was, of course, the site of the largest battle in the Pacific Theater of World War II.

The SR-71A detachment in Okinawa was in precisely the right spot. It was near enough to North Vietnam to conduct the reconnaissance flights and flew high enough to elude even the most sophisticated surface-to-air missiles.

Ounce of Prevention

The Blackbirds' base on Okinawa was far enough away from the enemy to keep it out of harm's way. The North Vietnamese had no method of attacking.

With the SR-71A now available to military planners for use over North Vietnam, the first mission was planned. On May 31, 1967, an SR-71A, flown by Major Mele Vojvodich, took off from Kadena Air Force Base in Okinawa and headed toward North Vietnam.

The aircraft refueled from a KC-135 tanker over the South China Sea and then entered North Vietnamese air space at 80,000 feet flying at a speed of Mach 3.1. The aircraft flew across Haiphong and Hanoi with its cameras noting everything on the ground. The pilot noted that enemy fire control radars were tracking his aircraft.

However, the speed of the aircraft was too great for the radars and the enemy fired their surface-to-air missiles in salvos—that is, groups or bursts of shots—in a vain attempt to knock the Blackbird down. None of the missiles got close.

The SR-71A exited North Vietnam in the vicinity of Dien Bien Phu. The mission was a complete success. Photos had been taken. During its brief visit over North Vietnam, the Blackbird had captured on film 70 of an estimated 190 enemy surface-to-air sites. After the first mission, 15 other missions were planned but only seven of them were ever flown. The North Vietnamese continued to try to shoot the SR-71A down, but they were getting no closer. However, the missions were not without their problems.

Problems Pushing the Envelope

Problems are to be expected whenever you are pushing the envelope of what is possible the way the Blackbird was. Especially when you are attempting to perform functions while flying an aircraft at faster than 2,000 miles per hour at 80,000 feet. On one flight, for example, the side panels of the SR-71A ripped loose in flight. The left side of the aircraft disintegrated. Luckily, the pilot was able to execute an emergency landing at Kadena Air Force Base in Okinawa.

More flights followed. Between August 1967 and the end of that year an additional 26 sorties were planned, with 15 of them actually flown. The enemy continued to try downing the SR-71A as it flew through its skies, taking high-resolution photographs of the military installations below. Using the photos taken by the Blackbird, the U.S. Air Force knew where to drop their bombs.

The aircraft continued to cause its crews much more trouble than the anti-aircraft fire from the enemy did. On one flight, piloted by a fellow named Frank Murray, the Blackbird's left engine experienced excessive vibration while flying over enemy territory. Murray successfully shut down the engine, but in the process of maneuvering the aircraft, he inadvertently pointed his camera across the Vietnamese border into Red China. When the aircraft landed back at Kadena and the film was analyzed, it revealed a trainload of 152mm self-propelled artillery pieces preparing to cross into North Vietnam. The unintended intelligence windfall allowed military planners to find, track, and eventually destroy the big guns before they got into operation against United States forces.

Can't Catch Me

The reconnaissance flights had an immediate effect on North Vietnam. The SR-71s were simply too fast. They appeared on the radar and were gone before any kind of concentrated attack could be made against them.

The North Vietnamese asked their Soviet allies for help. Using a system of agents on the island of Okinawa and intelligence-gathering ships off the island, the Soviets were able to track the SR-71s when they took off and then alerted the North Vietnamese as to when to expect reconnaissance flights.

Even with this early-warning information, however, the North Vietnamese defenses were unable to knock down one of the spy planes. By 1968 there were three SR-71As on Okinawa dedicated to making overflights of North Vietnam. As the war intensified, so did the number of flights. The aircraft flew a mission a week to determine what the enemy was planning and which enemy forces were moving toward South Vietnam.

Double-Loop Missions

The missions were so important that the crews began to fly "double-loop" missions. On these missions the crew would fly across North Vietnam, taking pictures of key targets and installations. Then the crew would fly out of enemy air space, refuel in the air from a waiting KC-135 tanker and then fly back over North Vietnam for another look-see. A two-fer.

The double loop missions were long and arduous. They lasted approximately six hours apiece. One aircraft racked up 48 missions during the operation's first 18 months. During the heavy B-52 bombing raids against North Vietnam, the Blackbirds were given a new mission. Now they flew in support of the big bombers.

On these missions, the SR-71As were sent aloft over North Vietnam while the B-52s were over their targets. The sensors on the reconnaissance plane could detect enemy radar. The Blackbirds could listen in on North Vietnamese radio transmissions, which proved to be tremendously helpful as we rained bombs onto the enemy.

Capturing this data allowed the U.S. intelligence agencies to dissect the enemy's battle plan and give the bomber crews new ways to defeat enemy tracking and firing radars. The SR-71As also found that their immensely successful electronic countermeasures systems could be used to help shield the B-52s from enemy missile attacks.

Tempo Takes Its Toll

The more bombing missions that were flown over North Vietnam, the more missions were ordered for the reconnaissance aircraft. By 1970, the Blackbirds out of Okinawa were averaging two missions per week apiece.

The increased tempo of operations soon took its toll on the complicated aircraft. On May 10, 1970, after completing one reconnaissance flight over North Vietnam, both engines of an SR-71 flamed out immediately following refueling. Both crewmen ejected safely and the aircraft disintegrated when it plunged into the South China Sea.

Heroes in the Sky

In the late spring of 1972, the SR-71s were called upon to carry out one of their most unusual missions. They were ordered to "buzz" the infamous "Hanoi Hilton." The plan was to keep up the morale of the soon-to-be-released American prisoners of war being held there.

On May 2, 4, and 9, two SR-71s left Kadena, flying mission profiles that would follow them to set off two sonic booms within 15 seconds of one another. The twin booms would almost certainly convince the pilots that American aircraft were still out and about over North Vietnam. All three missions were successful.

Security Factoid

The SR-71s were used to gather information on the Son Tay Prisoner of War Camp, prior to the U.S. raid on that facility. The aircraft's ability to stay high in the air and still bring back detailed photos allowed them to shoot pictures at will without worrying about giving away their target.

As the war wound down in Southeast Asia, so did the number of SR-71A flights. When the Paris agreement was signed on January 27, 1973, the number of flights dropped off radically. The number of SR-71As stationed on Okinawa also decreased. By the spring of 1973 there were only two SR-71As left on the island and they were restricted to stand-off reconnaissance of Vietnam.

The A-12 and improved SR-71A played an important part in gathering intelligence over North Vietnam during the war. Their efforts are classified and generally unknown. However, the few missions that have been revealed show that the pilots executed their missions with great courage and skill.

Their high-flying aircraft, loaded with sophisticated equipment, brought back loads of important photographs and electronic intelligence that saved hundreds of American lives during the course of the war. The SR-71A's pilots, flying at 80,000 feet on grueling reconnaissance missions that were often too classified to even talk about with their families, are truly the unsung heroes of the air war over Vietnam.

CIA in Vietnam

During the peak of the U.S. involvement in the war in Vietnam, more than 500,000 American soldiers were in Southeast Asia. But the number of CIA officers working in the area never got much higher than 700, which is still a tremendously large number by CIA standards.

Security Factoid

The U.S. embassy in Saigon, the capital of South Vietnam, was practically taken over by CIA personnel during the late 1960s. A full three floors of the building were needed to house the CIA. Of course, the sign on the door did not say, "CIA." It said, "Office of the Special Assistant to the Ambassador." The head of the Office of the Special Assistant was William Colby, who was in reality in charge of the CIA's efforts in Vietnam and who would later become DCI.

For example, operation *Phoenix* was a CIA program designed to root out civilians in South Vietnam who were supporting the Vietcong army or the army of North Vietnam, with whom we were at war. Once the Vietcong supporters were identified, the information was passed along to the South Vietnamese.

What started out as a perfectly sound plan turned into a major black eye for the CIA a few years later. The CIA, of course, had no control over what the South Vietnamese government would do with the information after they received it. They arrested and interrogated some of the suspects, but others were promptly killed.

The Least You Need to Know

◆ The war in Vietnam was similar to the Korean conflict in that it was a fight between an ally and a Communist country adjacent to Red China.

- Aerial reconnaissance missions over North Vietnam were one of the key factors in that conflict.

- The Lockheed SR-71A, nicknamed the Blackbird, performed the aerial reconnaissance over North Vietnam, and its pilots were the unsung heroes of the air war over Vietnam.

- The Vietnam War was the U.S. military's most frustrating endeavor, and its only loss.

End of the Cold War

In This Chapter

- ◆ "Tear down this wall"
- ◆ Summits
- ◆ The curtain opens
- ◆ Who do we spy on now?

In the national security game, you can never tell who your friends, or your enemies, are. The global situation is always fluid. As the twentieth century wound down and the twenty-first began, it wasn't always easy to tell who our enemies were.

The Soviet Union, which had been our number-one enemy since the end of World War II, gave up on communism and became Russia and a group of smaller countries, who were all friendly toward the United States.

Friends vs. Enemies?

During the last decades of the last century, the Soviet Union fought a war in Afghanistan against the ruling government there known as the Taliban.

Since the enemy (the Taliban) of our enemy (the Soviets) was considered a friend, we supported the Taliban in that battle. That was then. Times changed.

Security Speak

Terrorism is defined in the Code of Federal Regulations as "the unlawful use of force and violence against persons or property to intimidate or coerce a government, the civilian population, or any segment thereof, in furtherance of political or social objectives."

Today the Taliban is known as the government who gave the *terrorist* group Al Qaeda a home in Afghanistan—and Al Qaeda is the group responsible for the 9/11 attacks. Now, the Taliban is the friend of our enemy (Al Qaeda) and so has become our enemy. Indeed, our military and paramilitary have spent the last few years trying to wipe the Taliban out.

During the 1980s a bloody war was fought between Iran and Iraq. We supported Iraq and their leader Saddam Hussein in that conflict and today, as this is written, the United States has just finished the major phase of a war against Iraq. The next phase is the reorganization and rebuilding of that country as a democratic nation. The point is, when it comes to preserving our national security, trusting no one is always the best idea, because information you share today might be used against you tomorrow.

Terror Didn't Start on 9/11

America's problems with terrorism did not begin on September 11, 2001. Terrorists from the Middle East repeatedly struck against Americans during Reagan's time in office. And intelligence alone was not enough to stop it.

The worst of these attacks came on October 23, 1983, when a suicide bomber from the Hezbollah Islamic terrorist group drove a truck packed with more than 2,000 pounds of explosives into the U.S. Marine barracks in Beirut, killing 241 U.S. military personnel.

Fifty-eight French soldiers were killed that same morning in a separate suicide terrorist attack. The Marines were part of a multinational force sent to Lebanon in August 1982 to oversee a Palestinian withdrawal from Lebanon.

From its inception, the mission was plagued with problems. Four months after the bombing of the Beirut barracks, on February 7, 1984, Reagan announced the end of the American role in the peacekeeping force.

A National Security Agency phone tap recorded a September 24, 1983 call from the Iranian ambassador in Syria to his foreign minister, in which the ambassador relayed orders he'd given to Abu Haidar, leader of the Husaini Suicide Forces Movement.

The ambassador told Haidar to get weapons from Yasir Arafat's Fatah group to "undertake an extraordinary operation against the marines" in Beirut. A CIA source says U.S. military officials had the intercept in hand a month before the bombing, which killed 241 Marines and other U.S. servicemen, but failed to prevent it.

But taking raw intelligence, interpreting it, and then taking the correct action is more difficult than it might seem. There is so much intercepted message traffic, it is often difficult to determine which is most important or timely. Some of the messages are false and are actually planted in an effort to force reactions or direct attention away from actual plans. Intelligence must face these problems and cannot always provide what leaders need in time.

Reagan Plays Rough with Communism

Ronald Reagan, as president, was the fiercest opponent communism had ever known. On June 8, 1982, before the House of Commons in London, England, Reagan called the Soviet Union "evil." In that same speech he said, "Our military strength is a pre-requisite to peace, but let it be clear we maintain this strength in the hope it will never be used, for the ultimate determinant in the struggle that's now going on in the world will not be bombs and rockets but a test of wills and ideas, a trial of spiritual resolve, the values we hold, the beliefs we cherish, the ideals to which we are dedicated. The British people know that, given strong leadership, time, and a little bit of hope, the forces of good ultimately rally and triumph over evil."

When President Reagan called communism evil, he meant it in a religious sense. He truly believed that communism was the work of the devil. He told the world that the Soviets were liars and cheaters and not to be trusted.

Point/Counterpoint _____

Reagan wrote a letter early in his presidency to Soviet president Leonid Brezhnev in which he tried to explain to the Soviet leader the errors of his ways: "[The people] want the dignity of having some control over the individual destiny. They want to work at the craft or trade of their own choosing and to be fairly rewarded. They want to raise their families in peace without harming anyone or suffering harm themselves. Government exists for their convenience, not the other way around."

During Reagan's presidency, the Soviet Union went through four leaders. The first three had been old and sick. Leonid Brezhnev died in 1982 and was replaced by Yuri Andropov. Andropov died in 1984. He was replaced by Konstantin Chernenko, who died in 1985. He was replaced by Mikhail Gorbachev. "How can I be expected to make peace with them if they keep dying on me?" Reagan complained. The dead leaders had all been old men, but the new leader, Gorbachev, was only 54 and appeared healthy indeed. He wasn't going to die soon; together he and Reagan would make history.

Gorbachev did not trust Reagan's Strategic Defense Initiative (SDI) plan any more than his predecessors had. In one of his first speeches as Soviet leader, he warned that World War III could result if the United States attempted to put a space shield in place. U.S. intelligence learned that the Soviet Union soon thereafter began research into developing their own SDI system.

Reagan and Gorbachev met in person four times, the first being during the cold winter of 1985 in Geneva, Switzerland. At their first meeting, Reagan stepped outside their hotel to greet Gorbachev as he got out of his car.

 Point/Counterpoint

At that Geneva, Switzerland, meeting, Reagan said to Gorbachev, "What a unique position we are in. Here we are, two men born in obscure rural hamlets in the middle of our respective countries, and now, together, we can forestall a World War III ... and don't we owe this to mankind?"

Reagan was hatless and wore no overcoat. He was photographed shaking hands with the shorter Gorbachev who was bundled up for the weather. The photo gave the impression that the American leader was made of stronger stuff. The image was completely unintentional, but Reagan made sure that he wore an overcoat the next time he and the Soviet leader were photographed outside.

The two men developed a relationship, not quite of friendship—they were political enemies with the fate of the world in their hands, after all—but of mutual respect. After the meeting, their relationship grew still warmer as Reagan and Gorbachev exchanged a series of personally written letters.

They next met in person in Reykjavik, Iceland, during the summer of 1986. This summit got off to a strong start as Gorbachev told Reagan he was prepared to drastically reduce his arsenal of nuclear weapons.

It was only as the meeting was about to come to an end that Gorbachev told Reagan that he would only do this if Reagan gave up on his SDI plan. This angered Reagan, who knew the Soviets were working on their own SDI.

Reagan walked out on the meeting and next addressed Gorbachev indirectly, during his famous speech at the Berlin Wall in 1987 when he said, "We welcome change and openness, for we believe that freedom and security go together, that the advance of human liberty can only strengthen the cause of world peace. This is one sign the

Soviets can make that would be unmistakable, that would advance dramatically the cause of freedom and peace. General Secretary Gorbachev, if you seek peace, if you seek prosperity for the Soviet Union and Eastern Europe, if you seek liberalization: Come here to this gate! Mr. Gorbachev, open this gate! Mr. Gorbachev, tear down this wall!"

The whole world could hear the anger in Reagan's voice. Two years later, the wall came down.

Reagan and Gorbachev met for a third time in Washington, D.C. in December 1987. This was the meeting during which the most was accomplished. Gorbachev did not bring up SDI (he realized it was a lost cause) and the pair agreed to both greatly reduce their nuclear arsenal.

They met for a fourth time in the spring of 1988 in Moscow. This meeting came near the end of Reagan's presidency, and not much was done. Gorbachev invited Reagan as a matter of courtesy. The highlight of the trip was the standing ovation Reagan received after giving a speech explaining the virtues of democracy to the student body of Moscow State University.

Although communism fell in the Soviet Union during the administration of George Bush the elder, several years after Reagan left office, Reagan's unyielding anticommunist attitudes deserve much credit toward winning the Cold War. The vigilance of the U.S. intelligence community gets a lot of credit, too.

One Berlin Once Again

The Berlin Wall, which had been for so many years the front line of the Cold War, came down on November 9, 1989. Berlin became a single city, undivided—and Germany became a single country for the first time since the end of World War II.

Suddenly, the CIA and the NSA found themselves slightly behind the times. For years they had set up camp in West Berlin to try and see and hear everything that happened on the other side of the *Iron Curtain*.

The Iron Curtain tumbled along with the Berlin Wall. As we now know, militant Muslims have replaced Communists as the number-one enemy to U.S. security, but there was a period of floundering when American spies were trying to determine just whom they should be spying on.

Security Speak

The **Iron Curtain** was the common expression used during the Cold War for the barrier that prevented people from crossing back and forth between Communist Europe and Free Europe.

Picking Up the Pieces

The United States' national security force had been predominantly anticommunist organizations for more than 40 years. They didn't change overnight. It took the U.S. intelligence community time to adjust to the new enemies that were developing in the world and replacing the old enemies.

And, as one might think, the end of the Cold War did not increase our national security. The unfortunate truth, as modern times have made all too clear, is that national security suffered when the Soviet Union collapsed. There are three reasons for this:

- Security discipline suffered with the loss of the prime "enemy."

- Technology has made security much harder.

- Senior officials were slow to react to the changing global situation.

When the Soviet Union dissolved and Russia stopped being the archenemy of the United States, there was of course concern that all of the military might and technological capabilities that had been developed during the Cold War would fall into the wrong hands. Steps were taken to keep Russia's military secrets from going anywhere.

Point/Counterpoint

Former DCI Robert M. Gates said during the Clinton administration, "Perhaps most importantly, tone and attitude at the top are vital. From the outset of the current administration, whether by allowing people to work at the White House before security clearances were approved by the FBI or showing indifference to and even disdain for security as a manifestation of a Cold War mindset, a message has been sent that these issues are no longer very important. Individual senior officials in various departments and agencies have reinforced that message, partly with arrogant attitudes conveying the idea that the rules do not apply to them. Good security still starts and ends with trust, integrity, and seriousness of purpose. Agencies need more resources. But simply observing the rules that already exist, from the top down, would go a long way."

Just because the Russians are no longer our archenemies does not mean that they are not still spying on us. Not long ago a Russian diplomat was detained after he was found loitering in a park across the street from the State Department.

The diplomat was identified by federal authorities as a technical expert for the Russian foreign intelligence service. In searching the man, investigators found a remote switching device hidden in his clothing. The device turned on a receiver and tape recorder in the car and a device designed to detect electronic surveillance signals.

He probably used the radio devices in his car to activate the eavesdropping device and would wait nearby, hoping to overhear meetings in the seventh-floor conference room.

Treason Is Treason

Not all of the spies who have been caught have been working for our enemies. Jonathan Pollard, who is currently serving a life sentence for treason, was a former U.S. Navy civilian intelligence analyst who spied for Israel.

Should Pollard be shown leniency because he spied for an ally rather than an enemy? Most people in the national security community do not think so. He passed tens of thousands of highly classified documents to his Israeli handlers.

Back in 1986, then-Secretary of Defense Caspar Weinberger said the damage was immense, "impossible to overstate." Once a secret is out, it is impossible to know who will learn it. The cat, as they say, is out of the bag.

> **Author's Corner**
>
> Wilson: Efforts to reduce or change the sentence against Pollard have been ongoing. In the intel community we still believe a spy is a spy is a spy. The damage they do is the same so each should be treated as a spy against us.

In his 1991 book, *The Samson Option*, Seymour Hersh wrote that Israel used U.S. intelligence information to target their nuclear deterrent forces on Soviet targets and to plan their 1985 raid on the PLO's headquarters in Tunisia—neither of which were in the U.S. interest. Israel, according to the book, shared some of the U.S. secrets with the Soviets in order to curry favor, including increased Jewish immigration from the USSR.

The Least You Need to Know

- The Cold War ended, to everyone's relief, without a shot being fired between the United States and the Soviet Union.

- National security had to be redefined in the 1990s as communism, the old enemy, crumbled, and new enemies emerged to take its place.

- Many important military secrets, including how to build an atom bomb, were lost to the Communists during the Cold War because of failures in our counter-intelligence system.

- The unfortunate truth, as modern times have made all too clear, is that national security suffered when the Soviet Union collapsed.

New Enemies

In This Chapter

- ◆ Saddam I
- ◆ Political terrorists
- ◆ Al Qaeda
- ◆ Saddam redux

When the Cold War ended, many thought that the world had been made a safer place, and the tendency was for Americans to relax about their national security. But, as time has shown, the end of the Cold War merely revealed other deadly dangers. From countering the "evil axis" of Iran, Iraq, and North Korea to a genocidal dictator in Europe, to an international web of terrorists seeking to destroy our way of life, the U.S. intelligence community has not only been unable to relax, it has been forced to be more vigilant than ever. In this chapter, we will look at America's new (that is post-Cold War) enemies.

The Gulf War

The United States engaged in its first full-fledged war since Vietnam in 1991 under the leadership of President George Herbert Walker Bush. Iraq had invaded Kuwait to annex that country and take their oil fields. The move threatened to destabilize the region.

In response, the United States led an international force to kick Iraq—which was led by an evil dictator named Saddam Hussein—out of Kuwait. President Bush called the war Operation Desert Storm. It was a quick affair, over in a matter of weeks.

The United States and her allies had a great technological advantage and inflicted hundreds of thousands of casualties upon the enemy while taking casualties that numbered less than a thousand. Because of sophisticated aerial surveillance and the first use of the so-called "smart bombs," the United States was able to locate military targets and take them out while causing a minimum of civilian casualties. It was the most lop-sided war in the history of the world.

Security Factoid _____

At the outset of the first Gulf War, an Iraqi intelligence agency attempted unsuccessfully to carry out terrorist bombings against U.S. embassies and other facilities, including targets in Manila, Bangkok, and Jakarta. Pairs of agents were sent to many countries where they were to pick up explosives or weapons that had already been sent abroad. According to former DCI William Webster: "These teams were picked up; they were interrogated; they were arrested where there was cause to do so; and when there were no legal grounds for arrest, they were deported."

Troubles in Bosnia

During the early 1990s, trouble was brewing in Eastern Europe. With the fall of the Soviet Union, the newly independent nation of Yugoslavia, formerly under Soviet rule, became lacking in cohesiveness. Yugoslavia soon fell into civil war, dividing into ancient factions based on ethnicity. Yugoslavia ceased to exist, separating into Slovenia, Croatia, Serbia, Montenegro, and Bosnia-Herzegovina.

Among the warring factions, the Serbs had been historically dominant in Yugoslavia's politics and military. They were Orthodox Christians who were friendly with Russia. Mixed into the cities of Bosnia were Muslims, who were hostile to both of the other groups.

All of the groups wanted independence from—and sometimes dominance over—the others, but the land they claimed overlapped.

Trying to Overthrow Milosevic

During the early 1990s CIA agents, who had penetrated the Yugoslav government at its highest levels, presented a plan to overthrow the genocidal Serbian president

Slobodan Milosevic, whose murderous campaigns came to be known as "ethnic cleansing." The CIA allegedly infiltrated the Serb hierarchy in Belgrade, bugging key buildings and obtaining valuable information on Serb plans and intentions.

Additionally, agents identified an individual to lead a coup against the government. A top-level CIA officer was dispatched to Belgrade to establish contact with the turn-coat and other disillusioned members of Milosevic's inner circle.

The potential coup leader was then flown to CIA headquarters, where he outlined a coup strategy. Since he claimed to have the support of key Yugoslav generals, the plan was thought to be feasible. Perhaps the plan was canceled because then-DCI John Deutch was allegedly not a fan of covert operations, and, more likely, because Milosevic was then an integral part of ongoing Bosnian peace negotiations.

Keeping the Peace

In 1992 the United Nations placed 14,000 peacekeeping troops in Croatia. That same year Bosnian Serbs laid siege to the Bosnian capital of Sarajevo. In 1995 a cease-fire was declared, peace talks commenced, and a peace agreement was signed by Croatian, Bosnian, and Serbian leaders.

A 60,000-troop NATO force, many of them American soldiers, entered the region to help keep the pace, and that force has remained there ever since.

Enter the Political Terrorists

The intelligence community had become staid and needed a figurative kick in the pants in order to adjust to the post-Cold War new world. That kick came in an extremely deadly form, with the 9/11 attacks.

If ever there was a clear indication that the Cold War was over, this was it. To the credit of our national security force, despite the shock that was felt in the United States and around the world, the intelligence community's reaction to the crisis was immediate and appropriate.

After 9/11, our national security force had to deal with the fact that our number-one enemy in the world was no longer a country, or a form of government, but rather *political terrorism*.

Security Speak

Political terrorism (as distinguished from criminal and psychotic terrorism) is generally a tool of desperation by states or groups that are militarily and economically weak but ideologically, religiously, or nationalistically fanatic.

Al Qaeda

The terrorist group behind the terrorist attacks on the Pentagon in Washington, D.C., and the World Trade Center in New York on September 11, 2001, is Al Qaeda, which means "the base" in Arabic.

According to a U.S. government indictment handed down against the organization in November 1998, almost three years before the 9/11 attacks …

- In approximately 1989, Osama bin Laden and codefendant Muhammad Atef founded Al Qaeda, "an international terrorist group … which was dedicated to opposing non-Islamic governments with force and violence."

- "One of the principal goals of Al Qaeda was to drive the United States armed forces out of Saudi Arabia (and elsewhere on the Saudi Arabian peninsula) and Somalia by violence."

- "Al Qaeda had a command and control structure which included a *majlis al shura* (or consultation council) which discussed and approved major undertakings, including terrorist operations." Both Atef and bin Laden sat on this council.

- Al Qaeda had ties to other "terrorist organizations that operated under its umbrella," including: the al Jihad group based in Egypt, the Islamic Group, formerly led by Sheik Omar Abdel Rahman, and other jihad groups in other countries. "Al Qaeda also forged alliances with the National Islamic Front in Sudan and with representatives of the government of Iran, and its associated terrorist group Hezbollah, for the purpose of working together against their perceived common enemies in the West, particularly the United States."

- The named defendants, plus other members of Al Qaeda, "conspired, confederated and agreed to kill nationals of the United States."

- In furtherance of this conspiracy, bin Laden and others "provided training camps and guesthouses in various areas, including Afghanistan, Pakistan, Somalia and Kenya for the use of Al Qaeda and its affiliated groups."

- Bin Laden and others provided currency and weapons to members of Al Qaeda and associated terrorist groups in various countries throughout the world.

- Bin Laden established a headquarters for Al Qaeda in Khartoum, Sudan, in 1991, and established a series of businesses, including two investment companies, an agricultural company, a construction business, and a transportation company, all of which were "operated to provide income and support to Al Qaeda and to provide cover for the procurement of explosives, weapons and chemicals and for the travel of Al Qaeda operatives."

- Bin Laden issued a number of fatwahs (rulings on Islamic law) stating that U.S. forces stationed in Saudi Arabia, Yemen, and the Horn of Africa, including Somalia, should be attacked.

- Al Qaeda members "provided military training and assistance to Somali tribes opposed to the United Nations' intervention in Somalia … On October 3 and 4, 1993, in Mogadishu, Somalia, persons who had been trained by Al Qaeda (and trainers who had been trained by Al Qaeda) participated in an attack on United States military personnel serving in Somalia as part of Operation Restore Hope, which attack resulted in the killing of 18 United States Army personnel."

Security Factoid

The 1993 events in Mogadishu, Somalia, were dramatized in an award-winning Hollywood movie called *Black Hawk Down* which was released in 2001. Applauded for its graphic realism, it was released by Columbia Pictures and directed by Ridley Scott.

- Bin Laden and others attempted to procure components of nuclear and chemical weapons.

And that was *before* the events of 9/11. It is important to focus on that fact. Those dedicated members of the intel community had seen these threats developing. Fortunately, we had begun to correctly assay the rapidly changing situation, as it grew around the world.

U.S. Policy Regarding Terrorism

Here is the U.S. Counterterrorism Policy:

- First, make no concessions to terrorists and strike no deals;

- Second, bring terrorists to justice for their crimes;

- Third, isolate and apply pressure on states that sponsor terrorism to force them to change their behavior; and

- Fourth, bolster the counterterrorism capabilities of those countries that work with the United States and require assistance.

Regarding the taking of American hostages:

- The U.S. Government will make no concessions to individuals or groups holding official or private U.S. citizens hostage.

♦ The United States will use every appropriate resource to gain the safe return of American citizens who are held hostage.

♦ At the same time, it is U.S. Government policy to deny hostage takers the benefits of ransom, prisoner releases, policy changes, or other acts of concession.

Hezbollah

Al Qaeda wasn't the only terrorist group threatening national security during the first years of the twenty-first century. According to a Justice Department letter to a Senate committee released to the press in November 2002, the Iranian-backed jihad group Hezbollah had cells in the United States and was prepared to make an attack on U.S. soil. The terrorist group had been called the most sophisticated in the world.

The letter stated, "They're here. FBI investigations to date indicate that many Hezbollah subjects based in the United States have the capacity to attempt terrorist attacks here, should this be a desired objective of the group. [Hezbollah members] have been tasked with surveillance of potential targets in the United States."

> ### Ounce of Prevention
>
> During the winter of 2003, the FBI identified Hezbollah members inside the United States and, concerned about domestic homicide bombings, kept them under surveillance. FBI agents were even sent to Israel to learn how to profile the killers. Said one FBI official: "We're always watching."

Hezbollah was responsible for driving the Israelis from southern Lebanon. They are also responsible for the 1983 truck bombing of the Marine barracks in Beirut that killed 241 U.S. Marines. They have provided explosives training to Al Qaeda.

The FBI has twice busted Hezbollah members in the United States, both times for illegal money-making schemes, the selling of bootleg cigarettes and videotapes.

In reaction to the 9/11 attacks, the United States committed military forces to the overthrow of the Taliban, the ruling government of Afghanistan who were playing host to Osama bin Laden and the Al Qaeda terror training camps. The Taliban was removed from power but Osama bin Laden apparently survived the war, much to the chagrin of President George W. Bush, who had called for the capture of bin Laden "dead or alive."

A Dangerous New Alliance

According to senior intelligence officials in February 2003, elements of Al Qaeda and Hezbollah had joined forces and were planning a series of attacks using unconventional weapons. Best bet was that the plans involved chemical weapons.

The report said that groups of Al Qaeda and Hezbollah activists from the Sidon area of Lebanon met in Africa during December 2002 to set up a joint operation at that location. Leading operatives from the terrorist group led by Abu Jaffar, a bin Laden associate connected with the bombings of American embassies in Kenya and Tanzania, were also on hand.

The meeting was used to coordinate final details for a joint chemical weapons lab in a safe house, possibly in Somalia. The two groups have to overlook religious differences in order to work together because Hezbollah is Shi'ite Muslim, a branch of Islam that differs and disagrees with the Sunni Muslims who make up Al Qaeda.

Point/Counterpoint

According to *Daily News* columnist Richard Chesnoff: "[In 2002], America's counterterrorism strategy in Africa reportedly was strengthened when the Pentagon established a special antiterror force to focus on the Horn of Africa countries, including Somalia. Now's the time to put it to work—before it's too late."

The Shi'ite and Sunni factions of Islam divided soon after the death of the prophet Muhammed in 632 A.D. Muhammed died unexpectedly without leaving instructions as to who should replace him as the leader of the faith. The Sunni faction, considered the more moderate of the two, has become more widespread, dominating North Africa and most of Asia. The Shi'ites, who are more conservative, live predominantly in Iran and Lebanon.

North Korea: Threat to Global Stability

Another threat to global stability is North Korea. As was the case 50 years ago, once again U.S. intelligence collection efforts are concentrating on events there. During December 2002, North Korea announced that it would resume operations at its Yongbyon nuclear reactor, which is located 50 miles north of P'yongyang. The former Soviet Union provided North Korea with a five-megawatt reactor. The reactor was completed before being placed in an inactive status because of a 1994 agreement, under which the United States was to provide fuel oil to North Korea. But, as restrictions were tightened on North

Security Factoid

Direct U.S. exposure on the Korean Peninsula may be reduced. Studies are underway to have South Korea assume an increasingly dominant role in its national security, and will "review" the location and strength of U.S. forces in South Korea (39,000 as of Summer 2003).

Korea, these supplies were cut off. North Korea also has two larger reactors, currently unfinished, which the government says will now be completed.

Of concern is the fact that North Korea has in storage approximately 8,000 spent fuel rods. These contain sufficient plutonium to construct several plutonium nuclear weapons. With the reactor back in operation, additional plutonium can be produced for nuclear weapons construction.

North Korea also ordered U.N. inspectors out of the country and disconnected the video surveillance and monitoring equipment in the reactor. North Korea reopened its reprocessing plant, which takes the spent fuel rods from the reactor, extracting the weapons-grade plutonium. Without on-site inspectors, the United States must now use its various intelligence collection tools. Some surveillance could be conducted by satellites, but there is no substitute for on-site inspections.

Security Factoid _____

A number of North Korean nuclear scientists have reportedly defected through a smuggling operation involving the tiny Pacific island of Nauru. The defections started in October 2002 and were made possible with the help of 11 countries that agreed to provide consular protection to smuggle the targets from neighboring China. Among those believed to be in a safehouse in the West is the father of North Korea's nuclear program, Kyong Won-ha, who left his homeland late last year with the help of Spanish officials.

Just before the overthrow of Saddam Hussein's regime, a North Korean freighter, supposedly loaded with bags of cement on the way to Yemen, was also found to contain hidden cargo of Scud missiles and related spare parts. Supposedly, these had been ordered by the government of Yemen, but what if they had been reshipped into Iraq?

While North Korea has further inflamed matters by test firing missiles—some of which reportedly could be armed with nuclear weapons and which have the range to reach the West Coast of the United States—there is diplomacy underway to solve the crisis.

Both North Korea and the United States talk tough in public, but diplomatic progress may be underway behind the scenes. North Korea believes its military is its best means of influencing the international community. According to the country's Foreign Ministry, the American-led war in Iraq has taught North Korea that "it was necessary to have a powerful physical deterrent force."

Third Member of the "Evil Empire": Iran

Along with Iraq and North Korea, the third member of President George W. Bush's "evil empire" is Iran. All indications are that Iranian support to Middle Eastern terrorists hadn't decreased at all during the first years of the twenty-first century—in fact, there are indications that it had increased.

Iran had increased shipments of guns and explosives to the Palestinian extremist group *Hamas*. Both U.S. and Israeli intelligence believed Iran had accelerated its deliveries of arms—including long-range *Katyusha rockets*—to Hezbollah, whose military arm was fighting to oust Israeli forces from the strip of South Lebanon occupied as a buffer against attacks on Northern Israel.

Although out of the news for a while, Iran did push its way back into the headlines during March of 2003 when it was revealed that a nuclear complex near the town of Natanz in Central Iran was close to being up and running. Iran, if left alone, is now expected to be capable of producing several nuclear bombs per year by 2005. The discovery of the complex caught U.S. intelligence by surprise. U.S. surveillance had been busy keeping an eye on a location further to the south near the port city of Bushehr.

Security Speak

Hamas (Islamic Resistance Movement) is the outgrowth of the Muslim Brotherhood. This terrorist group believes in establishing a Palestinian state through violent means. It is known for its suicide bombers. The **Katyusha rockets,** capable of delivering warheads four times as powerful as those delivered by Scud missiles, have enough range (12.7 miles) to strike the suburbs of Haifa from Southern Lebanon.

Back to Iraq

Although the first war in Iraq was to liberate Kuwait, the second was to kick Saddam Hussein out of Baghdad and Iraq. This purpose, as U.S. policy, was first stated in 1998 during a speech at Stanford University by then-National Security Advisor Sandy Berger.

His words committed the White House (then occupied by Bill Clinton) publicly to the overthrow of Saddam Hussein by supporting the Iraqi opposition, including a threat "to use effective force if necessary."

Security Factoid

In the 1980s, American intelligence and tacit support for Iraqi chemical warfare and ballistic missile operations against Iran turned the tide in favor of Iraq in its war with Iran—one of this century's bloodiest wars. At the time Saddam was considered the great hope of holding back the militant Islamic tide. In the national security business, you never can be sure who your friends are.

Berger was not referring to an all-out U.S. war against Iraq, however. He wanted to topple the Baghdad regime by using intelligence assets to focus on instigating a *coup d'etat* (the violent overthrow of a government), as well as sponsoring an insurrection from the outside.

Bush Changes the Tone

The tone of our foreign policy toward Iraq changed as soon as Bill Clinton was replaced by George W. Bush in the White House. Saddam Hussein and his weapons of mass destruction were not to be tolerated for much longer. The United Nations sent weapons inspectors into Iraq to rout out the weapons, which—of course—were well hidden.

President Bush, whose father had led the first war against Iraq, has made it increasingly clear that he intends to change the regime in Iraq with or without help from the United Nations. Great Britain has agreed to help but other allies have been hesitant.

Surveillance

President Bush signed directives okaying the missions during the summer of 2002. The U.S. forces were reportedly working in conjunction with Israeli and British forces.

Security Speak

Rivet Joint is a converted Boeing 707 that has the ability to intercept and track radio and cell phone signals.

In addition to covert operations, there were huge intelligence-gathering operations designed to facilitate the capture or assassination of the Iraqi ruler. One method used was monitoring the communications of Hussein's bodyguard in an attempt to fix the leader's location. The forces were being aided from above by a surveillance airplane known as *Rivet Joint*.

In addition to these attempts to hunt down Saddam, the U.S. forces inside Iraq were also assembling a guerrilla force of Kurdish dissidents, attempting to woo Iraqi tribal and military leaders to defect, and monitoring the movements of the Iraqi National Guard.

Inspections

At the start of 2003, U.N. weapons inspectors were in Iraq, unsuccessfully looking for weapons of mass destruction while the Iraqis seemed reluctant to cooperate. War was beginning to look inevitable, but there were also reports that, in some ways, the war had already begun—a clandestine war designed to keep bloodshed to a minimum.

In his 2003 State of the Union address, President George W. Bush said, "Today, the gravest danger in the war on terror … the gravest danger facing America and the world … is outlaw regimes that seek and possess nuclear, chemical, and biological weapons. These regimes could use such weapons for blackmail, terror, and mass murder. They could also give or sell those weapons to their terrorist allies, who would use them without the least hesitation …. Twelve years ago, Saddam Hussein faced the prospect of being the last casualty in a war he had started and lost. To spare himself, he agreed to disarm of all weapons of mass destruction. For the next 12 years, he systematically violated that agreement …. Almost three months ago, the United Nations Security Council gave Saddam Hussein his final chance to disarm. He has shown instead his utter contempt for the United Nations, and for the opinion of the world …. The dictator of Iraq is not disarming. To the contrary, he is deceiving."

During the winter of 2003, the Pentagon and the CIA were working together to maximize the possibility that Saddam Hussein could be removed from power without a full-fledged war being necessary. Commandos from Special Forces and CIA paramilitary squads were reportedly using an abandoned presidential palace in the mountains of Northern Iraq as headquarters for clandestine missions designed to disrupt Hussein's regime.

During the early stages of U.N. weapons inspections, Saddam Hussein declared that his 12 square miles of presidential palaces, close to 50 locations, were off-limits. Naturally, these were considered a potential hiding place for weapons of mass destruction. Saddam did open his palaces for a one-week period in December 2002 for brief and incomplete inspections. When the war finally came, these sites were prime targets for U.S. smart bombs and missiles. Although U.S. law prohibits the assassination of foreign leaders, the Bush administration clearly would not have been heartbroken had one of those bombs reduced Saddam to smithereens.

In February 2003, the Bush administration announced that Saddam Hussein was hiding mobile biological weapons laboratories from international weapons inspectors in violation of U.N. Security Council demands.

One of the U.N. demands that Iraq absolutely refused to meet was to persuade Iraqi scientists to submit to private interviews with U.N. arms controllers. Canada tried to lend a helping hand during January of 2003 by offering asylum to any Iraqi scientists who were willing to discuss Iraqi weapons programs with U.N. inspectors.

Another demand not being met was permission for the United States to fly U-2 reconnaissance planes to assist the inspection effort.

Iraqis in the United States

Back on the home front during the winter of 2003, the FBI was questioning as many as 50,000 Iraqis living in the United States in a search for potential terrorist cells, spies, or people who might provide information helpful to a U.S. war effort.

According to the Iraqi-American Council, about 300,000 people of Iraqi origin live in the United States. More than 50,000 Iraqis came to the United States after the 1991 Gulf War, and many became U.S. citizens. The largest Iraqi communities are in Michigan, California, Texas, Illinois, Pennsylvania, and Tennessee.

Agents across the country interviewed Iraqis in their homes and where they work, study, and worship. The FBI was looking for three things:

Security Factoid _____

During the first weeks of 2003, the CIA placed ads in newspapers in New York, Washington, Los Angeles, Detroit, and Tampa—cities with large Arab-American populations. The ads read: "For over 100 years Arab-Americans have served the nation. Today we need you more than ever." The ads—designed to recruit Arab-Americans to help the fight against terrorism—had results, but the need for Arabic-speaking Americans still exists.

- Potential terrorists (they are looking for any links between Iraqis in this country and possibly sympathetic radical Muslim groups, such as Al Qaeda and Hezbollah)

- Aliens whose visas have expired

- Those who might be interested in helping the United States overthrow Saddam Hussein

FBI agents are given sensitivity instructions from headquarters to stress that the interviews are voluntary and to assure people the government will protect them from any anti-Iraqi backlash. Still, many of the interviewees are afraid—fearing that they will be sent back to Iraq. Their worries were in vain. No lawful Iraqi was ever deported.

Plots to Kill Saddam

Some might ask, "Why can't the war with Iraq be won with one bullet?" That bullet, of course, would go through the temple of Saddam Hussein. Well, it has been considered, but for one reason or another, it hasn't happened.

Israel's Operation Bramble called for the killing of Saddam Hussein on the night of November 7, 1992. Premier Yitzak Rabin had approved Bramble, and the final rehearsal took place in the Negev desert on November 5. Unfortunately, a live missile was mistakenly used in the exercise and five Israeli soldiers were killed. The operation was canceled.

The idea remained alive, however, and in 1998 the operation was revived, this time called Bramble II and approved by Premier Netanyahu. Special Israeli forces trained to kill Saddam during one of his regular visits to his mistress.

Once they received information that Saddam was on his way, about 40 soldiers would be flown to Iraq and divide into two units. Ten soldiers would move within 200 meters of the relevant site; the other group would wait six miles away with special television-guided missiles, code-named *Midras*. The forward group would target Saddam with a video monitor. At the right moment, the main group would fire three Midras missiles. After the firing the troops would immediately evacuate.

The operation was canceled because the schedule for the attack coincided with the American and British bombardment of Iraq, and because Ariel Sharon and Yitzak Mordechai doubted the accuracy of Mossad's information. Remember from Chapter 4, Mossad is Israel's ultra-secret intelligence agency.

Anti-War Groups Infiltrated

There is evidence that at least some of the Iraqis who have recently entered the United States are up to no good. According to a report issued by the intelligence unit of the Homeland Security Department in January 2003, Iraq sent spies who had been living in Canada into the United States to New York City and Washington, D.C.

The spies were assigned to stir up anti-war demonstrations. They were also assigned to recruit Arabs and other foreigners for other unspecified espionage missions inside the United States.

The report stated that spies had been sent to the United States from the Iraqi Embassy in Ottawa, Canada, with instructions to "intensify spying activities and to carry out anti-U.S. demonstrations to stop a war against Iraq."

The same report apparently established a clear link between the United States' top two enemies: Iraq and Al Qaeda. It stated that there was a plot by Al Qaeda-linked militants in Africa to carry out terrorist attacks upon targets of American interest in Zimbabwe should the U.S. attack Iraq.

The group involved, called Tablik Ja'maat, is suspected of being the go-between for Al Qaeda and Iraq. The group was also planning attacks in Nigeria, Turkey, South Africa, and Israel.

Powell Goes to the United Nations

As a second war against Iraq approached in February 2003, the United States had a difficult decision to make. Our intelligence sources had come up with the evidence that Saddam Hussein's Iraq was merely toying with U.N. weapons inspectors, and that they indeed were hiding weapons of mass destruction.

The problem was, many countries in the world did not believe Iraq to be a sufficient threat to warrant a war. So a decision was made to, at the risk of exposing our intelligence systems, go public with the gathered intelligence in an attempt to convince the world that a war with Iraq was necessary.

The messenger was Secretary of State Colin L. Powell, and the forum was a special meeting of the Security Council of the United Nations. Powell's presentation took place on February 5, 2003, and was shown on live television to much of the world (although not Iraq).

The secretary of state offered raw intelligence, including intercepted telephone calls, satellite photographs, diagrams, and eyewitness accounts, all selected to show that Iraq was harboring and hiding weapons of mass destruction. (To prevent compromising future sources of intelligence, a special "sources and methods" committee was convened before Powell's presentation weighing the risk of disclosing each piece of information.)

Powell's presentation displayed the substantial array of U.S. intelligence capabilities, including intelligence received from defectors and from in-country agents from 10 foreign intelligence services. The unspoken message of the presentation was that the United States and its allies were already operating within Iraq.

Point/Counterpoint

"I cannot tell you everything that we know, but what I can share with you, when combined with what all of us have learned over the years, is deeply troubling," Secretary of State Colin L. Powell said to the United Nations Security Council. "Iraq has now placed itself in danger of serious consequences. Unless we act we are confronting an even more frightening future. Saddam Hussein and his regime will stop at nothing until something stops him."

Iraq's U.N. ambassador, Mohammed Aldouri, attended the Security Council meeting and accused Powell of fabricating the evidence presented.

Iraq, if it ever had any doubts, knew for sure after Secretary Powell's presentation at the United Nations that we have the technological capability to intercept their cell phone communications and maintain an invisible aerial surveillance presence over their nation.

During the middle of March 2003, the second war against Iraq began, both in the air and on the ground. With a minimum of casualties, Saddam Hussein's regime was toppled by military force. The prolonged house-by-house fighting to capture Baghdad that had been feared did not materialize. The reason: the solid work of U.S. intelligence. Our spies had been in Baghdad long before the war began, contacting religious, military, and governmental leaders, explaining the benefits of nonresistance once the war started.

How did our spies get into Baghdad? Therein lies a tale. Perhaps you recall a news story regarding anti-war Americans who traveled to Iraq to serve as "human shields." Well, at least some of those human shields were CIA agents armed with cell phones, lap-top computers, and an impressive rolodex. Once in Iraq they began what amounted to a telemarketing campaign, calling Iraqi leaders and selling them on the benefits of surrender.

The Least You Need to Know

- On September 11, 2001, the United States' feeling of security was rattled, perhaps forever, by terrorist attacks in New York City and Washington, D.C.

- What is known generically as the "War on Terrorism" actually focuses on one terrorist group, Al Qaeda, which was responsible for the 9/11 attacks.

- Clandestine operations by U.S. forces, in conjunction with allies, inside Iraq were seeking the location of Saddam Hussein during the winter of 2003.

- Some of the United States' national security methods and means were exposed in an effort to convince the world that a second war against Iraq was necessary.

- Because of some clever intelligence work, the war to overthrow Saddam Hussein was short, with a minimum of casualties.

Chapter 8

9/11: How Did It Happen?

In This Chapter

- ◆ Who's to blame?
- ◆ The evil exiled Saudi
- ◆ Global warfare
- ◆ Buffalo cell

As everyone knows, September 11, 2001 is a date that will live in infamy, every bit as much as the day the Japanese bombed Pearl Harbor, or the day President John F. Kennedy was assassinated. It was a day that turned American life upside down.

Americans who thought themselves safe because the mainland of the United States had not been attacked in close to 200 years suddenly realized that they were not safe at all—and they were not apt to feel safe anytime soon.

Finger Pointing

In the days following 9/11, while attention should have been focused on protecting us from future attacks, all too much time was spent trying to find someone in the U.S. intelligence community to blame for the attacks.

Although no clear scapegoat ever emerged, we did learn that there was evidence that such an attack was about to take place. Unfortunately, one agency had one piece of data, and another agency had another piece of data, and a third agency had a third piece of information. Only when the pieces of evidence were put together would the ability to predict 9/11 come into focus.

Security Factoid

The 9/11 terrorists were led by Mohamed Atta, who was the leader of a group of student recruits. He and two of those recruits planned the attacks while based in Hamburg, Germany, and went on to pilot three of the four hijacked planes.

Unfortunately, the members of the U.S. intelligence community have been all-too-frequently slow to share the information they have. Instead of working as a team, the members of the community often behave as competitors for Congressional dollars. With a new and vicious War on Terrorism underway, it is clear that the intelligence community can no longer afford this sort of behavior. It must work together to protect us, for we Americans truly are in danger.

Hindsight Is 20/20

In 1999, the House Armed Services Committee was told by the joint heads of the "U.S. Commission on National Security/Twenty-First Century" that America will become increasingly vulnerable to hostile attack on our homeland, and our military superiority will not necessarily protect us. Regarding technology, the committee said, "We believe that some new technologies, benign as they may be for the most part, could have a dramatic leveling effect, allowing an increasing array of states, and even small disaffected fanatical groups, to inflict enormous damage on unsuspecting civilian populations, including our own."

Also in 1999, Senators Warren Rudman and Gary Hart led an all-star Commission on National Security that warned that a major terrorist attack on the United States was inevitable. Subsequently, in February 2001 they called for the creation of a Department of Homeland Security. What happened to the report? According to former PFIAB Chairman Rudman, "we printed 100,000 copies of the report, and 99,800 were stored in a warehouse until September 11th. On September 12, they were all gone."

On August 6, 2001, a month before the 9/11 attacks, President Bush told DCI George Tenet, "Give me a sense of what Al Qaeda can do inside the U.S." Unfortunately, much of Tenet's response was based on intelligence gathered three or four years earlier. According to Condoleezza Rice, there was just a sentence or two on hijacking. The possibility that a hijacked plane would ever be flown into a building was not addressed. This, despite the fact that a plot to crash a plane into the Eiffel Tower had been foiled in 1994, and that, since that time, there had been additional threats of "kamikaze" attacks.

Author's Corner

McLean: Pay attention to what the leaders of the U.S. intelligence community say. There are times when it really does seem that they have a crystal ball. Back in 1999, the Director of Central Intelligence, George Tenet, peered into his crystal ball and testified before the Senate Armed Services Committee. He said that there was sufficient information to believe another attack by terrorists associated with Osama bin Laden was imminent. Then he threw in that North Korean missiles were a concern as well.

Kissinger/Kean Committee

President George W. Bush, in an attempt to answer all of the unanswered questions, appointed an independent commission to investigate all of the events of 9/11. The commission was designed to find out:

- Why the terrorist attacks were not prevented

- How our response to those attacks could be improved

- How we can better prevent similar attacks from occurring in the future

The commission was originally to be chaired by Henry Kissinger, the 79-year-old diplomat who served as secretary of state under Presidents Richard Nixon and Gerald Ford, and as Nixon's national security adviser. After a brief time, however, Kissinger withdrew from the position because of potential conflicts of interest.

Kissinger was replaced by the former governor of New Jersey, Thomas H. Kean. The commission met for the first time, out of public view, on January 27, 2003. Other subjects the commission was expected to explore were foreign affairs, aviation security, immigration policy, and border patrol.

Osama bin Laden

In 1994, Saudi Arabia stripped Osama bin Laden's citizenship, citing his opposition to the Saudi king and leadership, and expelled him from the country. He, the son of one of Saudi Arabia's wealthiest families, then went to Khartoum, Sudan (where he owns numerous businesses), but under U.S. pressure was expelled in 1996 and relocated to Afghanistan. In Afghanistan, he and his terrorist organization received protection from the predominant Afghani government, known as the Taliban. Bin Laden used his money to finance a campaign against the Saudi rulers and U.S. presence in Saudi Arabia.

Links to Other Attacks

The attacks on the World Trade Center and the Pentagon may have been Al Qaeda's largest attacks on the United States, but they were not the first.

Security Factoid _____

One of the ways the United States and its allies have combated bin Laden is by, to the best of their ability, separating him from his money. The United Nations imposed economic sanctions on the Taliban regime in Afghanistan in 1999 for harboring bin Laden, and many nations, including the United States, have frozen assets belonging to bin Laden and his senior associates.

Point/Counterpoint _____

"Our terrorism is a good accepted terrorism because it's against America, it's for the purpose of defeating oppression so America would stop supporting Israel, who is killing our children."
—Osama bin Laden

Bin Laden has been linked to the following:

- Killings of Western tourists by militant Islamic groups in Egypt

- Bombings in France by Islamic extremist Algerians

- Maintenance of a safehouse in Pakistan for Ramzi Ahmed Yousef, the convicted mastermind of the 1993 World Trade Center bombing

- Sheltering Sheikh Omar Abd Al-Rahman (the Blind Sheikh), who was also convicted in the World Trade Center bombing

He has also been linked to …

- The 1992 bombings of a hotel in Yemen, which killed two Australians, but was supposedly targeted against American soldiers stationed there.

- The 1995 detonation of a car bomb in Riyadh, Saudi Arabia.

- The 1995 truck bomb in Dhahran, Saudi Arabia, that killed 19 U.S. servicemen.

- The 1995 assassination attempt on Egyptian President Hosni Mubarak.

- The October 2000 bombing attack of the USS *Cole* in Yemen.

Attacks on U.S. Embassies

On May 28, 1998, bin Laden announced the establishment of "The International Islamic Front for Holy War Against Jews and Crusaders," an umbrella organization linking Islamic extremists in scores of countries around the world, including Egypt, Bangladesh, and Pakistan. The group issued a religious edict upon its establishment: "The ruling to kill the Americans and their allies, civilians and the military, is an individual duty for every Muslim who can do it in any country in which it is possible to do it …. This is in accordance with the words of Almighty God, and 'fight the pagans all together as they fight you all together,' and 'fight them until there is no more tumult or oppression, and there prevail justice and faith in God.'"

On August 7, 1998, bomb blasts damaged the U.S. embassies in Dar es Salaam, Tanzania, and Nairobi, Kenya. The bombings were investigated by teams of FBI, CIA, and State and USMC antiterrorist professionals, along with British and Israeli experts. Both bombs were delivered by truck. Al-though the bombings are now widely believed to have been the work of Osama bin Laden's Al Qaeda, at the time an obscure organization called the Islamic Army for the Liberation of Holy Places took responsibility for the bombing.

> **Point/Counterpoint**
>
> According to one retired FBI official, before 9/11: "Nobody was looking domestically. We didn't think they had the people to mount an operation here."

U.S. intelligence had received several reports prior to the East African bombings—these out of thousands of reports of possible threats received each month. Three of those reports were:

◆ One that indicated a sudden departure of Osama bin Laden's deputies from hideouts in Afghanistan.

◆ One that warned of action against American installations in retaliation for the Jihad fighters apprehended and extradited by Albania (at U.S. request) to Egypt—which resulted in increased security measures for the U.S. Embassy in Cairo by both U.S. and Egyptian authorities.

◆ One that consisted of a warning passed by the Israelis to the United States in Kenya, but with an Israeli caveat to "take the information with a grain of salt."

President Clinton met with his top security advisors to discuss ways in which the United States could best defend U.S. installations around the world, and how to take a more offensive strategy against terrorism.

Aside from political and policy measures, the challenges for the United States were to improve intelligence coordination with other nations, to further enhance American counterterrorist intelligence operations (both through technology and human resources), and to focus and refine real-time analysis.

Coded Video Tapes?

When Osama bin Laden made videotaped messages for the world and publicized them over the Arab broadcasting network Al Jazeera, U.S. media never put out these tapes immediately—although it certainly has the technological capability to do so. That's because the tapes must be screened carefully before being broadcast in the United States, in case they contain coded messages for sleeper cells of terrorists inside the United States.

Author's Corner

McLean: Interesting observations regarding the videotapes of Al Qaeda leader Osama bin Laden that were broadcast over the Al Jazeera network during 2002: "In three videos released, watch Osama's hands. Each video is different. The watch switches from left wrist to right wrist and back, and there are, or are not, rings on the finger, and the finger positions are markedly different. This is signaling."

To give you an idea of just how well U.S. intelligence technology has tapped into terrorist communications, Secretary of State Colin Powell had a transcript of an audio tape of Osama bin Laden (or someone pretending to be bin Laden) before that tape was even broadcast by the Arab network Al Jazeera on February 11, 2003.

The Afghanistan War

Two days after the 9/11 attacks President Bush received a briefing from his chief of staff. The CIA had just sent over a warning from a foreign intelligence service that Pakistani jihadists—Muslim extremists—were planning an attack on the White House.

The director of the Secret Service advised that the president be evacuated, but President Bush refused to leave. The nonessential employees at the White House were allowed to go home but government activity continued. It was agreed that Vice President Cheney should not be in the White House, and this was when Dick Cheney was first moved to his now famous "undisclosed location."

The CIA briefing had been given to the president that morning by DCI George Tenet. It took place in the White House Situation Room, one floor below the chief of staff's office in the southwest corner of the West Wing. At that meeting Tenet mapped out what was to become the U.S.'s War on Terrorism.

Security Factoid

The current DCI, George Tenet, was born in New York City in 1953. Tenet received a Bachelor's degree in 1976 from the School of Foreign Service at Georgetown University and a Master's degree from the School of International Affairs at Columbia University in 1978. He began government work at age 29, working on the staff of Pennsylvania senator John Heinz. In 1985, Tenet began work on the staff of the Senate Intelligence Committee, and, in 1989 he became that committee's staff director. Tenet was only 44 years old when he was appointed DCI, which makes him the youngest ever. It has been said that he quietly let the CIA know that there would be a return to CIA tradition when, on his first day on the job, he moved the portrait of Richard Helms from the hallways and put it up in his private office. When President George W. Bush took office, Tenet was the only survivor from the Clinton administration to remain on the president's national security team.

Tenet and the Paramilitary Operations

Tenet told the president on the morning of September 13, 2001 that there must be a combined usage of the CIA's *paramilitary operations*, covert action, and technology. And they had to maximize their usage of Afghanistan forces already in place who were battling the Taliban.

There were about 20,000 soldiers in what was being called the Northern Alliance. That alliance was made up of about 25 factions, out of which five were powerful enough to have a say in things. With CIA money and training, it was hoped that these troops could be turned into a strong enough army that most of the ground fighting could be done without U.S. personnel. (This was not entirely successful as the Northern Alliance remained a hesitant lot.)

Security Speak

Paramilitary operations are operations undertaken by military forces separate from the regular armed forces of a nation. Often used in an effort to hide source of control.

George Tenet has now been DCI under two presidents. He submitted his reports to President Clinton in writing and the two men rarely spoke. In contrast, he meets in person with President Bush every morning, and the two have become close allies in the War on Terrorism.

The task of unifying the Northern Alliance figured to be a difficult one right off the bat. Two days before the 9/11 attacks, the Northern Alliance's most charismatic leader, Ahmed Shah Massoud, was assassinated by two suicide bombers who had been posing as journalists.

The United States, as it turned out, was already giving some aid to the Northern Alliance in their ongoing fight against the Taliban for control of Afghanistan. For four years CIA paramilitary teams had been meeting in secret with the leaders of the Northern Alliance. But that aid was going to have to be greatly increased now that the United States was eager to have the Taliban vanquished, along with Al Qaeda, and especially Osama bin Laden.

Each warlord of each faction would be accompanied by a CIA team, Tenet told the president. These men would be the United States' "eyes on the ground" and help coordinate attacks.

Black Says "We'll rout 'em out!"

When Tenet's briefing of the president was through, President Bush was briefed by Cofer Black, head of the CIA's counterterrorism center. Black told the president the benefits of covert action. The more U.S. personnel on the ground in Afghanistan, the better.

Cofer Black is famous among CIA employees, a hero. It was the hulking Cofer who captured one of the world's most deadly terrorists, Carlos the Jackal. Carlos is now serving a life sentence in France. He was one of the most famous of early terrorists. "You give us the mission," Black said to the president, "and we can get 'em! We'll rout 'em out." The president gave Black the nod to make it so, and the war had begun.

On September 15, Tenet again met with Bush, this time at Camp David. The briefing concerned Osama bin Laden. Bush wanted to know all there was to know about the world's most dangerous terrorist and Tenet had four years' worth of intelligence to report. The briefing lasted for a half hour: Tenet again outlined the need for a global war on terrorism focusing initially on Al Qaeda, Osama bin Laden, and the Taliban government in Afghanistan.

Attack Matrix

Tenet's global "Attack Matrix" involved combating terrorism through covert action in 80 different countries. These actions sometimes involved no more than the dissemination of propaganda, but in other countries, plans called for preliminary CIA strikes in preparation for larger military actions. The ground war in Afghanistan, it was agreed, would begin with six or so CIA paramilitary teams on the ground.

A full-scale attack on the finances of organized terrorism was also outlined in Tenet's plan. He suggested clandestine computer surveillance and electronic eavesdropping to locate the assets of Al Qaeda and other terrorist groups.

This included clamping down on the assets of charitable groups who had been supporting Al Qaeda. Bush pretty much gave the CIA a standing order to destroy Al Qaeda wherever they encountered it, anywhere in the world. The CIA was given an unprecedented amount of power, including permission to use deadly force.

So CIA officers would now be full-fledged soldiers in the War on Terrorism. This fact became all too clear when the first American fatality in Afghanistan was a CIA man. Tenet brought with him a draft of the presidential intelligence finding that Bush would have to sign to give Tenet formal permission to carry out the plan. Also proposed was that the CIA make maximum use of cooperative foreign intelligence services. Again, as had been true in the past, this would put the CIA in a working relationship with people of questionable character, including past human rights violators.

Tenet told the president that the CIA had somewhat of a head start in Afghanistan because it had already been doing a great deal of work in the area and already had officers in place. Tenet said that, because the Predator robot surveillance plane was equipped with Hellfire missiles, they not only could be used to find Osama bin Laden but to kill him as well.

The DCI told the president that cooperation from the former states of the Soviet Union—Tajikistan and Turkmenistan—as well as Pakistan, would be necessary to restrict the travel of fleeing terrorists. Tenet then described in detail how money, weapons, and advisors could be used to coagulate the noncohesive "Northern Alliance" into a successful fighting army.

Finding Targets

While the great bulk of news coverage regarding the war against terrorism featured the aerial attack of selected sites in Afghanistan, the greatest achievement of the war was the precise selection of those sites.

Given the circumstances, finding adequate targets was much like finding a needle in a haystack. Afghanistan is a large country and very easy to hide in. In order to wage an air campaign that would be effective, it was essential that the U.S. pilots know where to drop the bombs and for the sailors to know where to point the missiles.

Determining targets for the hundreds of sorties flown in Afghanistan was the job of the CIA, working behind the scenes and in the shadows, with the effort being run from CIA headquarters in Langley, Virginia.

Obviously, the CIA alone on the ground in Afghanistan was not going to gather the kind of intelligence that brought about the downfall of the Taliban in that government.

Author's Corner

McLean: A 1999 CIA plan to train and equip a secret Pakistani unit to snatch Osama Bin Laden from his Afghanistan hideout never got off the ground because of foot-dragging by Pakistan, probably on purpose.

In order to accomplish this, CIA operatives in Afghanistan forged relationships with anti-Taliban leaders, as well as with Pakistani, Russian, and other intelligence operatives.

These relationships between the CIA men and others in the region were not only important because of the extremely high quality of the intelligence that was being gathered, but because it created the sort of war in which it has been possible to keep U.S. combat fatalities, as of January 2003, to remain minimal.

And, of course, the fewer terrorists there are over there, the fewer that can come over here and terrorize our homeland.

Prisoners to Guantanamo

During the first weeks of the War on Terrorism in Afghanistan, 5,000–6,000 Taliban troops and Al Qaeda fighters were captured or surrendered. Those prisoners were taken to Guantanamo, Cuba, and interrogated as part of an intelligence-gathering program by U.S. Special Forces and CIA officers.

U.S. forces also seized and examined Al Qaeda documents, computer hard drives, videotapes, and telephone books. That material produced names and phone numbers of Al Qaeda members in other countries and led to additional arrests.

Problems in Indonesia: The Bali Explosion

Al Qaeda's deadliest attack after 9/11 came on October 12, 2002 when a man named Ali Imron drove a van packed with explosives beside a nightclub in Bali. When the explosives ignited, most of the nightclub blew up and 192 people, many of them Australian tourists, were killed. Seven Americans were killed in the Bali bombing.

Imron and 16 others were arrested by Indonesian police. Those arrested are members of Jemaah Islamiyah, an extremist Islamic group that is believed to be linked to Al Qaeda. The Indonesian terrorist Ali Imron confessed to assembling the bombs that were used. "Our target is America and its allies," he said in his confession.

The same group carried out a series of church bombings across Indonesia in 2000, done as revenge for the killings of Muslims by Christians during communal conflicts in the Maluku Islands and Central Sulawesi in 1999 and 2000. Jemaah Islamiyah began with a goal of creating an Islamic state, and then grew into a terrorist organization.

The terrorist arm of Jemaah Islamiyah operates through cells and has an ad hoc structure. Below two tiers of leaders are young men who carry out the attacks, driving the cars and delivering the bombs. They are often not selected until shortly before the attack.

> **Security Factoid**
>
> Now that the United States and its interests are the target of terrorist attacks, our sources of energy have been under attack as well. In recent years, Exxon Mobil was forced away from the world's largest natural gas fields in Indonesia because of threats of violence from local nationalist extremists.
>
> In Aceh, Northern Sumatra, Exxon Mobil vehicles were hijacked 50 times and Exxon aircraft were fired upon as they tried to land. The Indonesian government responded to this loss of revenue by sending in troops and ordering an offensive against the local Muslim insurgents.

Problems in the Philippines

Most of the unrest in the Philippines is domestic in nature and has primarily to do with various long-standing—and probably legitimate—economic and political grievances against dominant elites and the national government, either on the part of a disenfranchised and impoverished rural peasantry (in the case of the NPA, or New Peoples Army), or the part of various Muslim peoples of the Southern Philippines (in the case of the MNLF, or the Moro National Liberation Front, and cognate groups).

Both sets of grievances will require political, not military, solutions, if the unrest is to subside. This excludes the much-in-the-news Abu Sayyef, who have been aptly described as "social bandits" and who are indeed criminals in need of capture.

Do the Philippines "harbor" terrorists of the Al Qaeda sort? Surely they do, but in much the same fashion that, say, Spain and (alas) even the United States do—leastwise I'd put the Philippines closer to those two countries than, say, to Afghanistan before or to Pakistan now.

That is, there are terrorists living in the Philippines, just as surely as there are some (hopefully, few) living in the United States, but for the very great majority of Filipinos—as for the very great majority of Americans—these are individuals not seen as part of, or somehow springing from, the social fabric. They are seen rather as individuals surely foreign in origin and motive. Filipinos have the same gamut of (sometimes-conflicting) opinions and emotions that Americans have about terrorism, and about their own national security.

Ounce of Prevention

In 2002, 1,300 U.S. troops were sent to the Philippines because of the terrorist problem there, but they were limited to an advisory role.

Even though the problem of extremist Muslims in the Philippines was not intrinsic to their government, the problem was still severe enough to necessitate the sending of 1,700 more American troops, in addition to the 1,300 that had been sent in 2002, during the last days of February 2003. The troops were assigned to "disrupt and destroy" members of the extremist group Abu Sayyaf in the southern part of the country.

Cells in the United States/Canada

One of the toughest jobs facing federal, state, and local law enforcement today is routing out Al Qaeda terror cells that may already be in place in the United States and Canada.

The Buffalo Six

On September 13, 2002, just two days after the first anniversary of the 9/11 attacks, five Yemeni American residents of Lackawanna, New York, were arrested, suspected of operating an Al Qaeda terror cell. Two days later, a sixth suspect was arrested in the gulf Emirate of Bahrain, and brought to Buffalo, where he was arraigned in federal court.

During the late spring and early summer of 2001, the Lackawaana Six allegedly traveled to Pakistan to attend religious training. They are alleged to have traveled to Kandahar, Afghanistan, and attended a nearby Al-Farooq Training Camp. Bin Laden reportedly visited the camp and gave a speech to attendees there. During June 2001, the U.S. government received information that first raised suspicions regarding the defendants. During the spring of 2002 Lackawanna Mayor John Kuryak was informed of an FBI investigation of the Lackawanna residents, and that September the arrests were made.

According to prosecutors, the six men were awaiting orders from Al Qaeda to carry out a terrorist attack in the United States. No evidence that an attack was imminent was found, however. While attending the camp in Afghanistan, the men were taught to use numerous weapons, including M-16s, rocket grenades, and rocket-propelled grenade launchers. They also received training in explosives and tactics.

A standard law enforcement technique to get arrests and secure convictions is to make a deal with one of the accused to tell his story, or in other words, squeal on the

others. In the case of the Buffalo Al
Qaeda cell, the songbird turned out to be
26-year-old Faysal Galab. Following a
long series of negotiations with prosecutors during the first days of 2003, Galab
pleaded guilty to supporting Al Qaeda by
attending one of its training camps in
Afghanistan. He then testified against his five
codefendants in exchange for a lesser sentence.

Security Factoid

An antiterrorist law was passed
by Congress in 1996 in the
aftermath of the Oklahoma City
bombing, calling for a 10-year
sentence for anyone convicted
of providing funding, weapons,
or safe haven to terrorists.

According to Galab's lawyer Joseph LaTona, "[Galab] has not admitted to being a
member of Al Qaeda. He has not admitted planning or preparing or agreeing to
engage in any acts of terrorism whatsoever."

Leader Killed in Yemen

The alleged leader of the Lackawanna sleeper cell was a Yemeni American named
Kamal Derwish. Derwish is believed to have been killed on November 3, 2002, during a CIA air strike in Yemen. The air strike was carried out by the CIA's Predator spy
plane built by General Atomics Aeronautical Systems of San Diego. The drone plane
located six members of Al Qaeda in a car and fired a Hellfire missile, killing all of the
terrorists in the car.

Reports say that one of the terrorists gave away their position by using his cell phone,
and that it was the signal from the phone that allowed the Hellfire missile to home in
on the car. (It should be noted that U.S. forces in both Afghanistan and in Iraq, if
necessary, will be forbidden from using cell phones so that enemy missiles will not be
able to home in on their signal.)

Sources say that Al Qaeda members have used their cell phones more since
learning—through harmful leaks in the U.S. press—that U.S. antiterrorist forces
have the capability of reading their e-mail. By the winter of 2003 Al Qaeda operatives
were using disposable cell phones and special "one-time-only" e-mail accounts.

Reports out of Yemen a few weeks after the Hellfire attack said that one terrorist got
out of the car and ran away moments before the missile struck. This was the first
American military strike against Al Qaeda outside of Afghanistan since the 9/11
attacks.

The United States scored a major victory in the War on Terrorism on March 1, 2003
when Pakistani authorities, acting on a tip from neighbors, captured Al Qaeda king-
pin Khalid Shaikh Mohammed, who was suspected of planning the 9/11 attacks. He

was arrested in Rawalpindi, the old city adjacent to the modern capital of Islamabad, in the middle of the night. The world got to see a photo of him disheveled, sleepy and angry, being led to his interrogators in a white tee-shirt.

The Yemeni news agency SABA said the dead also included Ali Qaed Sinan al-Harithi, also known as Abu Ali. Harithi was a chief operative of Al Qaeda in Yemen. He was an associate of Osama bin Laden's since the early 1990s in Sudan. He and another operative still at large, Mohammed Hamdi al-Ahdal, are believed to have played the key on-the-ground role in the October 2000 bombing of the USS *Cole*.

The dead terrorists were also believed responsible for the strike by an explosive-laden boat on a French tanker off Yemen's coast that killed one sailor and spilled 90,000 barrels of crude oil into the Arabian Sea.

> **Ounce of Prevention**
>
> As the capture of Khalid Shaikh Mohammed during the winter of 2003 demonstrated, the War on Terrorism continued long after military action in Afghanistan stopped topping the daily news broadcasts. In the Arabian Sea, the coalition of the United States and eight allies continued to intercept hundreds of vessels in the search for terrorists, with four members of Al Qaeda being captured.

Remember the Technology

Wars are often best remembered for the new technology they introduce. World War II will forever be remembered because of the atomic bomb. The 1991 Persian Gulf War will best be remembered for the introduction of smart bombs. In that same vein, the war in Afghanistan will be remembered as the war in which integrated military ISR (Intelligence, Surveillance, and Reconnaissance) and smart precision weapons came of age.

Pilotless Predator drones, satellites, reconnaissance and surveillance planes, and human ground spotters were networked together, enabling forward air controllers on the ground or distant commanders to direct warplanes to targets with stunning speed and accuracy. One result has been a relentlessly accurate bombardment, conducted day and night, under clear and cloudy skies alike. Taliban and Al Qaeda prisoners have confirmed that the precise bombing, from planes that they often could neither hear or see, broke the will of their troops.

The Least You Need to Know

- The United States would have had a better chance of preventing the terrorist acts of 9/11 if there had been a better system of information sharing between the members of the U.S. intelligence community.

- The Director of Central Intelligence's global "Attack Matrix"—devised not long after the 9/11 attacks—involved combating terrorism through covert action in 80 different countries.

- A terrorist cell in suburban Buffalo, New York, was busted up by U.S. law enforcement in 2002.

- Terrorists have adapted to U.S. capabilities to listen in to cell phone and e-mail communications.

Chapter 9

Thwarted Attacks

In This Chapter

- ◆ Terrorists rounded up
- ◆ The fuse that wouldn't light
- ◆ List of terror
- ◆ Major arrests

Don't think that 9/11 "woke up" U.S. intelligence to the threat presented by Osama bin Laden and his Al Qaeda network. A spectacular three-country attack in January 2000 that would have included multiple bombings in Jordan and the United States and the sinking of a U.S. destroyer in Yemen was thwarted by good intelligence and subsequent arrests.

According to the director of the Defense Intelligence Agency, Vice Admiral Lowell E. Jacoby, more than 100 terrorist attacks planned against the United States and its allies have been thwarted since September 11, 2001, in part based on information gained from the continuing interrogation of enemy combatants and other captives ensnared in the War on Terrorism.

Al Qaeda Operatives Detained

On January 22, 2003, Italian police arrested five men from Morocco with ties to Al Qaeda in a farmhouse 30 miles west of Venice. The terrorists were in possession of more than two pounds of deadly C-4 explosives and maps of both London and NATO bases in Italy. The arrests were the result of a joint effort by Italian police and British intelligence officers from MI5.

Security Factoid

One of the most disturbing and gruesome stories of 2002 was the murder and videotaped beheading of *Wall Street Journal* reporter Daniel Pearl in Pakistan. A year later the story became even more disturbing when it was discovered that the man who kidnapped Pearl, Khalid Shaikh Mohammed, a Kuwaiti of Pakistani descent, was also a key organizer of the 9/11 attacks.

It was becoming evident that not only had Al Qaeda dug in all around the world, but that the civilized world was united in their attempt to root them out.

More than 3,000 Al Qaeda operatives and associates have been detained in dozens of countries since 9/11. U.S. embassies appear to have been a particular focus of terrorist targeting. The plots were in various stages of development when disrupted.

Other threats have been aimed at airports and the aviation industry. Some attacks were reportedly deterred by newly installed protective measures. The most valuable information has come from senior Al Qaeda operatives in custody, particularly Abu Zubeida, a top lieutenant captured in Pakistan in 2002.

Shoe Bomber

The most famous of the thwarted terrorist plots after 9/11 is the case of the "Shoe Bomber." The Shoe Bomber was 29-year-old Richard C. Reid, a disciple of Osama bin Laden who, using explosives in his ankle-high hiking boots, attempted to blow up an airliner over the Atlantic Ocean with 197 passengers and crew members aboard on December 22, 2001.

The flight was on its way from Paris to Miami. Reid tried furiously to light a match to his shoes but he was unable to ignite the fuse. Authorities have speculated Reid's shoes may have been too moist from sweat. Three flight attendants and several passengers struggled with and immobilized Reid after they smelled sulfur from the matches he was using.

They used his seat belt and their own belts to strap him to his seat. Two doctors who were passengers on the plane injected him with sedatives, and the flight was then diverted to Boston.

Flight attendant Hermis Moutardier told authorities Reid put a lit match in his mouth when she confronted him. Moutardier told the captain and returned to see Reid with a match held to the tongue of his sneaker and then noticed a wire protruding from his right shoe.

She said she tried to grab the shoe, but Reid pushed her to the floor and she screamed for help. Another flight attendant, Cristina Jones, told authorities she saw Reid hunched over in his seat, trying to light something.

 **Point/Counterpoint**

"I believe that Richard Reid was on a mission of evil, a mission of destruction and a mission of murder. Richard Reid put all of us on this flight under great stress and trauma."
—Flight attendant Carole Nelson.

She said Reid bit her hand when she tried to stop him. Attendant Carole Nelson said that many passengers jumped up from their seats and headed for Reid when they saw him struggling with flight attendants.

A Terrorist Conspiracy

Officials knew immediately that the Shoe Bomber was not a lone nut, but part of a terrorist conspiracy. The kind of the explosive charge, its preparation, and the way it was concealed in Reid's shoes required the skills of professionals, not the work of an amateur.

Reid passed through the United Kingdom recruiting centers and mosques, including the mainstream Brixton mosque. With a history of petty crime, he was influenced by the Islamic extremist doctrines of Islamist ideologue Abu Qutada.

Reid traveled to Pakistan and Afghanistan, where he went through a process of recruitment, indoctrination, and training. He swore allegiance to bin Laden and may have had some connections to Zacarias Moussaoui, one of the suspects in the 9/11 attacks.

"I'm a follower of Osama bin Laden"

In October 2002, Reid surprised prosecutors by pleading guilty to the following eight charges:

- Attempted use of a weapon of mass destruction
- Attempted homicide
- Placing an explosive device on an aircraft
- Attempted murder

- Two counts of interference with flight crew and attendants

- Attempted destruction of an aircraft

- Using a destructive device during a crime of violence

> **Security Factoid**
>
> CIA and MI6 investigators have been examining files, travel tickets, and financial transactions to determine if Richard Reid is one and the same as Al Qaeda agent Abdul Rauff, whose name was found on a computer in Afghanistan. Both Reid and Rauff flew to Holland, Israel, Egypt, Turkey, and Pakistan. Both men, it is reported, obtained their British passport from the consulate in Amsterdam.

At that time, U.S. District Judge William Young asked Reid, "Did you intend to blow that plane up and kill the people on that plane and yourself?"

Reid replied, "Yeah" and smirked. "I'm a follower of Osama bin Laden. I'm an enemy of your country and I don't care. Your government has sponsored the torture of Muslims in Iraq, and Turkey, and Jordan and Syria with their money and weapons."

Almost a year after the Shoe Bomber's attack was foiled, in November 2002 French police arrested eight Islamic militants and charged them with being Reid's coconspirators. Six were Pakistanis and one was an imam in a mosque north of Paris.

Life Sentence

On January 30, 2003, Judge Young sentenced Reid to life in prison. At the sentencing, Reid told the judge, "I am at war with your country. I further admit my allegiance to Sheik Osama bin Laden, to Islam, and to the religion of Allah. You're not going to stand me down. You'll go down. You will be judged by Allah. Your flag will come down and so will your country."

This statement angered Judge Young who replied, "You are not an enemy combatant. You are a terrorist. You are not a soldier in any army. You are a terrorist. To call you a soldier gives you far too much stature. You are a terrorist, and we do not negotiate with terrorists. We hunt them down one by one and bring them to justice. We have been through the fire before. You are a species of criminal guilty of multiple attempted murders."

The judge continued, "It seems to me that you hate the only thing that to us is most precious. You hate our individual freedoms, our individual freedom to come and go as we choose and to believe—or not to believe—as we individually choose. We are not afraid. We are Americans. You see that flag, Mr. Reid? That's the flag of the United States of America. That flag will fly there long after this is forgotten."

Assassination Attempt

Many of the thwarted Al Qaeda plots can be credited to the effectiveness of foreign intelligence and law enforcement. For example, in January 2003 Italian police arrested 28 Pakistani members of Al Qaeda, between the ages of 20 and 48, who are believed to have been plotting the assassination of Admiral Sir Michael Boyce, Britain's most senior military man, who had been planning a visit to Naples in March 2003 to visit NATO installations.

The terrorists were arrested in a Naples apartment. Also found were 28 ounces of explosives, 230 feet of fuses, and electronic detonators. Photos of Boyce were found along with maps that had potential targets marked on them. The marked locations included the headquarters of NATO's southern European command on the outskirts of Naples, the U.S. Consulate in that city, and a U.S. Navy air base at nearby Capodichino.

> ### Author's Corner
>
> McLean: In the world terrorism battle, America has had allies dating back some years in what many may think unlikely places … like Jordan. The Jordanian intelligence agency, the Mukhabarat, has recently grown in stature as the CIA's partner in the fight against terrorism. In December 2002, Jordan arrested 13 people associated with Osama bin Laden, in connection with a plot to attack Christian and American targets in Jordan. Last year the Mukhabarat is said to have alerted the CIA to at least three plots by Bosnia-based Islamic terrorists to attack U.S. targets in Europe.

The JFK Airport Plot Revealed

In January 2003, it was revealed that a terrorist group known as Algerian Tahir bin Ammar al-Yusifi was plotting to infiltrate the United States through Ontario, Canada, and—using Albany, New York, as their launching pad—blow up a terminal at JFK Airport in New York City, a nearby gas station, and a city clerk's office.

The plan involved parking three explosives-packed cars, possibly in underground parking areas. U.S. Customs uncovered the plot, and it was foiled with the help of the FBI and the New York Police Department. Each car would hold 100 kilograms of explosive. The group was to meet at a grocery store before the attacks, and then return to Albany after the attacks were complete.

Catalonia Arrests

In January 2003, Spanish police arrested 16 militants with suspected ties to Al Qaeda and the Algerian Salafist group. Confiscated were electronic material and containers of unidentified chemicals. The 16 arrests were made during 12 separate raids in the eastern provinces of Catalonia.

According to the Spanish ministry, the suspects "had explosives, used chemical products and maintained connections to terrorist cells established in the United Kingdom and France." Two of the 9/11 hijackers, Mohamed Atta and Marwan al-Shehhi, met with other Al Qaeda conspirators in the Catalonia area two months before the attacks, according to American and Spanish authorities.

Terror Bigwig Busted in Indonesia

In February 2003, Indonesian police arrested one of the most hunted terrorist suspects in Southeast Asia. Mas Selamat bin Kastari was accused of involvement in plots to attack U.S. facilities in the region.

Kastari was arrested on the Indonesian island of Bintang, just off Singapore. He was the leader of the Singaporean cell of Jemaah Islamiyah, a radical Islamic group based in Indonesia.

He'd been on the run since December 2001, after his plot to blow up the American Embassy in Singapore was uncovered and more than a dozen of his cell members were arrested. He had threatened to retaliate by hijacking an American jet and crashing it into Singapore's airport.

The Capture of Khalid

Khalid Shaikh Mohammed was a key planner of the 9/11 attacks, as well as many other terrorist attacks. The evil genius was captured in Pakistan in February 2003 by U.S. and Pakistani agents. Captured along with the man were his computer and files.

One senior American intelligence officer said, "Other than (Osama) bin Laden, there is practically no one we would have liked better to have in custody. It's pretty damn significant."

Khalid's capture apparently came in the nick of time, as there were Al Qaeda plans in the works to attack U.S. suspension bridges and gas stations. The bridges were to be felled by snipping their support wires, while the gas stations were to be destroyed by crashing into them with hijacked fuel trucks, driven by suicide terrorists.

On March 15, 2003, Al Qaeda's financial supply was disrupted by the arrest of Al Qaeda financier Yasser Al Jazeeri in Pakistan by Pakistani police with the help of the FBI. Follow the money, as they say ….

Next stop: Osama?

Key Arrests Inside the United States

Here is a list of some of the key terrorist arrests inside the United States since 9/11:

- ♦ In August 2001, the so-called "twentieth hijacker"—Zacarias Moussaoui—involved in the planning of the 9/11 attacks is arrested in Eagon, Minnesota.

- ♦ In September 2001, four members of a sleeper operational combat cell for militant Islamic movement allied with Al Qaeda are arrested in Detroit and Dearborn, Michigan.

- ♦ In December 2001, in Peoria, Illinois, Ali Saleh Kahlah al-Marri is arrested. He has ties to Mustafa Ahmed al-Hawsawi, one of the 9/11 organizers based in the United Arab Emirates.

- ♦ In December 2001, in Ann Arbor, Michigan, Rabih Haddad is arrested, accused of funneling money to terrorists through the Global Relief Foundation.

- ♦ In April 2002, Enaam Arnout is arrested in Justice, Illinois, and accused of funneling money to Al Qaeda and other terrorist organizations.

- ♦ In April 2002, in New York City, three associates of Sheikh Omar Abdel Rahman are arrested. Abdel Rahman is serving a life sentence for plotting to blow up New York landmarks.

- ♦ In May 2002, Jose Padilla is arrested in Chicago, Illinois, for plotting to release a "dirty bomb" in the United States.

- ♦ In September 2002, six men are arrested in Lackawanna, New York, just outside Buffalo, and accused of providing material support to Al Qaeda.

- ♦ In October 2002, six people are arrested in Portland, Oregon, and Detroit, Michigan, and are accused of forming an Al Qaeda terrorist cell.

- ♦ And in December 2002, six people are arrested in Seattle, Washington; Phoenix, Arizona; and Roanoke, Virginia, and accused of sending $12 million in cash to Iraq.

Guide to Other Terrorist Groups

Here's a list of the major known terrorist groups in the world, and a little about each of them. Be aware that many of these groups overlap, and some go by various names. Source: Warzone Magazine.

Abu Nidal Organization (ANO)—Militant Palestinian group split from the PLO in 1974. Has carried out terrorist acts in twenty countries—including the United States, United Kingdom, and Israel—claiming 900 lives.

Abu Sayyaf Group (ASG)—Islamic group fighting for an Islamic state on the island of Mindanao in the Philippines.

Algerian Tahir bin Ammar al-Yusifi—Group responsible for plotting to blow up a terminal at JFK Airport in New York City, as well as other targets, during the winter of 2003.

Armed Islamic Group (GIA)—Islamic extremist group fighting to replace the current regime in Algeria with an Islamic state.

Aum Shinrikyo (Aum)—Japanese religious sect. Carried out Sarin gas attacks in the city of Matsumoto, Japan in 1994.

Security Factoid

The State Department maintains an updated list of terrorist organizations and has details about them. It is a useful list for all interested in terrorism to visit periodically for the latest information.

Euzkadi Ta Askatasuna (ETA)—Basque group fighting Spain for an independent Basque state.

Democratic Front for the Liberation of Palestine—Hawatmeh Faction (DFLP)-Marxist-Leninist group supporting the birth of a Palestinian state through revolt of the masses.

HAMAS (Islamic Resistance Movement)—Outgrowth of the Muslim Brotherhood. Terrorist group believes in establishing a Palestinian state through violent means. Known for its suicide bombers.

Harakat ul-Ansar (HUA)—Islamic group based in Pakistan and operating in Kashmir against Indian troops.

Hezbollah (Party of God)—Group of Lebanese Shi'ite Muslims fighting Israel since the 1982 Lebanon War.

Gama'a al-Islamiyya (Islamic Group, IG)—Militant Islamic group seeking Islamic rule in Egypt by force. Leader of this group arrested for 1993 World Trade Center bombing.

Islamic Jihad—Group headed by Ayman Zawaheri, who used to reside in Khartoum, but was pressured to leave in 1996. He moved to Afghanistan, where he was linked to Osama bin Laden.

Japanese Red Army (JRA)—International terrorist group dedicated to the overthrow of the Japanese government and world revolution. The leader lives in Lebanon and supports militant Islamic causes.

Jemaah Islamiyah—An extremist Islamic group that is believed to be linked to Al Qaeda, responsible for the bombing of a nightclub in Bali in 2002 that killed 192 people.

al-Jihad-Militan—Islamic group operating in Egypt against the Egyptian government, as well as Christian, Israeli, and Western targets on Egyptian soil.

Kach—Radical Israeli group seeks overthrow of Israeli government and restoration of the biblical state of Israel.

Kahane Chai—Offshoot of Kach (see above).

Khmer Rouge—Radical Cambodian political group. Their attempt to purify the "Khmer race" resulted in millions dead.

Kurdistan Workers' Party (PKK)—Communist group of Turkish Kurds seeking an independent Kurd state in southeastern Turkey.

Liberation Tigers of Tamil Eelam (LTTE)—Revolutionaries in Sri Lanka.

Manuel Rodriguez Patriotic Front Dissidents (FPMR/D)—Armed wing of the Chilean Communist Party has attacked U.S. businesses in Chile, mostly fast food restaurants.

Mujahedin-e Khalq Organization (MEK, MKO)—Radical Iranian revolutionaries based in Iraq.

National Liberation Army (ELN)—Marxist guerrilla group operating out of Colombia. They kidnap foreign businessmen for ransom.

Palestine Islamic Jihad—Shaqaqi Faction (PIJ)—Militant Palestinians originally based in the Gaza Strip, now operating throughout the Middle East.

Palestine Liberation Front—Abu Abbas Faction (PLF)—Conducts attacks against Israel. Attacked cruise ship *Achille Lauro* in 1985, murdering U.S. citizen Leon Klinghoffer.

Popular Front for the Liberation of Palestine (PFLP)—Group based in Syria, Lebanon, and Israel. They attack Israeli and moderate Arab targets.

Popular Front for the Liberation of Palestine—General Command (PFLP-GC)—
Based in Syria, and active since 1968. Believes in the violent destruction of Israel.

Revolutionary Armed Forces of Colombia (FARC)—Military wing of the
Colombian Communist Party, which has since 1964 committed terrorist acts against
Colombian targets.

Revolutionary Organization 17 November (17 November)—Based in Greece,
named after the 1973 student uprising in Athens. Supports radical causes in Greece
through assassinations and bombings.

Revolutionary People's Liberation Party/Front (DHKP/C)—Offshoot of the
Turkish People's Liberation Party/Front. This radical anti-United States group
attacks Turkish military targets (as well as U.S. targets during the Gulf War).

Revolutionary People's Struggle (ELA)—Greek leftist group. Bombs Greek government and economic targets.

Shining Path (Sendero Luminoso, SL)—Maoist group in Peru. Conducts bombings and assassinations. Has claimed 30,000 lives in Peru.

Tablik Ja'maat—Based in Zimbabwe, this group is suspected of being a "conduit of
communication" between Al Qaeda and Iraq.

Tupac Amaru Revolutionary Movement (MRTA)—Radical Peruvian group seeking to rid Peru of imperialism through kidnapping, assassinations, and commando-
style military operations.

Remember that organizations change their names and shapes, and members move
between groups and organizations. It is very much like the American Far Right and
Far Left. Lots of groups, same goals, and they affiliate with each other when it suits
them.

The Least You Need to Know

- Many terrorist plots since 9/11 have been thwarted by intelligence-gathering
  services and law enforcement organizations throughout the world.

- Many of the thwarted Al Qaeda plots can be credited to the effectiveness of foreign intelligence and law enforcement.

- The "Shoe Bomber" attempted to blow up a commercial airliner over the
  Atlantic Ocean but was stopped by vigilant flight attendants and passengers.

- Al Qaeda is only one of many terrorist organizations around the globe that are a
  threat to the Free World.

Part 2

National Security Today

Many people of diverse abilities interact in this curious intelligence business. There is a natural and healthy tension between the multitude of disciplines as they interact to provide our government with the information it needs to succeed. There are more than 20 serious intelligence functions. Nearly every cabinet department has its own intelligence service. Each department approaches intelligence from the perspective of its own needs. Coordination of these efforts can be a daunting task as each struggles to provide for perceived needs. In this section, we will look at the components of today's national security envelope, starting with the National Security Agency.

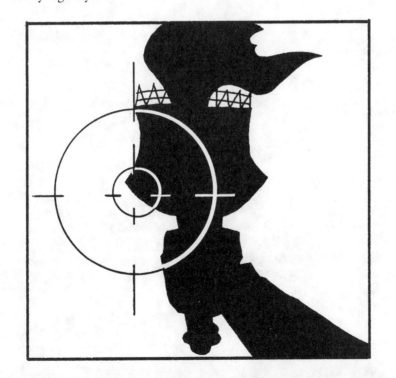

Chapter 10

The National Security Agency Today

In This Chapter

- ◆ No Such Agency (NSA)
- ◆ Codes, codes, codes
- ◆ Learning the latest
- ◆ Team players

According to Executive Order 12333 of December 4, 1981, the resources of NSA are organized for the accomplishment of two national missions:

> "The Information Assurance mission provides the solutions, products and services, and conducts defensive information operations, to achieve information assurance for information infrastructures critical to U.S. national security interests."

> "The foreign signals intelligence or SIGINT mission allows for an effective, unified organization and control of all the foreign signals collection and processing activities of the United States. NSA is authorized to produce SIGINT in accordance with objectives,

requirements and priorities established by the Director of Central Intelligence with the advice of the National Foreign Intelligence Board."

The NSA is the United States' most secret organization, and the subject of this chapter.

Security Speak

Cryptologic means having to do with enciphering and deciphering messages in secret code.

Security Factoid

Because of interest in weapons of mass destruction and cyber-warfare, the CIA and other U.S. intelligence organizations are recruiting more and more biologists, computer scientists, and other technical experts to be both analysts and intelligence collectors.

On the Frontiers ...

The NSA collects, processes, and disseminates intelligence information from foreign electronic signals for national foreign intelligence and counterintelligence purposes and to support military operations.

The NSA, according to its own website, "coordinates, directs, and performs highly specialized activities to protect U.S. information systems and produce foreign intelligence information. A high technology organization, NSA is on the frontiers of communications and data processing. It is also one of the most important centers of foreign language analysis and research within the Government." It is what is called a *cryptologic* organization.

The NSA's headquarters are located at Fort Meade, Maryland. The nickname for the HQ is the Puzzle Palace. This was originally the moniker for the Pentagon by its critics, but has since been attributed to NSA.

Two Missions: Making and Breaking

To put it in the simplest language possible, the NSA's two missions are (1) making codes, and (2) breaking codes. To be more specific, those two missions are ...

◆ To design cipher systems that will protect the integrity of U.S. information systems.

◆ To search for weaknesses in adversaries' systems and codes.

If you are an excellent mathematician but are hesitant to work for the NSA because you don't know much about codes, do not worry. The NSA has its own school, called the National Cryptologic School. And the NSA employs more mathematicians than any other organization in the United States—and perhaps in the world.

Schooling is essential to the NSA's efforts. Because the organization functions are the very cutting edge of technology, even veterans of the NSA have to go back to school again and again to keep up with the latest developments.

NSA schools are not available solely to NSA employees. They also serve the entire U.S. Defense Department. According to the Agency: "NSA sponsors employees for bachelor and graduate studies at the nation's top universities and colleges, and selected Agency employees attend the various war colleges of the U.S. Armed Forces."

Security Factoid

Intelligence jargon is synonymous with spookspeak, which really means the slang or jargon used in the intelligence community (spies are sometimes called "spooks") to describe activities, projects, methods, and otherwise confound outsiders.

Point/Counterpoint

In a 1999 interview with *Signal* magazine, the Director of the NSA, Lt. Gen. Michael V. Hayden, USAF, noted the change in the role of the NSA: "The role traditionally had been one of support to the decision maker and to the warfighter. Now, 'support' as a verb no longer works. We have to view ourselves as participants in the fight. This implies a far greater degree of responsibility for the final outcome than simply producing a good intelligence product and throwing it over the transom. We are now in an era where, although target focus and continuity are still important, the ability to be agile and to move from one area of focus to another quickly, fully and competently has a greater premium."

If you have always been fascinated by codes—both making them and breaking them—then perhaps a job with the National Security Agency (NSA) is for you. If you are in the U.S. military or a student, and you are interested in a career with the NSA, follow one of these career or study paths:

◆ Mathematics

◆ Computer science

◆ Electrical engineering

◆ Cryptoanalysis

◆ Foreign languages

◆ Intelligence analysis

◆ Signals analysis

NSA Director and Deputy Director

The director of the NSA is Lt. Gen. Michael V. Hayden. He is responsible for a combat support agency of the Department of Defense with military and civilian personnel stationed worldwide.

According to his official bio on the NSA website (www.nsa.gov): "The General entered active duty in 1969 after earning a bachelor's degree in history in 1967 and a master's degree in modern American history in 1969, both from Duquesne University. He is a distinguished graduate of the Reserve Officer Training Corps program. The General has served as Commander of the Air Intelligence Agency and Director of the Joint Command and Control Warfare Center, both headquartered at Kelly Air Force Base. He also has served in senior staff positions in the Pentagon; Headquarters U.S. European Command, Stuttgart, Germany; the National Security Council, Washington, D.C., and the U.S. Embassy in the People's Republic of Bulgaria. Prior to his current assignment, the General served as deputy chief of staff for United Nations Command and U.S. Forces Korea, Yongsan Army Garrison."

As of 2003, the Deputy Director of the NSA was Bill Black, who joined the agency in 1959. After three years in the army, he joined the NSA as an operational linguist/ analyst. During his time with the NSA, he had a variety of jobs, working his way up to Senior Cryptologic Executive Service, where his primary focus was on building new organizations and creating new ways of doing business.

Bill retired from the NSA in 1997 and became assistant vice president and director of Information Operations in the Advanced Technologies and Solutions Group of the Science Applications International Corporation (SAIC).

At SAIC, Bill led Information Operations (IO) research and worked with the Information Operations Technology Center (IOTC) to establish an Institute for the Analysis of Complex Systems to develop advanced techniques for the analysis of networks and critical infrastructures. He rejoined the NSA in 2000 as deputy director.

Intelligence Community, Working Together

The NSA doesn't just work alone, but also as part of a team involving officers of other national security organizations. In 1998, a new type of intelligence unit— composed of analysts from the CIA, DIA (Defense Intelligence Agency), NSA, and the State Department's Bureau of Intelligence and Research (INR)—called the Support of Diplomatic Operations (SDO), was given its first field trial during elections in Bosnia.

Security Factoid

According to www.intelligence.gov: INR functions as the "'eyes and ears' of the State Department and provides continuous real-time intelligence support to both senior policymakers and working-level officials. INR analysts evaluate, interpret, and disseminate nearly two million reports and produce more than 6500 written assessments each year. INR also works continuously with the Secretary and the entire Department to ensure that intelligence and intelligence activities support America's foreign policy priorities."

The experiment was rated highly successful. According to Jeffrey Smith of the *Washington Post*, while U.S military command posts routinely have access to top-secret information, "only half of the U.S. embassies around the world have secure facilities and equipment to gain similar access."

The SDO team, using only off-the-shelf computers and portable encryption gear, was able to access satellite reconnaissance photography and sensitive materials about possible civil disturbances obtained from extensive U.S. and Allied collection facilities in the region.

They successfully monitored potential threats to the safety of U.S. personnel involved in the Bosnian elections. The field test went so well that team members were honored with the James R. Killian prize for "excellence in the performance of foreign intelligence activities" in a closed ceremony at the White House.

Author's Corner

McLean: Saddam Hussein planned, during the 1991 Gulf War, to execute hundreds of terrorist acts using as many as 200 agents. The scheme was foiled, however, when the NSA intercepted communications regarding the agents. Two terrorists blew themselves up in Manila near a U.S. citizen–frequented center, and one bomb was defused outside the U.S. ambassador's residence in Indonesia. All other agents were arrested, detained, or deported from country to country.

Search for Columbia's "Secret Government Property"

Everyone realizes that it was a terrible tragedy when the space shuttle Columbia crashed while returning to Earth on February 1, 2003—but it was also a bit of a national security emergency. Along with the rest of the wreckage that rained down across a swath of the American South, there fell a top-secret communications device.

Many days after the crash, hundreds of National Guardsmen, federal agents, and local police were scouring an area near the Texas town of Bronson, near the Louisiana border, trying to find the device before it could fall into the wrong hands.

On the device's face plate were written the words "Secret Government Property." The device handled encrypted messages between the spacecraft and Mission Control in Houston, Texas.

The equipment was categorized as TSEC, which stands for Telecommunications Security. These devices are used for defense and other classified communications. The device was keyed to be used with mathematical algorithms. Whether or not the device was ever found has not been made public.

The Least You Need to Know

- ◆ The NSA is the United States' most secret organization.

- ◆ The NSA's two missions are making codes and breaking codes.

- ◆ The NSA doesn't just work alone, but also as part of a team involving officers of other national security organizations.

- ◆ A top-secret communications device was among the debris that rained down over Texas when the space shuttle Columbia crashed in February 2003.

The CIA Today

In This Chapter

- ◆ The directorates
- ◆ Spy planes
- ◆ Spy satellites
- ◆ The new CIA

The CIA, which is the subject of this chapter, employs about 22,000 people full-time and maintains stations in more than 130 countries. Eighty-five percent of those employees work in the Washington, D.C. area. The CIA does more than spy. It also determines what needs to be spied on, interprets the information its intelligence gathering has brought, and makes sure that the agency stays on the cutting edge of technology.

Structure of the Agency

The head of the U.S. intelligence community and the CIA is called the Director of Central Intelligence, or DCI. Below him are the four "directorates" or divisions of the CIA. The office of the Director of Central Intelligence is considered a fifth equal part of the organization. They are as follows:

- Directorate of Operations (DO), the part of the CIA that does the actual spying. It puts officers into the field to recruit agents and acquire intelligence.

- Directorate of Intelligence (DI), the analytical arm of the CIA, provides timely, accurate, and objective intelligence analysis on the full range of national security threats and foreign policy issues facing the United States.

- Directorate of Science and Technology (DS&T), the arm of the CIA in charge of technical operations and tradecraft. In that capacity, it has a hand in all phases of the intelligence process. And

- Directorate of Administration, which functions as the CIA's office manager, makes sure that everyone has enough paper clips and that their phones are working.

The DCI is not just the head of the Central Intelligence Agency. His role is actually much bigger than that. He oversees the entire U.S. intelligence community, so is therefore the supervisor of the National Security Agency, the military intelligence services, and the intelligence-gathering wing of the FBI. In addition, four deputy directors report to the director, one from each directorate.

Point/Counterpoint

According to Vice President Dick Cheney, speaking at CIA headquarters in honor of the fiftieth anniversary of the Intelligence Directorate: "As we began the Presidential transition some two years ago, [Deputy Director for Intelligence] Jami Miscik came into my office with a CIA briefing. Since then, the President and I have begun every day, whether at home or abroad, with a CIA briefing. I probably spend more time with George Tenet than he spends with his own family. And that's as it should be … (laughter). For years, analysis informed the decisions that kept the Cold War from turning into a hot war, and helped lead to the Soviet Union's demise. Today, the nature of the threat to our country has changed dramatically and the challenge to you in many ways is even more formidable …. As the President has said many times, we have entered a different kind of war, which we fight with many tools: diplomacy, law enforcement, financial influence, and military power. And the effective use of all of these tools requires superior intelligence and analytic work—a product that is insightful, accurate, and timely. Much is asked of you. We rely on your expertise as analysts to sort through enormous volumes of information and put together the pieces of some very important and complex puzzles. We also rely on you to point out where you have doubts, to admit what you don't know, and to question your own conclusions. We will look to you for new ideas and for actions that reflect the highest principles of the American people …."

The DCI is hired and fired by the president of the United States. Before a president's choice may serve as DCI, there is a hearing and the choice must be approved by the U.S. Senate. The legal offices at the CIA— The Office of General Counsel—now have 125 employees and 60 of them are lawyers. Ever since 1990, the CIA's inspector general has been in a position of power almost equal to that of the DCI.

Adapting to the Post-9/11 World

If ever there were two organizations whose very existences—their *raison d'etre*—were geared toward upsetting the other, those two organizations were the CIA and the KGB. When the Soviet Union fell apart and the KGB was no more, the CIA suddenly found itself without a focus.

Of course, after 9/11, that was no longer a problem. The War on Terrorism has given all of the CIA's directorates plenty to keep it busy—both when it comes to gathering intelligence and carrying out covert actions.

Eye in the Sky

Eye-in-the-sky spy systems became necessary because human beings and electronic devices on the ground simply weren't doing the job. During the early days of the Cold War (which began pretty much as soon as World War II ended), Communist counterintelligence agents rounded up many of the Western intelligence agents and drove the remainder underground. Information was in short supply. The CIA attempted some desperate measures. They approached every American who was trav-

eling to the Soviet Union—and there were not that many of them back then— and asked them to look for missile sites during their visit. Not a single visitor stumbled upon any missile sites. The CIA even dropped paratroopers behind the Iron Curtain in hopes of learning something—but this, too, was ineffective. It became clear that the only way to get intelligence was from the air. Reconnaissance planes were needed to fly over the Communist bloc nations and determine the extent and location of their defenses, troop movements, industrial might, and thousands of other details.

Security Factoid

A CIA officer and a CIA agent are not the same thing, although these terms often are incorrectly treated that way in the common usage of the language. A CIA officer is a staff employee of the Agency, whereas an agent is an outsider hired by the officer to spy. The agent is often a citizen of the country being spied upon. Another term for agent is asset.

Security Factoid

Eyes in the sky are getting tinier all the time. The U.S. Defense Department is developing a 6-by-9 inch surveillance drone.

The first attempts by the CIA to photograph the Soviet Union from the air came from unmanned balloons—their cover story was that they were weather balloons—which the United States floated over the USSR (and Red China) with cameras mounted on them. The balloons floated at 50,000 feet. The balloons worked, but they were not efficient. Five hundred sixteen of the balloons were launched. Forty of them drifted all the way across the country so they could be recovered on the other side. An amazing 13,813 photos were taken, which amounted to about 8 percent of the land mass of the Soviet Union and mainland China. Unfortunately, the photography had been more or less random and little usable intelligence was gathered.

U-2: The Plane, Not the Group

To solve the problem, Lockheed developed a plane that could take pictures of the Soviet Union, yet fly so high that the Russians' antiaircraft guns could not touch it—or so it was thought. The plane made its debut in 1954. Flying reconnaissance missions on the U-2, of course, was a dangerous job. Conventional military reconnaissance aircraft could be intercepted and shot down by enemy aircraft.

This happened in 1960 when Francis Gary Powers was shot down during a U-2 mission over the Soviet Union, causing the Cold War to suddenly heat up. (If you recall, we learned about the U-2 incident in Chapter 4.)

The U-2 needed to be replaced by a new and better spy plane, but it was never completely retired. In fact, U-2s flew over Iraq through Operation Iraqi Freedom in 2003.

A New Spy Plane: The Blackbird

The replacement for the U-2 was the "Blackbird," the SR-71, which we learned about in Chapters 4 and 5. It was designed by Lockheed and helped the U.S. choose bombing targets in North Vietnam during the Vietnam War. The Blackbirds continued flying regular missions until 1990 when they were retired from active service—retired temporarily, at least. The aircraft were expensive to operate and maintain. The CIA's experts believed that satellite reconnaissance, which we'll discuss shortly, could provide the same coverage as the SR-71 but at a lower cost. With a touch of foresight, the Blackbirds were put in storage and carefully preserved. And it was a good thing, too, because they were called back into active duty.

Although the spy satellites in orbit around the earth provided adequate coverage, they were not always in the proper location to photograph a chosen target. To move a satellite to a new location could take days—and that was too long given the frantic pace of modern world events. In 1995, the Defense Department allocated $100 million to reactivate several SR-71s. They were equipped with the latest ASAR-1 synthetic aperture radar, broad-area optical bar and targetable tactical resolution cameras. The revitalized Blackbirds began active duty again in 1996 and have been used ever since.

Satellites

In August 1960, thousands of feet over the Pacific Ocean, a U.S. Air Force C-119 closed in on a parachute falling from the sky. Using a trailing nylon cable, the aircraft tried to snag the parachute to reel it in, but missed.

Point/Counterpoint

Sure, we use satellite surveillance to read the license plates of the enemy from space, but—disconcerting as it may be—we get watched too ... by whoever can rent the system. Images taken by the commercial satellite company Digital Globe, headquartered in Colorado, show that during the first half of 2002, the U.S. Al Udeid airbase in Qatar was quietly expanded and hardened to support war operations. The runway was enlarged to 13,000 feet to handle heavy bombers, and ammunition dumps, aircraft shelters, and storage buildings for tanks were constructed. All this is in the commercial public domain. What is available commercially is also available to the many states that have satellite imaging capabilities, including Japan, China, India, Israel, France, etc. Military planners now have to operate in a fishbowl.

The pilot tried a second time, and missed again. The parachute was at 8,500 feet altitude when the pilot tried for a third time and this time was successful. The retrieved parachute held a roll of 70mm film that had been taken by a satellite called Corona over the then-Soviet Union. These were the first reconnaissance photos ever taken from a satellite.

Corona

Corona was the result of a series of Air Force studies conducted from 1946–1956, when the Air Force formally began the satellite reconnaissance program called Weapons System 117L. It was originally intended to photograph a target, develop the film onboard, scan the images electronically, and then broadcast them down to Earth.

But with the launch of the Soviet Union's Sputnik, the first artificial satellite to orbit the earth, in 1957, the U.S. decided that it wouldn't be able to wait for the 117L to be developed and instead switched to an interim plan. This satellite would use a Thor rocket and return its unprocessed film to Earth. In early 1958 President Dwight D. Eisenhower ordered that the satellite be developed jointly by the CIA and the Air Force. (The CIA and the Air Force had previously teamed to build and operate the U-2 spy plane.) The project was named *Corona*, after the brand of the typewriter upon which the proposal was written. This was the classified name. The public knew only of a satellite called *Discoverer*.

Corona's camera had a 24-inch focal length and was designed by the Itek Corporation. As the satellite orbited, the camera would sweep a narrow slit over a long strip of film. The film would advance, and the camera would sweep over the next piece of film. When the individual strips of film were placed next to one another, they formed a mosaic of a vast area. The resulting photos were supposed to have a resolution of 25 feet, but the system endured two upgrades before this quality of resolution was achieved. The film from this camera was wound on a film cassette inside a re-entry capsule. The capsule re-entered the atmosphere, where its ablative coating shielded it from the heat of atmospheric friction. At 60,000 feet, the re-entry shield was jettisoned and a spherical "bucket" was yanked clear with a small drogue chute. A larger chute quickly opened and a radio beacon was activated. The beacon allowed a nearby aircraft to fly by and snag the film as it descended. The film was flown to Pearl Harbor in Hawaii, and from there was transported to Eastman Kodak in Rochester, New York, where it was developed. The Itek Corporation designed Corona's cameras and Fairchild built them. Lockheed was responsible for overall satellite integration.

Security Factoid

There were 11 failures before the system worked in 1960, and during this time the urgency to get the system up increased when Gary Powers was shot down over the Soviet Union in his U-2 spy plane.

That first successful spy mission, known to the public as Discoverer 14, photographed the Soviet bomber base at Mys Schmidta as well as other areas. Both the camera designers and the photo interpreters were somewhat disappointed with the quality of the initial photos. The first camera design, known as the model C camera, rocked back and forth as it scanned its film. It was redesigned to reduce vibration by separating the heavy lenses from the scanning arm that exposed the film. The lenses then rotated 360 degrees as the scan arm rocked back and forth. This version was named the model C Prime.

A second upgrade, the model C Triple Prime, created a camera that finally took photos with a resolution of 25 feet. The satellite reconnaissance system received another major upgrade in 1962. This involved the addition of a second camera, which rotated in the opposite direction of the first. Now two images of the same location could be taken from slightly different angles. When viewed through a stereoscopic microscope, the resulting images revealed a third dimension and could determine the height of objects. There were several upgrades to come as photos became sharper and sharper. The final Corona mission flew in 1972, at which time it was replaced by a new satellite reconnaissance program. There were 145 Corona missions in all. Those missions photographed strategic targets within the Soviet Union such as missile complexes, bomber bases, shipyards, and plutonium production facilities.

Soviet Satellites

The first Soviet reconnaissance satellite was adapted from the Vostik manned spacecraft that took the first man to orbit the earth, Yuri Gagarin, into space. The reconnaissance satellite was called Zenit (or, in English, Zenith). The satellite weighed five and a half tons, as opposed to Corona, which weighed just under one ton. The Zenit satellite contained four cameras, two high resolution and two low resolution. Like Corona, Zenit parachuted its exposed film back to Earth. The first attempt to put the Zenit satellite into orbit, on December 11, 1961, failed because of a malfunction in the third stage of the booster rocket. The second attempt, which lasted from March 16 until March 19, 1962, went better but still no cigar. On that mission everything worked except the orientation of the satellite, so, although the satellite returned beautiful photographs to Earth, none of those images were of the intended targets. The third try, which blasted off on July 28, 1962, was a winner and the first useful photographs were returned. Later Soviet reconnaissance satellites were called Resurs-F and Kometa.

Today's Satellites

Today's surveillance satellites transmit their images directly to receivers on Earth, and they do it in real time. The current U.S. satellites are called KH-11s and KH-12s. Using film that picks up the electromagnetic spectrum, these satellites can be set so that they could read a license plate from space. But that is not the most efficient way to read a license plate, and taking photos of larger areas is usually required, so a lower resolution, larger scope is usually used. KH-12 spy satellites cost more than $1 billion apiece. The KH-11s and KH-12s orbited hundreds of miles above the earth, in synch

Security Factoid

You don't have to be a master spy to have access to satellite surveillance photographs. Now you can purchase them on the Internet. GlobeXplorer Inc. has a website that allows consumers to access unusually detailed aerial and satellite photos. Users can enter addresses in most metropolitan areas, zoom down to view neighborhoods, buildings, and even individual homes, using maps that pop up to aid navigation.

with the earth's revolution so that they remained parked over a single spot on the planet. They were moved to a spot over Iraq during the first Gulf War.

The CIA spy satellites provided the first-ever real-time images of enemy movements taken from space. These images gave the United States a tremendous advantage, and saved hundreds of American lives on the ground. The United States got off to an early lead against the Soviets in surveillance from space, even if the Soviets were, for a time, winning the space race. When it comes to spies in the sky, it was a technological advantage that the United States never gave up. Right up until the fall of the Soviet Union, the United States had superior reconnaissance satellites in space.

Next Generation

In the years following 2003, a new generation of small imagery reconnaissance satellites will be launched. These satellites provide a capability for almost uninterrupted surveillance of target areas and much greater launch flexibility.

This contrasts with today's situation where imagery reconnaissance satellites are heavy and few in number, their orbits known, so that timely concealment measures can be taken. Some of these space reconnaissance systems may be equipped with stealth technology so that they cannot be tracked.

The National Imagery and Mapping Agency, which we will learn about in Chapter 12, will oversee a coordinated effort within the intelligence community to standardize transmission and display equipment so that future analysis of the imagery will be able to keep up with the new collection capability.

Orion

A new U.S. Orion SIGINT satellite, launched less than a week before the Indian nuclear tests, has been placed over the equator above western Malaysia and Sumatra at about 23,000 miles altitude. The six-ton NRO spacecraft is one of a series of Orions launched to monitor different regions of the world.

While able to detect signals from the India/Pakistan area, the bird could not become fully operational for weeks after being positioned. Operational as of 2002, the satellite, which cost about $1 billion (including its Titan 4B Centaur booster), is expected to aid in U.S. understanding of activities in the area because of its 24-hour coverage.

Three advanced KHG-11 type optical-imaging spacecraft and two Lacrosse infrared-imaging radar satellites are currently operated by the NRO for the intelligence community. These birds probably flew over the nuclear test site in northwest India no more than two or three times a day, a limited frequency that enabled the Indians to time and camouflage their test preparations as well as easing the deception challenge.

Since the U.S. has, for various reasons, made a number of nations aware of its SIGINT and Imagery capabilities, there is no guarantee that future targets of U.S. intelligence interest will cooperate with the newly positioned spacecraft.

It is anticipated that the failure to provide tactical warning of the Indian tests (in contrast to strategic warning, which had been given repeatedly over recent years) will intensify calls for a larger fleet of smaller imaging satellites able to make more frequent overflights. Typically, more sophisticated processing of the increased data and more analysts to make sense of the data will probably follow way behind the thrust of more metal in the sky.

Security Factoid

National Intelligence Daily is the former name of the CIA classified daily intelligence report in newspaper format for top national leaders. It eventually was renamed the *National Intelligence Digest,* most likely because it is, in reality, a digest of the most important and significant intelligence notes of the day.

Remote Pilotless Vehicles

The U.S. intelligence community now has remote pilotless vehicles to do their aerial spying for them. In other words, the planes work by remote control. If they are shot down, there is no loss of human life.

The system has worked so well that they now have guns attached to them. They can locate an enemy behind enemy lines, photograph it, and then blow it to smithereens, all without putting a single good guy at risk.

The Predator

The remotely controlled Predator, which in recent years had seen limited use in the Balkans and Iraq, carries radar that can see through cloud cover and infrared lenses that work in low light (night) conditions.

Its video camera can transmit live images to the command center in Saudi Arabia or directly to the cockpit of an AC-130 gunship. The Predator can stay aloft for nearly 24 hours, allowing it to fly from bases in Pakistan or Uzbekistan, hang over Afghan target areas for about 14 hours, and then return to base.

But the Predator is not without its problems. It is slow-moving and operates at relatively low altitudes, making it easy prey for antiaircraft fire. At least two Predators have crashed in Iraq this year, presumably shot down, officials said. They are also extremely vulnerable to icing, and it is not clear whether they can operate in the brutal Afghan winter.

Author's Corner

McLean: Peek a boo ... we see you—right through the walls! Word is that the U.S. Army is seeking through-the-wall imaging capabilities. According to the Army: "Systems should have capability to image through walls of varying construction, including: (a) Interior Walls—Standard sheet rock; plaster over lath; plaster over screening materials, wood, ceramic tile, brick, cinder block, stone (marble or granite). These materials are typically installed over interior framing that is either wood or metal; and (b) Exterior Walls—Wood, brick, cinder block, stucco, vinyl or aluminum siding, concrete, and reinforced concrete."

Global Hawk

Global Hawk, an experimental unmanned spy plane, is intended to address some of those problems. It can fly above 60,000 feet, well above antiaircraft fire, and its longer range and greater speed enable it to watch a much broader swath of country. But the Global Hawk also has its limitations.

Security Factoid

Global Hawk can fly 1,200 nautical miles and orbit the area of interest at 60,000 feet for 24 hours in a single 32-hour mission. The system can gather imagery of a 200 x 200 mile area in 24 hours, or alternately, up to 1,900 narrow-field-of-view spot observations. Narrow enough so that the information can be used to drop a smart bomb on one building without harming the building next door. System operators have demonstrated the capability to send imagery from Global Hawk to an F/A-18 in as little as nine minutes.

Video cameras are said to be not so effective at high altitudes, so the Global Hawk produces only still images, albeit very high resolution images.

In the year 2000, a Global Hawk took off from Eglin Air Force Base in Florida, flew non-stop along the East Coast, crossed the Atlantic to Portugal, and finally flew back to Eglin, a 29-hour test flight that set an endurance record. The entire mission to Portugal was programmed on a laptop and downloaded to the UAV's main controls. The vehicle's sensor suite took hundreds of detailed radar and infrared images en route and transmitted them via satellite to Ft. Bragg, North Carolina, and to the aircraft carrier *George Washington* underway in the Atlantic. Global Hawk took photographic images capable of distinguishing vehicle tire tracks from 65,000 feet.

Its digital images also cannot be downloaded directly to other aircraft yet, so they must first be analyzed by personnel far from the battlefield. That has reduced the aircraft's utility in providing intelligence on moving or changing targets.

CIA Expanding Clandestine Capabilities

Clandestine is just a big word that means secret. The CIA has sharply increased its recruitment of case officers as part of a strategic plan to improve U.S. espionage services by 2005, supported by increased Congressional funding. The CIA plans to hire more than five times as many potential case officers than in 1995, when the agency hit its post–Cold War low, and to reopen a number of posts that had been closed. Stations in the developing nations had been closed because the necessity to recruit Soviet KGB and political personnel was gone, but now there is renewed appreciation for the importance of these stations to produce intelligence on terrorists and other international criminals.

Security Factoid

Since 9/11, the CIA has been deluged with a record number of applications. Unfortunately, many of these applicants were reacting to a knee-jerk impulse. But if you seriously want to serve your country with the CIA, send your resumé to:

Recruitment Center
P.O. Box 4090
Reston, VA 20195

For more info on joining the CIA see the truly great book *The Complete Idiot's Guide to the CIA.* It details many types of exciting assignments available.

Intelligence officials have been cited for some time as complaining that the CIA's Directorate of Operations had lost much of its effectiveness in recent years, suffering a drain of talent—including many officers who complained about low morale, heavy-handed bureaucracy, and risk-averse policies. The scandals involving Aldrich Ames and Harold Nicholson, both D.O. officers, also had a negative impact. In addition, a number of CIA operatives have been embroiled in public accusations of spying by France, Germany, and other nations, producing allegations of possible shortcomings in tradecraft—that is, the methods used by intelligence officers, gained from training and experience, to do their special intelligence work.

The program to expand the CIA's clandestine services has strong support in the House, where Speaker Newt Gingrich pushed through supplemental financing in 1998 to enable the increased recruitment and expansion of stations.

The Chairman of the Senate Select Committee, Senator Richard Shelby, is leery of the budget increases proposed by the House, reportedly stating that problems cannot be fixed by simply throwing money at the agency, and that he is more concerned about "quality, not quantity, at the CIA."

Recruiting New Personnel

The CIA recruiting brochure headline reads: "Our business is the future. Your workplace is the world." Here's the latest pitch the CIA is using to recruit personnel: "Wanted, smart, clean-living college and graduate students, fluent in non-Romance languages. Minority group members and Turkish and Iranian citizens especially welcome."

Rather than Ivy League males, the call is out to women and ethnic minorities, particularly Asian and Arab Americans. Advanced degrees and foreign language proficiency are a big plus. Experience living abroad helps. A taste for foreign intrigue is required.

> **Ounce of Prevention**
>
> To enhance CIA training, a "CIA University"—offering 11 different schools, some new, some not—has been established. There is a three-week teamwork course culminating in a Crisis Task Force simulation. A popular course is "Writing for the President." And there are courses in economic trends, international banking, the world oil market, and how the International Monetary Fund, World Bank, World Trade Organization, and other nongovernmental organizations work. In-house language-training courses are offered and security awareness training is being upgraded and expanded.

Help From Abroad: Interpol

The CIA (or the entire U.S. intelligence community, for that matter) are not alone out there. They are not the only good guys in the battle against terrorism. Among the CIA's allies is Interpol, an international police force based in Europe and representing 181 countries.

Interpol collects, stores, analyzes, and disseminates intelligence about suspect individuals and groups and their activities. This data is provided by its member countries and public sources of information that it also monitors. All terrorist-related information has to be shared in a systematic, timely, and accurate manner.

Change of Pace

We conclude this chapter on today's CIA with this darkly humorous anecdote:

A few months ago, there was an opening with the CIA for an assassin. These highly classified positions are hard to fill, and there are a lot of testing and background checks involved before you can even be considered for the position. After sending some applicants through the background checks, training, and testing, they narrowed the possible choices down to three persons: two men and one woman, but only one position was available. The day came for the final test to see which one would get the extremely secretive job. The CIA men administering the test took one of the men to a large metal door and handed him a gun. "We must know that you will follow your instructions no matter what the circumstances," they explained. "Inside this room, you will find your wife sitting in a chair. Take this gun and kill her." The man got a shocked look on his face and said, "You can't be serious! I could never shoot my own wife!" "Well," says the CIA man, "you're definitely not the right man for this job then."

So they bring the second man to the same door and hand him a gun. "We must know that you will follow instructions no matter what the circumstances," they explained to the second man, "Inside you will find your wife sitting in a chair. Take this gun and kill her." The second man looked a bit shocked, but nevertheless took the gun and went in the room. All was quiet for about five minutes, then the door opened. The man came out of the room with tears in his eyes. "I tried to shoot her, but I just couldn't pull the trigger and shoot my wife. I guess I'm not the right man for the job." "No," the CIA man replied, "You just don't have what it takes to be an assassin for the CIA. Take your wife and go home."

Now they turn to the woman for her test. They lead her to the same door to the same room and hand her the same gun. "We must be sure that you will follow instructions no matter what the circumstances. This is your final test. Inside you will find your husband sitting in a chair. Take this gun and kill him." The woman took the gun and opened the door. Before the door even closed all the way, the CIA man heard the gun start firing. One shot after another for 13 shots. Then all hell broke loose in the room. They heard screaming, crashing, banging on the walls. This went on for several minutes, then all went quiet. The door opened slowly, and there stood the woman. She wiped the sweat from her brow and said, "You guys didn't tell me the gun was loaded with blanks! I had to beat him to death with the chair!"

The Least You Need to Know

◆ The CIA has four directorates: the Directorate of Operations, Intelligence, Science and Technology, and Administration.

◆ The head of the U.S. intelligence community and the CIA is called the Director of Central Intelligence, or DCI.

◆ The end of the Cold War and the beginning of the War on Terrorism caused a major shift in CIA priorities in just a few short years.

◆ Much of the CIA's spying has been done from above, using spy planes and, later, spy satellites.

◆ Today there is a renewed focus on HUMINT, the human intelligence and linguists needed for the ongoing War on Terrorism.

The FBI Today

In This Chapter

- A look at the bureau
- What and who to protect first
- Five illegal men
- Arabic speakers wanted

For almost a century, the FBI has been the federal government's front line force protecting the public against crime and maintaining national security against spies, saboteurs, and terrorists.

Although there are more than 32 separate federal agencies responsible for performing law enforcement tasks, the FBI is the primary vehicle for the U.S. government. It is in charge of enforcing the more than 200 federal laws.

The FBI is not a national police force. Rather, it is primarily an investigative body. Its preeminent position of leadership as one of the world's great law enforcement agencies has put it at the center of an anticrime network of local and state police forces, other federal agencies, and international police organizations (such as Interpol, the International Criminal Police Commission based in Lyons, France).

Role Before and After 9/11

Even before the 9/11 attacks, the FBI was changing its very structure to better prepare it for the anticipated War on Terrorism.

In 1999, the FBI underwent a major reconstruction. The major operating divisions at the bureau increased from the original two—the Criminal Division and the National Security Division—to four, including two new divisions:

♦ A Counterterrorism Division, which includes the National Infrastructure Protection Center and its computer crimes unit.

♦ An Investigative Services Division that consolidates analysts who had worked in separate divisions, and includes the bureau's hostage rescue team and negotiators.

The objective of the new structure was to enhance information sharing between the divisions and improve communication between analysts and senior officials.

Because analysts were specialized, a suspect could be investigated separately for being a possible spy, terrorist, or criminal, and information gathered would not necessarily be shared. Also, the failure to share intelligence between divisions sometimes resulted in senior officials being "out of the loop" on critical information under investigation.

The new structure supported the growing FBI role in fighting terrorism worldwide, but also addressed an associated problem: that senior officials got so preoccupied with the focus on terrorist threats that they neglected counterintelligence. By separating the Counterterrorism unit from the National Security Division, the latter can focus more consistently on espionage threats and other foreign intelligence matters—in which the FBI works closely with the CIA and the Department of Defense.

The number of FBI intelligence officers has grown almost fivefold during the past ten years, from 224 to more than 1,000. The bureau, these days, is putting top priority on thwarting foreign spies and preventing terrorist attacks. Since 9/11, the FBI has received a record number of applications by citizens eager to fight terrorism.

Author's Corner

McLean: An Al Qaeda "sleeper cell" in the United States was poised to launch an attack, perhaps against the Capitol Building, soon after 9/11. The FBI, however, in its sweep against visa violators and other suspects of Middle Eastern backgrounds, picked up members of a "support cell" tasked with providing logistics help to the people actually carrying out the mission. The would-be terrorists then went underground or fled the country. Chalk another one up for the good guys.

"It's all part of our effort to play a larger role in the intelligence community in counterintelligence and counterterrorism activity, to identify, prevent and disrupt terrorists," said FBI Assistant Director John Collingwood.

Increasingly Global Bureau

Because drugs, terrorism, financial crime, and other international criminals are a global problem, the FBI has become as much a foreign as well as a domestic law enforcement and counterintelligence organization.

To say that the FBI is in charge of internal security and the CIA in charge of external security is too simplistic. By current law, the FBI has jurisdiction over cases of terrorist attacks on U.S. citizens worldwide.

The FBI's primary mission abroad is gathering information and evidence to serve as a basis for prosecution. In contrast, the CIA's role is to collect and evaluate intelligence for decision makers.

The agencies overlap in their counterintelligence missions and the pursuit of information about terrorism, however, and both act in diplomatic liaison capacities with foreign law enforcement and intelligence organizations. Although there are opportunities for competition, there has been productive FBI-CIA teamwork. Greater cooperation is being encouraged.

Until the year 2000, the FBI did not maintain offices abroad in which its agents served as full-time investigators. Until then agents were posted to American embassies as legal attachés (legats), serving in liaison or training capacities with their local counterparts. The FBI now has legats abroad in 44 countries.

Security Factoid

In addition to, and in support of, the Department of Homeland Security's alert system (see Chapter 16), the FBI has its own terror alert system. It is the FBI Awareness of National Security Issues and Response (ANSIR) report, and, when necessary, it urges all local law enforcement and private sector security to be on the highest state of alert.

That changed in March 2000 when the FBI opened an office in Budapest. The reason for the office was to combat the Russian mob, who consider Hungary as a convenient entrance to Western Europe and the United States.

"This will be truly a working squad," said Thomas V. Fuentes, chief of the FBI's organized crime division, at the time of the office's opening. "They will develop and operate criminal informants. They will gather intelligence. There is no precedent for that."

Says author Danny Coulson, this is technically accurate, but operationally untrue. Agents have been operational all over the world, first in South America during WW II and in Mexico working with Mexican authorities for some time. They were operational in the investigation of bombings in Africa and, of course, the USS *Cole* matter. We know they are operational in Pakistan, Afghanistan, and also in the Marine barracks investigation. They work with local agencies in the host country, but they are operational and in fact, they are armed.

The Marine barracks investigation refers to an attack on October 23, 1983, when a suicide bomber from the Hezbollah Islamic terrorist group drove a truck packed with more than 2,000 pounds of explosives into the U.S. Marine barracks in Beirut, killing 241 U.S. military personnel.

Protecting Targets

The FBI is in charge of identifying and supervising the protection of potential sites against future terrorist attacks. Predicting where and when terrorists might strike is a daunting task, since terrorists in the past have seldom repeated their methods of operation and resist the urge to commit signature attacks. Thus, the idea is to prioritize potential targets by the number of casualties that could be caused and the potential effect of an attack on the U.S. economy.

Some potential targets, if attacked, would involve neither great loss of life nor substantial economic loss. They would, however, if attacked, create great anguish and loss of national morale. They are the national landmarks.

What if an enemy laser weapon erased the faces of Washington, Lincoln, Jefferson, and Roosevelt from the face of Mount Rushmore? What if the Statue of Liberty were destroyed? Or if the dome of the Capitol Building were exploded? Even if there weren't a single injury, these potential happenings would be considered great national tragedies.

Security Factoid _____

One would have to think that New York City and Washington, D.C. remain very high on the list of potential targets by terrorists. The latter controls the U.S. government and the former controls the U.S. economy. It is interesting therefore to note that, despite the fact that millions of dollars were promised to New York City and Washington following the 9/11 attacks, the nation's capital has received $200 million to improve security in that city while the Big Apple has not received a dime.

Geometric Mapping (the Virtual Statue of Liberty)

But what if one of our national treasures is destroyed? What's the plan then? Well, the idea is to replace the treasure as quickly as possible. In order to do this, the federal government has been making "geometric maps" of some of our best-known icons.

High-powered, laser scanning technology has been used to make a map of each landmark from every angle, so that three-dimensional digital models can be created. These digital archives, if needed, would be able to recreate the landmark with accuracy down to a quarter of an inch.

Security Factoid

When it comes to mapping the 288-foot dome on the Capitol Building, two scans needed to be made, so that both the famous exterior and the ornate interior could be duplicated.

According to Don Striker, the superintendent of Mount Rushmore National Memorial in South Dakota: "If someone comes along with a suitcase bomb or a briefcase nuke and blows up a chunk of Thomas Jefferson and his nose falls off, the 3-D representation would allow us to perform major reconstructive surgery on the mountain."

The geometric mapping of the Statue of Liberty was performed by a team from Texas Tech University. What they did was called *reverse* engineering, which is when an object is used to create a blueprint, rather than the other way around, which is the norm. They used a Cyrax 2500 3-D laser scanner, which captures 1,000 images per second.

The statue was scanned from 13 locations, both on its pedestal and from various locations around Liberty Island in New York Harbor. The digital database created will be stored in the National Archives, where hopefully it will remain. But, if needed, it could be used to create a clone of the statue.

Officials note that there were plans to create such a database for national icons even before 9/11—because of the possibility of natural disasters—but these plans received greater funding and were pursued with greater urgency after the terrorist attacks.

Security around our national treasures is now just as tight as it is at the airports. And in some cases, visitation itself is restricted. To visit Liberty Island, for example, you have to go through the usual metal detectors and bag search—but once you get there, you're no longer allowed to climb up inside the statue.

Searching E-mail

As a method of keeping track of potential terror threats, the FBI has developed software that can search e-mail traffic for specific:

◆ Senders

◆ Recipients

◆ Keywords

The e-mail searching program was originally called Carnivore, but later the name was changed to the less ominous DCS 1000.

There is another program called Magic Lantern, which can record the number of keystrokes on targeted computers. This is useful in determining whether a computer is being used to send encoded messages.

Security Factoid

There are FBI-led terrorism task forces in every field division and in many resident agencies. Local police officers work these taskforces and they are very successful. All of the officers have security clearances, and sometimes they can't discuss their work with certain members of their brass.

Security Factoid

Until recently, when the FICA court ruled that there was no basis for keeping the intelligence and criminal arms of the Justice Department separate, the FBI was mandated to not share certain types of information. Many of the limits were placed on the FBI by the Justice Department without there being a mandate from Congress to do so.

Improving Databases

The FBI is currently working hard to improve its databases to better help rout out terrorists who are walking among us in the United States. Although the databases are very strong right now, there is room for improvement. The bureau needs to better be able to follow the finances of potential terrorists.

Because of changes in rules brought about by the passing of the Patriot Act (see "The Civil Rights Question"), the FBI, the State Department, the Bureau of Citizenship and Immigration Services (BCIS, formerly known as the Immigration and Naturalization Service), and the DEA now share information on 12.8 million people with records of law violations.

Some agencies want to share their databases with other agencies, but can't. Databases didn't and still don't fully communicate with each other. The information is there, it is just not readily retrievable, and there is no linkage between the systems. This problem is now being worked on, but they are not there yet.

Learning to Share

The FBI has taken steps recently to better share information. Three programs designed toward that end are as follows:

♦ Integrated Automated Fingerprint Identification System—Helps all law enforcement agencies, from local to federal, check fingerprints against a national file.

◆ National Crime Information Center (NCIC)—Computer system linking fingerprint and mug shot info for 80,000 law enforcement agencies. FBI Director
   Louis J. Freeh said when the system started in 1999: "This new system, NCIC
   2000, will make it possible for the FBI to continue to give valuable assistance to
   local, state, and federal law enforcement agencies in ways never before possible.
   Police agencies that are fully equipped with the new NCIC 2000 capabilities and
   technologies will now be able to obtain important investigative and identification information, such as single fingerprints and mugshots. At the same time,
   agencies will be able to use other new anti-crime services provided by NCIC
   2000, as well as continuing to take advantage of the valuable features of the
   NCIC system, that have been so useful to law enforcement throughout the
   nation. I believe that NCIC 2000 will foster a revolution in law enforcement. It
   will provide criminal justice agencies with tools of immense value against a variety of the worst kinds of crimes."

◆ Law Enforcement On-Line (LEO)—Computer system utilizing the Internet
   whereby the FBI can inform law enforcement agencies nationwide of details
   regarding a terrorist threat or other potential emergency quickly and effectively.

Not all information is being shared—yet. Many law enforcement agencies still maintain their own databases without allowing other organizations easy access. Existing
data-sharing systems need improvement as well. For example, the NCIC doesn't contain immigration status or include information regarding minor crimes.

Terrorist Threat Integration Center

A new "data-mining" Terrorist Threat Integration Center opened in January 2003.
The center was designed to close the "seam" between analysis of foreign and domestic intelligence on terrorism. Terrorist-
related material will be shared between
agencies.

The idea is that the right hand will know
exactly what the left hand knows, both
domestically and abroad. The center will
oversee shared databases and maintain an up-to-
date database of known and suspected terrorists
that will be accessible to federal and nonfederal
officials and entities.

Security Factoid _____

Here's the best example of the
FBI and the CIA learning to
share information and cooperate with one another: It was
decided in early 2003 that the
entire counterterrorism sections of
the FBI and the CIA will move
into a single complex as a way
of better coordinating the analysis and tracking of information.

The center functions under CIA direction, and is made up of elements of the Department of Homeland Security, the FBI's Counterterrorism Division, the CIA's Counterterrorist Center, and the Department of Defense.

Threat Assessment

Each morning President Bush receives a terrorist threat assessment that has been prepared by both the FBI and the CIA. The assessment usually presents raw intelligence—which is always terrifying—followed by analysis, which usually states that the quality of the intelligence is not that great.

For example: "Two separate sources have reported that Al Qaeda members have infiltrated an 'atomic device' into the U.S. This info comes from unsubstantiated discussions circulating within extremist circles."

Or: "Fifteen Al Qaeda operatives in the United States have hatched a scheme to dump sodium cyanide into public swimming pools. There is no info on the amount of sodium cyanide these operatives may have access to or their potential plans."

When there is a rush of frightening raw intelligence, the terrorist alert warning system tends to switch from yellow to orange, but this always means that the intelligence is vague. If the intelligence were specific, they wouldn't have to raise the alert level because they would be busy foiling the plot.

Tracking Potential Terrorists

Tracking potential terrorists who have entered the United States isn't easy. According to former FBI Special Agent Mike Hurm, "Many times people would come in the country and we would not have any idea they were here unless we were tipped off by either the State Department or the INS (Immigration and Naturalization Services, now part of the Department of Homeland Security and called the Bureau of Citizenship and Immigration Services) or one of the other elements of the intelligence community who somehow got some information that they were arriving."

If the FBI does know that a potential terrorist has entered the country, determining the location of that individual presents another set of difficulties. The bureau remains hampered by a scarcity of Arab American agents, a fact that will soon be remedied according to plans reported recently. We'll be discussing the effort to increase the number of Arab-speaking agents a little later in the chapter.

Strategic Information Operations Center

The FBI's Strategic Information Operations Center (SIOC) is one of the principal centers for the War on Terrorism. It is a 40,000-square-foot facility at FBI Headquarters where more than 500 lawyers, agents, intelligence officers, and support personnel work 12-hour shifts.

Working alongside agents from the FBI, Customs, Secret Service, and the Bureau of Alcohol, Tobacco and Firearms are personnel from the CIA, the Defense Department, and NSA. The center is headed by Director Bruce Gephart. Gephart took over from Tom Pickard, who was a deputy director from the CIA.

A typical SIOC day starts at 7:00 A.M. with an interagency coordination conference, necessary because the CIA and FBI are separate agencies. They are operating under different laws and using different methods. What may be legal for one to do, might be illegal for the other. Inter-agency meetings help resolve that situation. With inter-agency operations it is not just important, but essential, that the left hand knows what the right hand is doing.

Hoaxes Are Terrorist Attacks, Too

A terrorist doesn't actually have to explode a bomb or hijack a plane in order to carry out a terrorist attack. A false bomb threat can be a terrorist attack. That's because, simply put: Until it is exposed as a hoax, a certain segment of the population will be terrorized.

Take what we'll call "The Case of the Five Illegal Men." It started on December 29, 2002, when the FBI issued an alert to law enforcement agencies across the nation to help find five Middle Eastern men who were believed to have recently entered the country illegally. The bureau posted photographs of the men and said they had come to the attention of the authorities in connection with current investigations.

The five men identified as having entered the United States some time around December 24 are: Abid Noraiz Ali, 24; Iftikhar Khozmai Ali, 21; Mustafa Khan Owasi, 33; Adil Pervez, 19; and Akbar Jamal, 28.

By New Year's Eve, the FBI's website had the photos of the five illegal men with the words, in all uppercase letters, "SEEKING INFORMATION, WAR ON TERRORISM." On January 2, 2003, President Bush got into the act, saying that he had personally authorized the "all-points bulletin" for five men who might have been smuggled across the Canadian border in connection with a terrorist plot. In New York City, the police increased their counterterrorist efforts as a result of the warning.

The president said, "We need to know why they have been smuggled into the country, what they're doing in the country. And the American people need to know there's a lot of good people working hard, whether it be on New Year's Eve or any other time, to protect the American people."

" " **Point/Counterpoint**

Says Michael E. Rolince, a senior FBI counterterrorism official, "There's always conversation about whether we are overwarning, but I can't see that changing in the near future. You have to be worried about the Chicken Little syndrome, but the only way you will find [terror suspects] is by soliciting the help of the public."

The Case of the Five Illegal Men began to fall apart when a man in Pakistan said that one of the photos couldn't be of a terrorist who had illegally entered the United States, because the photo was of him, and he had the mole on his cheek to prove it.

A week later, however, authorities concluded that the tale was a fabrication, the invention of a man arrested in Canada on charges of trafficking in stolen traveler's checks and running a passport counterfeiting ring. In fact, no such group had attempted to enter the United States.

The man who had started the hoax was an alleged immigrant smuggler in Canadian custody. Michael John Hamdani had reported having knowledge of an attempt by a large group of Pakistanis to enter the United States on forged passports on or around December 24. He identified names and photographs, and passed a polygraph administered by a Canadian law enforcement agency. Information gleaned from Hamdani and other sources in Pakistan indicated 19 men might be involved, the same number of terrorists who hijacked airliners on Sept. 11, 2001.

One of the names had also been tied by U.S. intelligence to an Al Qaeda training camp in Afghanistan, further heightening the sense of alarm. It was a second examination of Hamdani's polygraph exam that led senior FBI officials to conclude that the entire episode had been false.

Wanted: Translators

On September 18, 2001, only one week after the 9/11 attacks, FBI Director Robert S. Mueller III put out one want ad in the form of a public call. The FBI desperately needed employees who could speak Arabic. The same was true of the CIA, the National Security Agency, and all other members of the U.S. intelligence community. Gathering intelligence that was in Arabic was useless if they did not have the personnel who could understand the language.

Author's Corner

McLean: The Defense Language Institute in Monterey, California trains intelligence linguists, primarily for signal intelligence duties. The institute has been in business for more than 50 years. Until 1990, more than half the students learned Russian, German, or Czech. Since then, of course, there has been a huge shift toward Middle Eastern languages. Military and economic concerns in China, Korea, and Japan have prompted a shift toward Asian languages, too. About 24 languages are now taught here. The Defense Department's Defense Language Institute Foreign Language Center is expected to graduate 500 Arabic speakers from its 63-week program in 2003.

The public call by Mueller spawned 20,000 inquiries. More than 70,000 resumes from Arabic-speaking people were received by the NSA, which listens in to conversations all around the world. But that deluge of early interest didn't last long. Fewer resumés are coming in but the need for translators continues.

The hiring of those who are qualified linguists in the various Middle Eastern languages is a slow process because filling jobs with the intelligence agencies requires extensive background checks and security clearance. In 2002, the NSA hired about 800 Arabic linguists, but many more are still needed. Although the FBI had hired about 100 people who speak Arabic for nonagent positions, they still have fewer agents who speak Arabic languages than they would like to have.

There are problems with the current system, however. Those who speak the language often lack the intelligence skills or clearance, and those who have the clearance and skills often do not speak the language. The lack of agents who can understand Arabic is a problem because, according to FBI agent John Bell, who at one time headed the Detroit FBI office, "Whenever an agent has to go through a translator there's always something lost."

Security Speak

Heritage speakers are native-born Americans whose parents were from a Middle Eastern country. They learn their parents' native language at home but speak English outside the home.

Many of the applicants are *heritage speakers*. These people have a limited knowledge of the language. According to one intelligence source: "Kitchen Urdu is not the same as how to make a bomb Urdu. The best intelligence recruits are academically trained and have lived abroad."

According to the FBI's Margaret Gulotta, "It takes 10 [potential Arabic translators] in the front door to get one person hired."

That's because six out of ten applicants fail the language test routinely given to translators. Another two fail the polygraph examination and another one is eliminated because he or she fails the background check. The fear, of course, is that a mole will be hired. The Defense Department has its own language training school and is in the process of teaching Arabic to employees who have already passed all security checks.

Don't Overlook Soldiers and Cops

Some agents of the FBI are concerned about the shift in recruiting emphasis. They are concerned that they are looking for more technical and language-qualified applicants. These are, of course, needed, but they can't overlook former military and policemen who are by nature more aggressive and have better people skills.

Remember, terrorism is a crime and you need aggressive agents out tracking them down. The best agents do not shy away from confrontations and enjoy developing informants and sources, and of course, that requires people skills.

We have heard from current agents that there is a tremendous backlog in conducting background investigations of language-trained applicants. They do not believe that these cases receive a high priority and that hurts their investigations because of the lack of translators.

Dirty and Clean Teams

In terrorism and espionage cases, the FBI will sometimes deploy two teams:

◆ One, a so-called "dirty team," that uses information that would not be admissible in court because it comes from sensitive intelligence sources or from foreign police services whose methods of interrogation are suspect, and

◆ One that works in parallel to develop evidence that can ultimately be presented in a U.S. courtroom. Members of the two teams avoid meeting with each other, but leads developed by the first team are checked by Justice Department lawyers to insure they won't "taint" a case before they are passed on to the so-called "clean" team.

Reaching Out to Militias

During the last years of the twentieth century, the FBI began a program designed to improve relations between the bureau and state militia groups. The FBI and the militias have not gotten along in the past. The militia movement believes in states' rights and a limited federal government. Federal agents and militia members both said that the FBI outreach program helps distinguish true constitutional militia members from hate groups and can change the public perception that all militias are "antigovernment."

"They are our FBI. We needed to get a face on them," said Raymond Smith, a commander with the Texas Freedom Fighters and a member of the National Militia Advisory Board. Smith and like-minded militia members said they believe they are fighting the same enemy as the FBI: people who want to undermine the Constitution and the American way of life.

This program was started by yours truly, co-author Danny Coulson who notes, "I started meeting with the Texas Constitutional Militia after the Oklahoma bombing and recommended it to the Director. I'm sorry to say that the program has not been as effective as I originally envisioned."

Domestic Terrorist Groups

Back in Chapter 9 we listed many of the known terrorist groups around the world, all of which were foreign in origin. Unfortunately, there are also terrorist groups right here in the United States. The most notorious example of domestic terrorism is the April 1995 truck bombing of the Alfred P. Murrah Federal Building in Oklahoma City, which killed 168 people and injured more than 500.

The FBI classifies domestic terrorist threats mostly by political motive, dividing them into three main categories: left-wing, right-wing, and special-interest. Religious sects, sometimes using what is called *leaderless resistance*, have also been connected with terrorist incidents.

Right-wing terrorism groups tend to be motivated by opposition to federal taxation and regulation, the United Nations, other international organizations, and the U.S. government itself, as well as by a hatred of racial and religious minorities.

Security Speak

Leaderless resistance entails a general endorsement of terrorist violence by movement leaders but leaves planning and executing operations to individuals or small groups.

Left-wing terrorism consists of anti-capitalist revolutionary groups. These groups were most active during the 1960s and the Vietnam era. The only such groups still active, experts say, are Puerto Rican separatists. There are also special-interest terrorists that focus on single issues such as abortion, the environment, or animal rights. (For details about domestic terror groups, consult the FBI website at www.fbi.gov.)

The Least You Need to Know

♦ The FBI reconfigured itself to be a better counterterrorist force, years before 9/11.

♦ A person who starts a hoax that terrifies a community is every bit as much a terrorist as one who explodes a bomb or hijacks a plane.

♦ The U.S. intelligence community is greatly in need of people who can speak Arabic languages—but that does not mean that there is less of a need for good law enforcement personnel.

♦ The FBI has a program designed to improve relations between the bureau and state militia groups.

Chapter 13

The National Security Council

In This Chapter

- ◆ Advice to the president
- ◆ Reflections of the chief's personality
- ◆ Key to big world events
- ◆ Coordinating the intelligence community

Another key organization that helps to develop the United States' national security strategy is the National Security Council (NRC). The NSC was created on July 26, 1947 by the National Security Act.

It advises the president on issues of foreign and defense policy. The council coordinates foreign and defense policy, and reconciles diplomatic and military commitments and requirements. According to the law, the NSC consists of the president, the vice president, the secretary of state, and the secretary of defense, with the Joint Chiefs of Staff and the Director of the CIA as advisors. The president can also request that other officials take part.

At the Center of the Foreign Policy System

The National Security Council is at the center of the United States' foreign policy coordination system. It has changed many times since its birth in 1947 (every four to eight years when a new president takes office), and usually reflects the attitudes, needs, and inclinations of the president, who changes the personnel on the council in an attempt to avoid the problems and deficiencies of his predecessors' council.

Security Factoid _____

The National Security Act that gave birth to the National Security Council also provided for a secretary of defense (who replaced the secretary of war in the president's cabinet), a National Military Establishment (commonly referred to as "The Pentagon," this includes all of the branches of the military and all that's under the domain of the secretary of defense), Central Intelligence Agency (see Chapter 11), National Security Agency (see Chapter 10), and National Security Resources Board (which advises the president concerning the coordination of military, industrial, and civilian mobilization).

The NSC is chaired by the president of the United States. Other key members include the secretary of state and the secretary of defense. Although the council was created to coordinate political and military questions, in practice it serves only the president, who uses it as a means of controlling and managing competing departments. In other words, agencies whose operations could, in theory, be redundant or conflict are more apt to stay on the same page because their directors regularly meet together to report to the president.

Regular Attendees

Other regular statutory and nonstatutory attendees are the vice president, the secretary of the treasury, and the assistant to the president for National Security Affairs (otherwise known as the "National Security Adviser").

The chairman of the Joint Chiefs of Staff is the statutory military adviser to the Council, and the Director of Central Intelligence is the intelligence adviser. The chief of staff to the president, counsel to the president, and the assistant to the president for economic policy are invited to attend any NSC meeting.

The attorney general and the director of the Office of Management and Budget are invited to attend meetings pertaining to their responsibilities. The heads of other executive departments and agencies, as well as other senior officials, are invited to attend meetings of the NSC when appropriate.

Author's Corner

McLean: Get out your books and sharpen your pencils: The Institute of World Politics is a graduate school of statecraft and national security affairs. They offer two Master's degree programs—Statecraft and World Politics and Statecraft and National Security Affairs, and also offer certificates of graduate study and continuing education courses. They are dedicated to helping develop leaders with a sound understanding of international realities and the conduct of statecraft—in other words, the use of the various instruments of power in service of national interests and purposes—based on knowledge and appreciation of American political philosophy and the Western moral tradition.

Shifting Shapes

As we said before, one can always tell a lot about the personality of a president by who dominates his NSC. Truman's NSC was pretty much run by the secretary of state, Eisenhower (being a retired general) had an NSC dominated by the military. Kennedy's easy style tended to blur the line between policy-making and operations.

Johnson distrusted the NSC structure and tended to rely more on the advice of trusted friends. Under Nixon and Ford, Secretary of State Henry Kissinger dominated the NSC, which concentrated on acquiring analytical information. Carter allowed his National Security Adviser to become a principal source of foreign affairs ideas.

Expansion Under Reagan ... Then Clinton

Under Reagan, the national security adviser was downgraded, and the chief of staff to the president exercised a coordinating role in the White House. The first President Bush—who was the Director of Central Intelligence himself from 1976 to 1977— brought his own considerable foreign policy experience to his leadership of the National Security Council, and reorganized the NSC organization to include a Principals Committee, Deputies Committee, and eight Policy Coordinating Committees.

Under Clinton the NSC membership was expanded to include the secretary of the treasury, the U.S. representative to the United Nations, the newly created assistant to the president for economic policy (who was also head of a newly created National Economic Council or NEC, parallel to the NSC), the president's chief of staff, and the president's National Security Adviser.

Security Factoid

The NSC played an effective role during such major developments as the collapse of the Soviet Union, the unification of Germany, and the deployment of American troops in Panama and Iraq (both times).

National Security Adviser

Security Speak

The official title of the **National Security Adviser** is Assistant to the President for National Security Affairs.

The position of *National Security Adviser* was created by President Dwight D. Eisenhower on March 23, 1953, in response to a report on NSC organization by Robert Cutler.

By design, the National Security Adviser has the president's ear when it comes to all matters of National Security. Just how much he or she dominates the president's ear, or shares it with other members of the NSC, depends on the president.

Here is a list of all of the assistants to the president for National Security Affairs (National Security Advisers):

- Robert Cutler   March 23, 1953–April 2, 1955
- Dillon Anderson   April 2, 1955–September 1, 1956
- Robert Cutler   January 7, 1957–June 24, 1958
- Gordon Gray   June 24, 1958–January 13, 1961
- McGeorge Bundy   January 20, 1961–February 28, 1966
- Walt W. Rostow   April 1, 1966–December 2, 1968
- Henry A. Kissinger   December 2, 1968–November 3, 1975 (served concurrently as secretary of state from September 21, 1973)
- Brent Scowcroft   November 3, 1975–January 20, 1977
- Zbigniew Brzezinski   January 20, 1977–January 21, 1981
- Richard V. Allen   January 21, 1981–January 4, 1982
- William P. Clark   January 4, 1982–October 17, 1983
- Robert C. McFarlane   October 17, 1983–December 4, 1985
- John M. Poindexter   December 4, 1985–November 25, 1986
- Frank C. Carlucci   December 2, 1986–November 23, 1987
- Colin L. Powell   November 23, 1987–January 20, 1989
- Brent Scrowcroft   January 20, 1989–January 20, 1993

- ◆ W. Anthony Lake   January 20, 1993–March 14, 1997
- ◆ Samuel R. Berger   March 14, 1997–January 20, 2001
- ◆ Condoleezza Rice   January 20, 2001–Present

Dr. Condoleezza Rice was born on November 14, 1954 in Birmingham, Alabama, and earned her Bachelor's degree in political science, *cum laude* and Phi Beta Kappa, from the University of Denver in 1974; her Master's from the University of Notre Dame in 1975; and her Ph.D. from the Graduate School of International Studies at the University of Denver in 1981.

Condoleezza Rice spent six years as Provost of Stanford University. As Provost she was responsible for a $1.5 billion annual budget and the academic program involving 1,400 faculty members and 14,000 students. Dr. Rice had been on the Stanford faculty since 1981 as a professor of political science.

As a teacher she won the 1984 Walter J. Gores Award for Excellence in Teaching and the 1993 School of Humanities and Sciences Dean's Award for Distinguished Teaching.

She has written several books, including ...

- ◆ *Germany Unified and Europe Transformed* (1995, Harvard University Press) with Philip Zelikow,

- ◆ *The Gorbachev Era* (1986, Stanford Alumni Association Press) with Alexander Dallin, and

- ◆ *Uncertain Allegiance: The Soviet Union and the Czechoslovak Army* (1984, Princeton University Press).

From 1989 through March 1991, during the final days of the Cold War, she served in the Bush administration as director, and then senior director, of Soviet and East European affairs in the National Security Council, and as special assistant to the president for national security affairs. In 1986, while an international affairs fellow of the Council on Foreign Relations, she served as special assistant to the director of the Joint Chiefs of Staff.

She has been the National Security Adviser since January 22, 2001.

Counterterrorism Security Group

Like everything else in the United States, the National Security Council had to change the way they viewed the world following the 9/11 attacks. The council's panel designed specifically to handle the War on Terrorism is the Counterterrorism Group. It is as assistant-secretary level group. It was originally chaired by a senior director on the NSC, and later by the national coordinator for national security issues.

The group receives reports from all members of the U.S. intelligence community and digests the information. This is another indication that the U.S. intelligence community is seeing itself more as a single team rather than separate factions competing for tax dollars.

The Least You Need to Know

- The National Security Council advises the president on issues of foreign and defense policy.

- The current assistant to the president for national security affairs is Dr. Condoleeza Rice.

- The National Security Adviser has the president's ear when it comes to all matters of National Security.

- The NSC's panel designed specifically to handle the War on Terrorism is the Counterterrorism Group.

The DIA and the Pentagon

In This Chapter

- ◆ Pentagon protection
- ◆ 9/11 changed everything
- ◆ DELTA and the SEALs
- ◆ Separating military and police
- ◆ Missile problems

Much of the envelope of security that surrounds our nation is provided by the U.S. military, which is, of course, headquartered in the Pentagon across the Potamic River from Washington, D.C. We are not only protected by our own military might, but by our ability to know more about our enemy than he does about us.

In this chapter, we will examine the various members of the U.S. intelligence community that work out of the Pentagon, and the ways in which they help make us secure.

Prepared for an Away Game

There can be no blunter way to put it: 9/11 changed everything. Countries always prepare their national security for the way they envision the threat. After the end of the Cold War, the chances of the U.S. mainland being attacked by a foreign enemy seemed highly remote. If it did occur, it would come in the form of missiles, not as hijacked commercial airliners.

Directors of the Defense Intelligence Agency:

- Oct. 1961–Sep. 1969: Lt. Gen. Joseph F. Carroll, USAF

- Sep. 1969–Aug. 1972: Lt. Gen. Donald V. Bennett, USA

- Aug. 1972–Sep. 1974: Vice Adm. Vincent P. de Poix, USN

- Sep. 1974–Dec. 1975: Lt. Gen. Daniel O. Graham, USA

- Jan. 1976–May 1976: Lt. Gen. Eugene F. Tighe Jr., USAF (acting)

- May 1976–Aug. 1977: Lt. Gen. Samuel V. Wilson, USA

- Aug. 1977–Aug. 1981: Lt. Gen. Eugene F. Tighe, USAF

- Sep. 1981–Sep. 1985: Lt. Gen. James A. Williams, USA

- Oct. 1985–Dec. 1988: Lt. Gen. Leonard H. Perroots, USAF

- Dec. 1988–Sep. 1991: Lt. Gen. Harry E. Soyster, USA

- Sep. 1991–Nov. 1991: Dennis M. Nagy (acting)

- Nov. 1991–Aug. 1995: Lt. Gen. James R. Clapper Jr., USAF

- Sep. 1995–Feb. 1996: Lt. Gen. Kenneth A. Minihan, USAF

- Feb. 1996–Jul. 1999: Lt. Gen. Patrick M. Hughes, USA

- Jul. 1999–Jul. 2002: Vice Adm. Thomas R. Wilson, USN

- Jul. 2002–Present: Vice Adm. Lowell Jacoby, USN

> **Author's Corner**
>
> McLean: I've seen what war devastation is, when Britain was bombarded by the Blitz during World War II and German cities were nearly obliterated as Allied Forces marched across that country. ... Many Americans also saw the destruction, but none could ever imagine two giant skyscrapers being obliterated in our own country. Now we know and our focus has changed.

Before 9/11, the United States had only been attacked once, and that was in Hawaii, far from the mainland. The Pentagon and the other organizations designed to protect us were concerned with foreign wars.

World War I, World War II, Korea, Vietnam, and the Gulf War had all been conflicts fought far, far from home. With 9/11, the concept of Homeland Security, keeping ourselves safe here at home, came to the fore.

Of course, that lone attack on American soil during the twentieth century was the Japanese attack at Pearl Harbor on December 7, 1941. That attack plunged the United States into a global war, fought both in the Pacific and in Europe.

Similarly, the 9/11 attacks in New York City and Washington, D.C. launched another global conflict, a War on Terrorism, that must be fought wherever terrorist cells may be in hiding. The trouble is that terrorism knows no patriotism, knows no boundaries, so fighting it will demand patience and, most of all, intelligence.

> **Point/Counterpoint**
>
> "North Korea's open pursuit of nuclear weapons is the most serious challenge to U.S. interests in the Northeast Asia area in a generation. While the North's new hard-line approach is designed to draw concessions from the United States, Pyong-yang's desire for nuclear weapons reflects a long-term strategic goal that will not be easily abandoned," Defense Intelligence Agency Director Admiral Lowell Jacoby said.

Getting Osama

Our national defenses are geared to fight other armies. This is why the War on Terrorism has been so different and initially difficult for us. Our primary goal, capturing Osama bin Laden dead or alive, proved to be difficult. We hoped that he would be under the mountain that we were bombing—a hit or miss strategy that, as this is written, appears to have not been effective. Finding DNA traces may tell a different story at some point.

According to a Saudi financier, Osama bin Laden had chosen a slightly more difficult, but maybe less treacherous, exit out of Afghanistan over the White Mountains and into the Parachinar area of Pakistan. Bin Laden, according to the Saudi financier, had arranged his escape with members of the Ghilzi tribe, whose villages straddle the Pakistani border. We had hoped to kill bin Laden by homing in on his cell phone signals, but he reportedly gave his cell phone to an aid before leaving Afghanistan and our attack got the wrong man.

Special Ops

As the ongoing War on Terrorism demonstrates, the best way to prevent terrorism at home is to kill the terrorists long before they get here. Toward that end, in

January 2003, Secretary of Defense Donald Rumsfeld granted the U.S. Special Operations Command (USSOCOM) authority to conduct global operations against terrorist networks. He also increased the Special Ops budget accordingly. USSOCOM, born in 1987, was previously a "supporting" command that provided personnel and equipment to regional Combatant Commands, which then plan and direct the missions. As of 2003, USSOCOM oversaw 47,000 personnel.

The Special Ops Command received a new battle-planning staff and "certain intelligence assets" were transferred to the Joint Special Operations Command at Fort Bragg, North Carolina, home of the DELTA and SEAL teams. Those teams, along with the Air Force's 160th Special Operations Wing, do the actual fighting.

Author's Corner

Allan: The word Operation with a second word includes a wide range of projects, from the past to present and projected activities by various intelligence and government organizations. You can find many of these by accessing the Department of Defense, various military services, or the CIA websites. Some are serious, others somewhat humorous, and all edifying. For example, Operation Choir was a code name for placement of a microphone bug into the wall of the Soviet Consulate in London. Operation Courtship was the code for a joint CIA and FBI operation to recruit then Soviet KGB officers, Operation Flypaper was a Navy code for antisubmarine warfare, Operation Moses was the Israel Mossad code for bringing Ethiopian Jews to Israel. Other odd codes included Operations: Oatmeal, Popeye, Rainbow, Samurai, Shampoo, Whip Worm, Yak.

Rumsfeld's plan is to create a global combatant command to assume responsibility for the worldwide war on terrorism, and thereby to have a mechanism for quickly deploying commandos to attack terrorists anywhere within hours of discovery. Special Ops now have the authority to plan and carry out certain missions, covert operations, and quick strikes with "hunter-killer" teams, independent of the currently established combatant commands. These missions, of course, will be tightly coordinated with CIA and FBI operations. Rumsfeld's plan also calls for prior diplomatic arrangements so that covert operators can enter countries quickly, carry out their mission, and promptly exit.

Posse Comitatus

In response to the military presence in the Southern States during the Reconstruction Era, on June 28, 1878 Congress passed the *Posse Comitatus* Act. The act stated that America's military is prohibited from acting as a domestic police force. But, in this post-9/11 era, has the concept of keeping our military from performing domestic policing duty grown outdated? That is a logical, perplexing question in today's strange world.

In 2002, Sen. John Warner invited the Pentagon to propose modifications to the *Posse Comitatus* Act. "Limited use [of military forces] beyond that permitted by existing law might strengthen the nation's ability both to protect against and to respond to events of the sort which we have recently undergone."

In the 2002 Defense Authorization Act, Congress has directed the secretary of defense to "conduct a study on the appropriate role of the Department of Defense with respect to homeland security."

Structure of the DIA

The Defense Intelligence Agency is the coordinating agency in the Defense Department that reports to the secretary of defense with intelligence collected from all military services, but also is subject to the coordinating authority of the DCI.

The DIA is considered one of the most important members of the U.S. intelligence community. It is the Defense Department's combat support agency.

A major portion of the United States' foreign military intelligence is gathered and processed by the DIA. This intelligence is provided to:

Security Factoid

The DIA employs 7,000 military and civilian personnel, who are stationed all around the world. The work force is skilled in military history and doctrine, economics, physics, chemistry, world history, political science, bio-sciences, and computer sciences. Among the DIA's personnel you can find expertise ranging from foreign military leaders to experts on interpreting the trajectory data of complex missile systems.

- Warfighters
- Defense policy makers
- Defense Department force planners
- Other members of the intelligence community

This intelligence supports U.S. military planning and weapon systems acquisition. The DIA's Director—always a three-star general or admiral—functions as the principle adviser to the secretary of defense as well as to the Joint Chiefs of Staff on all matters of military intelligence. He also is the chairman of the *Military Intelligence Board*, and, in that capacity, coordinates activities of the defense intelligence community.

Security Speak _____

The **Military Intelligence Board** is a decision-making forum that formulates defense intelligence policy and programming priorities.

The DIA is headquartered in the Pentagon in Washington, D.C. There are also major operational activities taking place at the ...

◆ Defense Intelligence Analysis Center (DIAC), Washington, D.C.

◆ Armed Forces Medical Intelligence Center (AFMIC), Frederick, Maryland.

◆ Missile and Space Intelligence Center (MSIC), Huntsville, Alabama.

If you were to become a DIA employee, you can rest assured that you'll always be working with the latest and greatest computer and technical equipment. If there is a new technological development after you are at work, you'll be trained to keep tabs on the most modern developments. And it's a great way to see the world, too.

Army Intelligence

Army intelligence is the oldest member of the U.S. intelligence community. As we learned in Chapter 1, Army intelligence is every bit as old as our nation and dates back to 1776 when Nathan Hale spied on the British under the command of Gen. George Washington.

Army intelligence is structured to provide military commanders with unique capabilities and a balanced, flexible force that can be tailored to meet any contingency. During the 1980s, the army created Combat Electronic Warfare and Intelligence Units—based at Fort Huachuca, Arizona—which were necessary to keep up with the increasingly sophisticated technology used on the modern battlefield. These units were first used in the 1991 Persian Gulf War.

Security Factoid _____

Despite the more than 225-year history of Army intelligence, it has only been less than 20 years that Army intelligence has functioned under the auspices of a single organization. That organization is the Army Intelligence Agency, which was formed in 1984.

The U.S. Army, as one of the four military services in the Department of Defense, is primarily concerned with the conduct of military operations. However, the Army's intelligence component does produce intelligence both for Army use and for sharing across the intel community. The primary mission of Army intelligence, according to the Army's own directives, is to facilitate Army transformation and support the warfighting combatant commanders by resourcing, fielding, and sustaining the world's premier military intelligence force.

In practical terms, this means providing commanders with the vital knowledge they need to successfully accomplish their multilevel mission. Army MI's first responsibility is to eliminate intelligence surprises by being engaged, around the world, on a daily basis to detect and uncover real and/or perceived threats to the U.S. and U.S. national interests.

To accomplish this, Army intelligence develops a variety of intelligence products, such as threat assessments, that are used by weapons systems developers and senior decision-makers. The Army intelligence component continually trains and prepares so that it will be ready to meet the span of contingencies from war fighting to peacekeeping. These efforts are conducted through such entities as the Headquarters Department of Army Office of the Deputy Chief of Staff for Intelligence—*G-2* and the U.S. Army Intelligence and Security Command.

Security Speak

G-2, at the Army General Staff level, is the term for intelligence—i.e., the Assistant Chief of Staff for Intelligence. It is the common term for intelligence at division and higher levels. At lower levels the term is S-2.

The Army's Chief Intelligence Officer is the Deputy Chief of Staff for Intelligence, called the G-2 Officer. Responsibilities include policy formulation, planning, programming, budgeting, management, staff supervision, evaluation, and oversight for intelligence activities for the Department of the Army. This individual has Army Staff responsibility for overall coordination of the five major intelligence disciplines: Imagery Intelligence, Signal Intelligence, Human Intelligence, Measurement and Signature Intelligence, and Counterintelligence and Security Countermeasures.

Then, the major commands such as the Army Intelligence and Security Command (INSCOM) located at Ft. Belvoir, Virginia, conduct dominant intelligence, security, and information operations for commanders and national decision-makers, and provide war fighters with the intelligence needed to understand and dominate the battlefield. At the corps level, the Senior Intelligence Officer (SIO), the G2, and an organic corps Military Intelligence (MI) Brigade provide intelligence support. The MI Brigade provides support to the corps across the full range of intelligence and counterintelligence disciplines and functions.

Army Military Intelligence accomplishes its mission in close coordination with the other services, the Air Force, Navy, and Marines, and with national intelligence agencies to ensure that ground component commanders and soldiers know what enemy forces they will face before, during, and after deployments. In addition, Army MI works to protect our nation's secrets, to protect the technology overmatch that the United States enjoys in the world, and to contribute to Homeland Defense.

There are today oversights in place because Army MI messed up a while back. Back in the 1960s and 1970s, there were some major demonstrations by U.S. citizens opposing the Vietnam War. When some top-level federal officials believed these demonstrations were beyond civilian authorities' ability to control, they called upon the military to assist in restoring order. The Department of Defense (DoD) gave responsibility to the Army for providing aid to civilian authorities. The Army asked the FBI for help. When the FBI was unable to provide the information commanders thought they needed, Army MI began collecting it. The senior federal officials did not object.

Unfortunately, the collection mushroomed beyond simple support to civilian authorities in civil disorder. As admitted in the Army's intelligence website, "Eventually, intelligence personnel collected information on some citizens' political views and expressions. MI personnel intercepted radio communications of civil rights and anti-war activists. Military CI agents infiltrated the 1968 Democratic National Convention under media cover and penetrated U.S. organizations such as 'Resistors in the Army' and 'Friends of Resistors in the Army,' and recruited informers. They placed under surveillance numerous people who were exercising their First Amendment rights. They stored the information in records repositories all over the U.S., sharing it with law enforcement authorities, whether or not there was evidence of criminal activity or relevance to that particular law enforcement agency's job."

What had begun as a simple requirement to provide basic intelligence to commanders had become an alleged massive intrusion into citizen rights according to legal records of that period. When Congress finally noticed problems in the early 1970s, it held investigations and public hearings that determined that the information collected and shared with law enforcement agencies had produced a chilling effect on those who were legally working for political change. At Congressional direction, the Department of Defense imposed severe restrictions on future surveillance of U.S. persons, ordered the repositories destroyed, and established a structure to regulate future intelligence activities.

According to the Army's report, Congress also recognized its own lapse in oversight. Up until then, total legislation covering the intelligence community was slim. Congress established the Senate Select Committee on Intelligence and the House Permanent Select Committee on Intelligence, which have been very busy ever since. President Ford signed Executive Order 11905 in 1976, which placed significant controls on all U.S. intelligence activities and made provision for an intelligence oversight mechanism. President Carter updated it in Executive Order 12036 in 1978. President Reagan signed Executive Order 12333 in 1981, and we operate under its policy guidance today. The goal of all these policies is to maintain the proper balance between the protection of individuals' constitutional and statutory rights and the legitimate information needs of the U.S. intelligence community.

Today, terrorism is on everyone's minds. At one point recently, a senior federal official said publicly that terrorism is so serious that U.S. citizens may well need to give up some of their rights so they could be properly protected. This is very much like the thinking that led to the 1960s' and 1970s' abuses. Had the intelligence oversight mechanism not been in place, we might have seen similar problems. How much

> **Author's Corner**
>
> McLean: Terrorists aren't stupid people. They may try to take advantage of these restrictions to set up activist groups aimed at harming America. Perhaps it is time to evaluate what our country needs to deter such threats, even those aimed at us from seemingly legal front groups secretly directed or manipulated by terrorists.

more deeply intelligence will be needed, including within the domestic arena, to find and uproot terrorist cells that may be in place already is another question. The fine lines between the need for intelligence to thwart terrorists and civil rights must be walked carefully, experts agree. Time will reveal how successfully that is done, without allowing terrorists to escape detection.

Air Force Intelligence

Since 1993, the U.S. Air Force has had its own organization assigned to intelligence. It is called, appropriately enough, the Air Intelligence Agency (AIA), headquartered at Lackland Air Force Base in Texas. Since 2001, the AIA has been under the structure of the Air Combat Command and the Eighth Air Force.

The AIA's commander also functions as the Eighth Air Force's deputy commander for information operations. The Eighth Air Force is the USAF's first operational force designed to achieve and maintain information superiority and has bomber and information operations capabilities.

Point/Counterpoint

The AIA's stated mission is: "To gain, exploit, defend and attack information to ensure superiority in the air, space and information domains. The agency's people worldwide deliver flexible collection, tailored air and space intelligence, weapons monitoring and information warfare products and services." Information warfare, we should note, involves attacking an enemy's information systems or attacking an enemy with information.

The AIA is not the only intelligence organization within the U.S. Air Force. There is also the National Air Intelligence Center (NAIC), which is the Defense Department's primary producer of foreign aerospace intelligence.

Headquartered at Wright-Patterson Air Force Base, near Dayton, Ohio, the NAIC analyzes all available data on foreign aerospace forces and weapons systems. Using this, they determine the intentions, capabilities, vulnerabilities, and performance characteristics.

Because they are our experts on foreign aerospace system capabilities, the NAIC has been extremely useful in supporting American weapons treaty negotiations and verification. The NAIC started out in 1961. Back then it was called the Air Force Systems Command's Foreign Technology Division—which is a mouthful and a half.

Office of Naval Investigation (ONI)

The Office of Naval Investigation recently was reorganized. ONI is now composed of the Director of Naval Intelligence and his staff, a chief of staff, and an assistant of Naval Intelligence, all of whom oversee eight directorates.

Those directorates are as follows:

◆ Human Resources, which manages both civilian and military personnel and training

◆ Intelligence, with a staff of over 800 people

◆ Services, responsible for operations and production support

◆ Installation Management, which is solely responsible for moving ONI's files into its new headquarters

◆ Security, which handles all physical and personnel security

◆ Collections, which handles technical collection efforts as well as those of the DIA's human intelligence activities

◆ Systems, which operates current communications systems while acquiring and implementing new laboratory, processing, and communications systems

◆ Resource Management, which handles matters concerning programming for funds and other matters of the budget

The Intelligence Directorate is divided into three divisions: SWORD (undersea warfare), SPEAR (air and strike warfare), and, the most recent addition, SABER (expeditionary and mine warfare). Each division is supported by civilian intelligence analysts, military intelligence analysts, and warfare specialist-qualified operators.

Marine Corps Intelligence

The intelligence wing of the U.S. Marines Corps is called the Marines Corps Intelligence Activity (MCIA). In their own words, the MCIA is "a vital part of the military intelligence 'corporate enterprise,' and functions in a collegial, effective manner with other service agencies and with the joint intelligence centers of the Joint Chiefs of Staff and *Unified Commands*."

MCIA not only helps to determine what missions will need to be carried out by the Marines, but who will need to be trained to accomplish those missions. MCIA is a full partner with ONI and Coast Guard Intelligence in the National Maritime Intelligence Center, and at Marine Corps Base Quantico in Virginia.

Security Speak

The **Unified Commands** coordinate and adjust the various U.S. military commands around the globe.

U.S. Coast Guard

Since 1790, the U.S. Coast Guard has been in charge of keeping our nation's territorial waters—including our ports and waterways—secure.

The Coast Guard maintains its existing independent identity as a military organization under the leadership of the Commandant of the Coast Guard, unless war is declared. In that case, the Coast Guard operates as an element of the Department of Defense.

The U.S. Coast Guard is charged with regulatory, law enforcement, humanitarian, and emergency response duties. It is responsible for …

- The safety and security of America's inland waterways, ports, and harbors.
- More than 95,000 miles of U.S. coastlines.
- U.S. territorial seas.
- 3.4 million square miles of ocean defining our Exclusive Economic Zones.
- Other maritime regions of importance to the United States.

The Coast Guard has broad authority in the nation's ports as "Captain of the Port." Recently the Coast Guard has worked to establish near-shore and port-domain awareness, and to provide an offshore force gathering intelligence and interdicting suspicious vessels prior to reaching U.S. shores.

Since 9/11 the Coast Guard has made many changes to adapt to the changing world situation. Among other things, it has …

◆ Created Maritime Safety and Security Teams (MSSTs), which are federal maritime SWAT teams that provide an extra layer of security to key ports, waterways, and facilities.

◆ Developed special "Sea Marshal" boarding procedures where Coast Guard law enforcement officers remain onboard certain ships as they enter and leave ports to ensure they stay safely on course.

◆ Escorted cruise ships in and out of port and enforced 100-yard "no sail" Security Zones around them.

◆ Established a new, centralized National Vessel Movement Center and required foreign ships to provide a 96-hour advance notice of arrival plus more information about the ship, cargo, and all people on board.

◆ Established and enforced Naval Protection Zones around all naval vessels.

◆ Enforced Security Zones around sensitive maritime areas and facilities.

◆ Used their pollution and hazardous materials expertise to prepare for bioterrorism threats.

◆ Worked to "push our borders out" by detecting threats before they reach our shores.

The Return of Star Wars

In order to better protect the United States, President Ronald Reagan was supportive of something officially known as the "Strategic Defense Initiative" (SDI) and commonly known as "Star Wars," after the popular movie.

This popular name was inaccurate, though. The plan was to build a system that would prevent wars, not start them. The plan called for a system of "antimissile" missiles that would shoot down any attacking missiles that might be coming from other countries.

Reagan's Dream

Reagan's plan was to build the system and then share it with all of the countries in the world. The system would build a sort of shield around the world so that no one could be hurt by missiles fired from another continent.

This would render nuclear weapons obsolete and therefore they could all be dismantled. The trouble was that the Soviets did not believe that we would share the technology. They thought the United States would attack them and then use SDI to prevent retaliation.

Bush's Version

The Strategic Defense Initiative, Ronald Reagan's dream that would, in theory, render intercontinental ballistic missiles obsolete, has been reintroduced as a planned defense strategy by President George W. Bush.

His plan calls for 20 interceptor rockets to be placed in Alaska and California by 2005. These rockets would have the capability of shooting down enemy ballistic missiles. The plan also includes an early-warning system.

The system would place infrared sensors both on the ground and in space that would be able to detect any missile launched at the United States. Ground radar would track the rogue missiles and automatically launch the interceptor rockets.

Sensors placed both on satellites and on the interceptor rockets would be able to distinguish between active and decoy missiles. The interceptor rockets would strike the incoming missiles at 16,000 miles per hour. Ground- and space-based sensors would then be able to determine if the interception had been successful.

Another problem: Cruise Missiles

There is increasing concern that terrorists will use shoulder-fired, heat-seeking missiles to shoot down commercial airliners. Information gathered from captured terrorists reveals that such attacks have been considered by Al Qaeda and other terrorist groups.

A recent attempt in Kenya by an unidentified group was aimed at shooting down a commercial El Al airliner. Fortunately, that effort failed but abandoned shoulder-held missiles attest to the fact that this threat is now one being tested and considered by terrorists.

In response to the threat, the U.S. Defense Department has accelerated programs designed to develop safeguards that will protect airliners from this type of attack. In November 2002, several terrorists linked to Al Qaeda were arrested in Hong Kong as they attempted to exchange drugs for Stinger missiles. Later that month two missiles were fired in a failed attack on an Arkia-Israeli Airlines Boeing 757 as it took off from Mombasa, Kenya.

Security Factoid _____

According to intelligence sources, there are a half million shoulder-held missile launchers in the world, and an unknown number of those may already be in the hands of organized crime and terrorist groups. The new system to protect commercial airliners from such attacks would cost about $2.5 million per plane. The system would detect an incoming missile and then deploy decoy flares that would trick the heat-seeking missiles.

A Somali extremist group with links to Al Qaeda was the prime suspect behind the failed attempt to shoot down the Israeli airliner with an SA-7 missile. It was known that Osama bin Laden had, in the past, provided financial support and military weapons to the Somali group, Al-Itihad al-Islamiya (Islamic Union). An unknown group calling itself the Army of Palestine took credit for the attacks.

"We assume that Al Qaeda carried out the attack," said a senior officer of Israel's internal security service. "An operation this complicated has to have a broad network."

The SA-7 missile used in the failed late-November attack is known as the *Strela* and is nearly identical to the Chinese-made *Red Cherry* missile. The missile has a range of 13,500 feet in altitude and three miles downrange. It is a heat-seeking missile with a high-explosive warhead, four feet in length. It weighs only 20 pounds and can be fired from a shoulder-held launching system.

Intelligence, as we have seen, can be a lot like detective work. You use the clues you have. In the case of this attack, a marking on the missile launcher tube gave intelligence officers a solid lead. Because the serial number on a Soviet-built missile launcher tube discovered near the Mombasa airport was similar to a tube found in Saudi Arabia in May 2002, it is theorized that the two missile launchers were purchased at the same time.

The Least You Need to Know

- We are not only protected by our own military might, but by our ability to know more about our enemy than he does about us.

- The 9/11 attacks in New York City and Washington, D.C. launched another global conflict, a War on Terrorism, that must be fought wherever terrorist cells may be in hiding.

- The best way to prevent terrorism at home is to kill the terrorists long before they get here.

- The *Posse Comitatus* Act states that America's military is prohibited from acting as a domestic police force.

- The Defense Intelligence Agency is the coordinating agency in the Defense Department that reports to the secretary of defense with intelligence collected from all military services.

- The Strategic Defense Initiative, Ronald Reagan's dream that would, in theory, render intercontinental ballistic missiles obsolete, has been reintroduced as a planned defense strategy by President George W. Bush.

Security Without and Within

In This Chapter

- ◆ Spaceborne reconnaissance
- ◆ Making maps
- ◆ Protecting the president
- ◆ Keeping secrets in/enemies out

We have learned that keeping America safe has been, for many years, a global task. Our security must be protected through operations both internal and external. We must hunt out enemies who are already inside our country and seek out those around the world who may one day try to attack us.

In this chapter we will look at some of the other organizations that contribute to the effort of national security: those that operate outside the country, those that function domestically, and one that patrols the edges of the United States, our borders.

National Reconnaissance Office (NRO)

The National Reconnaissance Office (NRO) is a lower-profile agency responsible for satellite and aerial overhead intelligence gathering.

It gathers intelligence through spaceborne reconnaissance. It reports to the secretary of defense with coordination by the DCI.

Its job is to make sure that the United States has the technology and spaceborne assets necessary to maintain global information superiority. The NRO, in conjunction with NASA, oversees the research and development, acquisition, and operation of our intelligence-gathering satellites.

Here's how the Department of Defense defines the NRO: "The NRO's assets collect intelligence to support such functions as indications and warning, monitoring of arms control agreements, military operations and exercises, and monitoring of national disasters and other environmental issues. The Director of the NRO is appointed by the President and confirmed by the Congress as the Assistant Secretary of the Air Force for Space. The Secretary of Defense has the responsibility, which is exercised in concert with the Director of Central Intelligence, for the management and operation of the NRO. The DCI establishes the collection priorities and requirements for the collection of satellite data. The NRO is staffed by personnel from CIA, the military services, and civilian Department of Defense personnel."

For many years the very existence of the National Reconnaissance Office was classified. The public did not become aware of its existence until 1992, when the Director of Central Intelligence recommended the declassification of that information.

National Imagery and Mapping Agency (NIMA)

Established in 1996, the National Imagery and Mapping Agency (NIMA) is a grouping of what was before that a bunch of smaller organizations in charge of the government's imagery and mapping. Those smaller organizations that now work under the structure of the NIMA are as follows:

Security Factoid

NIMA employees are trained in cartography (map making), imagery analysis, marine analysis, physical science, geodesy (determining the exact location of objects on the earth's surface), computer and telecommunication engineering, and photogrammertry (measuring distance using aerial photography).

- ◆ Defense Mapping Agency (DMA)
- ◆ Central Imagery Office (CIO)
- ◆ Defense Dissemination Program Office (DDPO)

And NIMA also took over much of the mission and many of the functions of the CIA's National Photographic Interpretation Center, and it works in conjunction with the DIA, the National Reconnaissance Office, and the Defense Airborne Reconnaissance Office (DARO).

Department of State

The State Department's intelligence wing is called the Bureau of Intelligence and Research (INR). Since 1946, INR has served as the State Department's primary source for interpretive analysis of global developments.

It reacts to policy priorities and gives early warning and analysis of events and trends that affect U.S. foreign policy and national security interests. INR ensures that intelligence activities abroad are in harmony with U.S. policy and that collection resources and priorities are in accord with our diplomatic interests and requirements.

The INR Assistant Secretary reports directly to the Secretary of State and serves as the Secretary's principal adviser for all intelligence issues.

Security Factoid

The Bureau of Intelligence and Research does not have to answer to other sections of the State Department and is not formally connected to other members of the U.S. intelligence community.

Department of Treasury and the Secret Service

As many readers may already know, the Secret Service—the organization in charge of protecting the U.S. president and his family—works under the structure of the Department of the Treasury. In addition to protecting present and past presidents— presidents and their families receive Secret Service protection even after they are out of office, for as long as they live—the organization is also in charge of the detection and prevention of counterfeiting.

Protecting the White House

All visitors to the White House are screened. The Secret Service, in theory, scrutinizes everyone who enters the White House grounds. Private contractors are required to provide their employers with personal histories. Background information and identification papers are checked.

The idea is that you don't even get past the front gate unless the Secret Service knows exactly who you are, where you've been, and what you might be up to. But, as was recently learned, the system in place can be fooled.

Illegal Alien in the White House

The Secret Service was given a fright near the end of 2002 when it was revealed that an illegal alien from Mexico with fake identity papers had gotten access to the White House—for *two years*! The illegal alien was a 30-year-old man named Salvador Martinez-Gonzalez.

Years ago, he acquired a phony U.S. passport under the name Kelvin Rodriguez and, using it, got a job with HDO Productions, Inc., a firm that supervises the installation of lawn tents for White House social functions. While doing his job, Martinez-Gonzalez had managed to be photographed with then-President Bill Clinton and, later, with Vice President Dick Cheney and his wife, Lynne.

Martinez-Gonzalez was caught in December 2002 after he returned to Mexico and attempted to re-enter the country using his forged passport. At that time it was discovered that he had been caught trying to enter the country under false pretenses once before, in Texas in February 2000, but had been set free.

Office of Intelligence Support

Since 1977, the Department of the Treasury has also been in charge of an organization known as the Office of Intelligence Support, which took the place of the Office of National Security (ONS), an organization formed to give the Department of the Treasury a presence on the National Security Council.

Security Factoid

Since 1972, the Treasury Department has also been represented on the National Foreign Intelligence Board to make sure that our economic policy makers are fully informed.

The Office of Intelligence Support alerts the secretary of the treasury and other officials to fast-breaking events, both foreign and domestic; provides intelligence reports and products to Treasury officials; oversees the intelligence relationships of Treasury offices and bureaus; and helps to prep are the National Intelligence Estimates and other community-wide intelligence products, developing and coordinating Treasury Department contributions.

Department of Energy

Since 1947, even the Department of Energy has had a presence in the U.S. intelligence community. The foreign intelligence program within the Energy Department provides the department and other government policy makers with timely, accurate, high-impact foreign intelligence analyses; and detects and defeats foreign intelligence services that are attempting to acquire the Energy Department's sensitive information.

Point/Counterpoint

According to Executive Order 12333, the Department of Energy is directed to: "provide expert technical, analytical and research capability to the Intelligence Community; to formulate intelligence collection and analysis requirements where the expert capability of the department can contribute; to produce and disseminate foreign intelligence necessary for the Secretary of Energy's responsibilities; and to participate with the Department of State in overtly collecting information with respect to foreign energy matters."

The program also provides technical and analytical support to the DCI and makes the department's technical and analytical expertise available to other members of the intelligence community. Its intelligence responsibilities include nuclear proliferation, nuclear weapons technology, and fossil and nuclear energy.

U.S. Border Patrol

The U.S. Border Patrol was officially established on May 28, 1924 by an act of Congress. It is the mobile uniformed law enforcement arm of the Bureau of Citizenship and Immigration Services (formerly known as the Immigration and Naturalization Service), and, until 9/11, its main purpose was to keep illegal immigrants out of the country. Now, although technically its mission has not changed, it has the additional responsibility of preventing terrorists from crossing our borders.

Security Factoid

Border Patrol agents spend 19 weeks in training at the Border Patrol Academy in Glynco, Georgia, or Charleston, South Carolina, which is a component of the Federal law Enforcement Training Center. Agents are taught immigration law, statutory authority, police techniques, and Spanish. Upon graduation, they spend an additional 24 weeks in on-the-job training, which includes weekly intensive instruction in immigration law and Spanish.

When the Border Patrol began in 1924, it consisted of 450 officers who combated illegal entries and alien smuggling. Now, the Border Patrol is in charge of patrolling the 6,000 miles of Mexican and Canadian international land borders and 2,000 miles of coastal waters surrounding the Florida Peninsula and the island of Puerto Rico.

And today, the Border Patrol is a force of 9,500, which seemed like enough before 9/11—and not nearly enough ever since.

The borders are protected using surveillance, following up leads, responding to electronic sensor alarms and aircraft sightings, and interpreting and following tracks. Traffic checkpoints are maintained along highways.

Security Speak

Signcutting is the detection and the interpretation of any disturbances in natural terrain conditions that indicate the presence or passage of people, animals, or vehicles.

Unlike on a map, the border is not a thick line across the ground. Our border crosses uninhabited deserts, canyons, and mountains. Because of this, the Border Patrol, when *signcutting*, utilizes a variety of equipment and methods.

Electronic sensors are placed at strategic locations. Video monitors and night vision scopes are used. Agents patrol in vehicles, boats, aircraft, and on foot. Horses, all-terrain motorcycles, bicycles, and snowmobiles are also used.

The U.S. Border Patrol uses about 125 aircraft to keep tabs on the borders. They employ approximately 100 pilots who work in conjunction with ground units to keep all unwanteds on the correct side of the border. Both fixed-wing aircraft and helicopters are used.

The Border Patrol watches the coastlines of the mainland, the shores of Puerto Rico, and the waterways that separate the United States and Canada with boats and ships. The patrol's 88 vessels range from blue-water craft to inflatable-hull craft.

The Border Patrol did an adequate job of keeping illegal aliens out of the country. Because the problem of sneaking unwanteds into our country was more severe in Mexico than it was in Canada, the great majority of Border Patrol agents were—and remain—stationed on our southern borders.

But times have changed, and the Border Patrol must change as well. Until 9/11, those who wanted to sneak into the United States were usually extremely poor and not terribly dangerous. They were merely looking for a better way of life.

Terrorists are an entirely different matter. They are dangerous, and they often have money. They don't care which border they sneak across. The Border Patrol is going to have to change the way it operates or another group will have to be brought in to give the Border Patrol support.

Clearance for the Chiefs

The other organizations that enhance our national security are local fire departments and law enforcement agencies. Many local and state police chiefs had difficulty getting information after terrorists struck on 9/11. Not long thereafter, the Justice Department decided to let police chiefs from cities, counties, and other municipalities apply for national security clearance.

Such a clearance puts them in the information-sharing loop during national emergencies. Barry McDevitt—chief of police for Attorney General John Ashcroft—made the decision.

Campus Cops and the FBI

Even university police have been brought into the national counterterrorism campaign. For example, at the University of Massachusetts at Amherst, a campus police detective reports to the Springfield office of the FBI nearly full-time. Other large public universities have similar relationships with the bureau, although most of them would describe their involvement as part-time.

The UMass-Amherst/FBI relationship became controversial when it came to light that a university police detective, working part-time for the FBI, helped a federal agent question an Iraqi-born economics professor about his politics.

This revelation caused the American Civil Liberties Union to demand that the FBI reveal the scope of its involvement on college campuses nationwide. In response to an initial request for information under the Freedom of Information Act, the ACLU received a form letter from the FBI acknowledging the inquiry.

Terror Training on the Local Level

Police forces, such as the New York Police Department, have received special counterterrorism training. Since local and state police (as well as firefighters) are most apt to be the first to respond to a terrorist attack, it is essential that police and firefighters know what to do.

Of course, not all local police have received such training and the reason they haven't is most often money—or the lack thereof. It is essential that all communities find within their budgets the funds necessary to teach their police forces and firefighters (many of whom are volunteers) the proper procedures in the case of a terrorist attack.

The Least You Need to Know

◆ The National Reconnaissance Office is a lower-profile agency responsible for satellite and aerial intelligence gathering.

◆ The State Department's intelligence wing is called the Bureau of Intelligence and Research.

◆ The Departments of Treasury and Energy also have intelligence wings.

◆ The U.S. Border Patrol was set up to prevent usually poor and harmless illegal immigrants from entering the country, and is an inadequate force for stopping terrorists.

◆ Since 9/11, government officials are re-focusing on ways to expand the Border Patrol for greater effectiveness.

Chapter 16

Department of Homeland Security

In This Chapter

- ◆ A new cabinet-level agency
- ◆ Governor turned secretary
- ◆ What to do in case
- ◆ Color-coded alert system

The bill creating the Department of Homeland Security (DHS) was signed into law by President Bush on November 25, 2002. The DHS is one of the cabinet-level departments—such as the Department of Defense, State, Interior, etc.—which comprise "the president's cabinet" and whose heads therefore are primary advisers to the president. The Department's job is to protect the United States from terrorism. It does this by analyzing terrorism intelligence and comparing it to the nation's vulnerabilities, developing new technologies to detect threats, coordinating the training and funding of state and local police and fire departments, and scrutinizing U.S. borders and ports of entry.

The First Agency Secretary: Tom Ridge

President Bush simultaneously nominated former Pennsylvania governor Tom Ridge as the agency's secretary. Ridge had been Bush's primary adviser on matters of homeland defense since the first days following the 9/11 attacks. Ridge took office on January 24, 2003, the day that the Department of Homeland Security became the nation's fifteenth cabinet department.

President Bush nominated two other senior members of his administration to assist Ridge in the new agency: Navy Secretary Gordon England as Ridge's deputy secretary; and Asa Hutchinson, then administrator of the Drug Enforcement Administration and formerly a House member from Arkansas, to head the division that oversees border and transportation security.

> **Point/Counterpoint**
>
> At the signing ceremony to create the Department of Homeland Security, President Bush said, "We're taking historic action to defend the United States and protect our citizens from the dangers of a new era. We're showing the resolve of this great nation to defend our freedom, our security and our way of life."

Bringing Together Other Agencies

The new agency helped to bring together previously separate agencies such as the Immigration and Naturalization Service, the Secret Service, the Customs Service, the Federal Emergency Management Agency, the Transportation Security Administration, and the Border Patrol. DHS brought together 22 federal agencies with 170,000 employees in the largest reorganization of the federal government since the Defense Department was created in 1947.

> **Author's Corner**
>
> McLean: DHS has its own analytical unit that examines intelligence gathered by the CIA, FBI, and other agencies to look for clues about terrorist plots.

On March 1, 2003, the Coast Guard, the Secret Service, Customs, the INS, and the Transportation Security Administration were transferred to the new department. On June 1, 2003, these agencies were joined by the Agriculture Department's Plum Island Animal Disease Center, among others, as part of the DHS.

Building Infrastructure

In December 2002, a month before the DHS was officially born, the first job was to build its infrastructure, so that it could be an organization capable of getting efficient results. The first step was to form working groups at the Office of Personnel Management who set about developing a personnel system. They planned to have the system in place by June 1, 2003. Six such groups were formed. They were in charge of:

- Performance appraisals

- Job classifications

- Pay

- Labor management

- Discipline

- Employee appeals

The job was not an easy one. The DHS is an amalgamation of 22 agencies, many of which function under a variety of pay, benefits, and hiring systems. The department will eventually employ in the neighborhood of 170,000 people, who will be represented by as many as 17 different unions.

Security Factoid

About the creation and design of the new DHS department, President Bush said, "Our objective is to spend less on administrators and offices and more on working agents in the field, less on overhead and more on protecting our neighborhoods and borders and waters and skies from terrorists."

Coast to Coast

Although the great majority of this early organizational work will take place in Washington, D.C., only a little more than ten percent of the DHS's employees will live in the D.C. area, with the rest scattered around the country.

One priority is to give the new DHS employees a maximum of security even as their new organization, and in some cases their jobs, are still under construction.

Employees will hold on to their current jobs and salaries for at least a year after their transfer, and they cannot be laid off during that period. Even after that, officials said, layoffs will be a last resort, with buyouts and transfers the preferred methods of shaping the workforce.

Security Factoid

DHS coordinates with two million police, firefighters, and medical personnel around the country.

Multiple Responsibilities

The DHS carries the following responsibilities:

- ◆ Preventing attacks

- ◆ Reducing vulnerability

- ◆ Minimizing damage and recovery

- ◆ Threat analysis and warning

- ◆ Border and transportation security

- ◆ Emergency preparedness and response

During February 2003, as the nation moved from a yellow to an orange alert status (the meanings of the color system designations are explained in the next section), Secretary of Homeland Security Tom Ridge offered a list of precautions that American families should take in this age of terrorism:

- ◆ Make a plan for contacting family members in an emergency. Designate a meeting place in case phone service is knocked out—or your home is destroyed.

- ◆ Find out where your spouse and children would be evacuated to in the event of an attack.

- ◆ Keep life, property, health, and other insurance policies current. Stash copies of important documents such as identification, deeds, and wills in a watertight container.

- ◆ Keep some cash handy.

- ◆ Have a plan for pets. Shelters do not allow them.

- ◆ Assemble a disaster supply kit. It should have bottled water, food, and emergency supplies. Also include prescription drugs, extra pairs of glasses, and a first aid kit.

- ◆ Learn about different types of attacks, so you will know what to do in an emergency.

- ◆ Do not cancel events or travel plans.

- ◆ Be especially aware of your surroundings and the events happening around you.

The Alert System: What the Colors Mean

The Homeland Security Advisory System was created to comprehensively and effectively disseminate information regarding the risk of a terrorist attack. The information is provided to federal, state, and local authorities—as well as to the American people. The development, implementation, and management of the system has been the responsibility of the Attorney General.

This advisory system is not the first national alert system to be set up by the United States. Transportation, defense, agriculture, and weather all have their own systems, and all have been uniquely tailored to their individual needs.

According to the Office of Homeland Security, "This advisory system characterizes appropriate levels of vigilance, preparedness and readiness in a series of graduated Threat Conditions. The Protective Measures that correspond to each Threat Condition will help the government and citizens decide what action they take to help counter and respond to terrorist activity. Based on the threat level, Federal agencies will implement appropriate Protective Measures. States and localities will be encouraged to adopt compatible systems."

The factors used to assess each threat are as follows:

◆ Is the threat credible?

◆ Is the threat corroborated?

◆ Is the threat specific and/or imminent?

◆ How grave is the threat?

It is believed that the advisory system in itself is an effective tool to help fight terrorism, because public announcements of terrorist threats not only help the government and the public respond accordingly to the threat, but act as a deterrent to terrorist activity.

Security Factoid

A good analogy for the deterrence factor of the terror alert system is this: When you turn on a light in a cockroach-infested apartment, all of the roaches scuttle quickly into the walls. The cockroaches are the terrorists and the alert system is the light. Antiterrorist personnel also are given a chance to capture the terrorists before they can do any harm, because they are the ones who are scurrying for cover.

Here are the various levels of alert, as defined by the system, and what they mean:

GREEN: Low Condition

Green means there is a low risk of terrorist attacks. During a green alert, the following measures are recommended:

- Refine and practice protective measures.
- Train appropriate personnel in protective measures.
- Assess vulnerabilities—and take steps to reduce that vulnerability.

BLUE: Guarded Condition

Blue indicates what the Office of Homeland Security calls a "general risk of terrorist attack." All of the protective measures itemized under the green condition also apply here. In addition to those, there are these:

- Check communications with designated emergency response or command locations.
- Review and update emergency response procedures.
- Provide the public with necessary information.

YELLOW: Elevated Condition

Yellow indicates that there is a significant risk of a terrorist attack. All of the above-itemized conditions also apply here. In addition, the following may be applied:

- Increase surveillance of critical locations.
- Coordinate emergency plans with nearby jurisdictions.
- Depending on what we know about the threat, adapt protective measures to best provide security.
- Implement, as appropriate, contingency and emergency response plans.

ORANGE: High Condition

While much of the nation has been kept at yellow or lower levels since 9/11, New York City and Washington, D.C. have been kept at orange, which designates a high risk of a terrorist attack. In addition to the previously outlined protective measures, the following may be applied:

- Coordinate necessary security efforts with armed forces or law enforcement agencies.

- Take additional precaution at public events.

- Prepare to work at an alternate site or with a dispersed workforce.

- Restrict access to key locations to essential personnel only.

During an orange alert, it is recommended that:

- Hotels inspect all cars.

- Malls and offices prohibit delivery trucks from entering underground parking garages.

- Office tower managers control access at the door and monitor their heating and air conditioning ducts for breaches. (Terrorists could use chemical or biological weapons in ductwork to attack an entire building.)

Many readers will remember that the entire nation was placed at the orange alert level for the first anniversary of the 9/11 attacks, and then again during February 2003. The second alert came because of a combination of factors, the upcoming war with Iraq, the Islamic season for pilgrimage, and information received from a defector. No terrorist attack materialized, and the defector later failed a lie detector test. Another reminder that a terrorist's goal is to cause terror, not necessarily death and destruction.

RED: Severe Condition

This level would indicate that a terrorist attack is imminent. In addition to the previous steps of readiness, the following would be applied to a red alert:

- Assign emergency response personnel and pre-position specially trained teams.

- Monitor, redirect, or constrain transportation systems.

Point/Counterpoint

Homeland Security Secretary Tom Ridge said, "When we raise the level of alert, we raise the national consciousness about the level of attack, that in itself, is a deterrence. ... Just being more ready, being more prepared, is a deterrent in and of itself."

◆ Close public and government facilities.

◆ Increase or redirect personnel to address critical emergency needs.

The Least You Need to Know

◆ The Department of Homeland Security's job is to protect the United States from terrorism by analyzing terrorism intelligence to match it against the nation's vulnerabilities, developing new technologies to detect threats, coordinating the training and funding of state and local police and fire departments, and scrutinizing U.S. borders and ports of entry.

◆ The Secretary of the Department of Homeland Defense is former Pennsylvania governor Tom Ridge.

◆ The new agency helps to bring together previously separate agencies such as the Immigration and Naturalization Service, the Secret Service, the Customs Service, the Federal Emergency Management Agency, the Transportation Security Administration, and the Border Patrol.

◆ The Homeland Security Advisory system was created to comprehensively and effectively disseminate information regarding the risk of a terrorist attack.

◆ The alert system is color coded from low to severe alert: green, blue, yellow, orange, and red.

Part 3

Types of Threats and How to Combat Them

One of the main tasks of the U.S. intelligence community is to combat the proliferation of weapons of mass destruction. Would-be proliferators—"rogue" states plus some 60 potential proliferator states or organizations—are practicing more and more denial and deception as awareness of U.S. intelligence sources and methods grows. In this section, we'll be looking at the various types of threats that the United States faces and what we can (and can't) do to prevent them.

Chapter 17

Terror in the Air: Making Sure 9/11 Never Happens Again

In This Chapter

- ◆ Proving you are you
- ◆ Canine detectives
- ◆ Machines that smell
- ◆ What you need to know

During the 1960s and 1970s, the concept of "airport security" first surfaced, to combat the problem of planes being hijacked to Cuba. But it had been decades since a U.S. airliner had been hijacked when, on September 11, 2001, four commercial airliners were hijacked, almost simultaneously.

Teams of terrorists, including some who were trained as pilots, hijacked the jets. Two were flown into the twin towers of the World Trade Center in New York City, one was flown into the Pentagon in Washington, D.C., and the fourth crashed into a field in Pennsylvania when the heroic passengers foiled the terrorists' plans.

Our concept of "airport security" would never be the same ....

New Airport Security

> **Author's Corner**
>
> McLean: Get to know and think like your enemy and you will have a major leap forward in intelligence. Understand your enemy's way of thinking and you will better anticipate his next move and prepare against it.

Remember what it was like traveling by air before the 9/11 attacks? It seems like a long time ago, huh? You got to the airport about 30 minutes before departure.

You checked your bags and waltzed through a metal detector that never went off. You placed your carry-on bags on a conveyor belt, and, if you were interested enough to check, you probably caught the security personnel looking at their fingernails rather than the scan of your carry-on bag.

Photo IDs

Well, those of you who have flown since the terrorist attacks on the United States know that things have certainly changed. You must now show up between one and two hours before your departure. When you check in you must show your photo ID.

While checking your bags you may be randomly selected to step behind a screened-off area, inside which both you and your bags will be searched. You may be pulled aside while going through the metal detector, and you may again face a search just before boarding your plane.

Carry-On Luggage

Before putting your carry-on luggage on the conveyor belt, you will be asked to empty all of your pockets into a plastic container, which will then go onto the conveyor belt as well. Jackets must be removed and placed on the belt. Randomly selected passengers (and those who appear suspicious, of course) will be asked to remove their shoes so those can be inspected. Anything suspicious will be scrutinized.

When your carry-on bags go through the screener on the conveyor belt, you can rest assured that no one will be examining their nails. The low-paid airport employees who formerly performed this function have been replaced by federally trained personnel who know exactly what they are looking for and will have a bag hand-searched if they see anything at all that they find suspicious.

Transportation Security Administration

On November 19, 2001, the president signed the Aviation and Transportation Security Act (ATSA) into law. The act established a new Transportation Security Administration (TSA) within the Department of Transportation.

The new security personnel at the nation's 429 commercial airports are employees of the TSA. From more than a million applicants, 23,000 baggage screeners and 33,000 passenger screeners were put in place during 2002.

Bomb-Sniffing Dogs: The Nose Knows

During the first year after 9/11, the predominant method of determining if explosives were hidden inside passenger baggage was the use of bomb-sniffing dogs. Dogs are far better at sniffing out the source of a particular odor than any machine yet developed, experts say. Scientists have estimated that a dog's nose has about 220 million mucus-coated olfactory receptors, roughly 40 times as many as humans. The dogs were not perfect, however.

According to explosives detection, the dogs often react to the mood of their handlers. When the dogs' handlers are excited and stressed, the dogs may overreact and falsely suggest that explosives are present when they are not.

Sniff-dog expert Dr. Lawrence J. Myers, from the Auburn University College of Veterinary Medicine, says that more rigorous training and certification standards, and more research into the way dogs detect scents and the relationship between them and their handlers are needed to avoid these problems. Poor handlers are the number-one reason for false positives.

"Dogs want rewards," he added, "and so they will give false alerts to get them. Dogs lie. We know they do."

Dogs are not the only animals capable of detecting bombs with their olfactory sense. Rats, for example, could do it. It's just that dogs are so much more socially acceptable and more human-friendly to work with.

Author's Corner
McLean: Despite overanxious dogs, I would still prefer that we do double checks than be lax. Let their nose sniff out whatever they can find and let's all stay safer.

Fire the Dogs: Bomb-Detecting Devices

The new bomb-detecting devices that are being installed in airports are about the size of an SUV. There are still a few bugs in these machines that need to be worked out. They trigger false positives about 30 percent of the time.

Security Factoid

The installation of the new bomb-detecting machines in America's airports has led to an unexpected rule. Commercial airlines passengers are no longer allowed to pack cheese in their bags. The type of cheese apparently doesn't matter. No limburger, no cheddar, no brie.

Of course, having a machine that finds explosives when there are none there is far more preferable than a machine that finds no explosives in a bag when a bomb exists. As these machines are installed in more and more airports, and the quality of the job they do approaches perfection, there will be a lot of dogs with sensitive noses looking for work.

The reason: Just as human nostrils sometimes have trouble distinguishing between a ripe piece of cheese and a pair of dirty socks, the new high-tech bomb-detecting devices have trouble distinguishing between cheese and bombs. Go figure.

Travel Rules

According to the Transportation Security Administration, here is a list of simple rules to follow to keep the hassle of airport security to a minimum:

♦ If you have jewelry in body piercings that are not visible when you are wearing your clothes, remove them before you go through airport security.

♦ Do not lock bags. If the bag is hand searched, the lock may need to be broken. If necessary, use cable or zip ties to assure bags stay closed.

♦ Do not pack food or drink in checked bags. An electronic scanning device could be triggered, in which case your bag will have to be hand searched.

♦ Put personal items in clear plastic bags—toiletries, dirty underwear, etc.—to reduce the chance that an airport screener will have to search them.

♦ If you must pack scissors, knives, or other sharp items, be sure to put them in your checked baggage and not in your carry-on baggage.

♦ Place all camera film in your carry-on baggage and not in your checked baggage. Scanning equipment could ruin both exposed and unexposed film.

- Do not over-pack a bag. If you have to sit on your luggage to get it closed, re-closing it after a hand search may be impossible.

- This is especially true during the holidays: Do not pack wrapped presents, as they will have to be unwrapped for searching. Wrap presents after you arrive at your destination.

Regarding new airport security, Transportation Security Administration spokesman Mark Hatfield said at the end of 2002, "With a combination of an appropriately sized security force, the right amount of equipment and superior training, we're hoping to minimize any delays for passengers. But we still ask people to get to the airport early. Anytime you add a new process to travel like this, there's the potential for additional time to go through the additional security process."

Leaving on a Jet Plane

Assume that a terrorist or a hijacker manages to get through the security at the airport and as your jet takes off, he is on the plane with you. Well, steps are being taken to make a jet in flight safer as well.

Flight crews are now trained in how to react to an emergency. Northwest Airlines flight attendants, for example, now take what is called Cabin Response Training, a counter-terrorism training course designed by an Israeli security firm called GS3.

GS3's president is the former security director at the Israeli airline El Al and is the author of many of that airline's anti-terror strategies. The training teaches flight attendants to take charge and defend their lives and their aircraft at all costs.

> **Point/Counterpoint**
>
> According to Air Tran Airways flight attendant Clarissa Zimmermann, "Before September 11, we were just completely oblivious that there were people who wanted to take us out."

In addition, many cockpits now have weapons to prevent terrorists from taking over the controls of the plane. As 9/11 proved, control of a cockpit can turn an airliner into a lethal weapon. Stun guns have been approved for use by pilots; whether regular guns will be allowed in cockpits is still under debate. Homeland Security Secretary Tom Ridge said, "Where do you stop? If pilots carry guns [then] railroad engineers and bus drivers could ask to do the same."

Also, there has been talk about equipping commercial airliners with antimissile defense systems. For more about the threat to airliners from shoulder-held missile launchers, see Chapter 14.

The Future of Airport Security

The frightening thing about the War on Terrorism is that it may never come to a satisfactory conclusion. There can be no "surrender," no ultimate "victory." Because of this, we should not look forward to a slackening of airport security anytime soon.

It is more likely, in fact, that future airport security will be more stringent than it is today, not less—as it continually tries to keep up with the evil ingenuity of global terrorism.

The Least You Need to Know

- It takes a lot longer to get through airport security than it used to, but the delays, in terms of increased security, make it more than worth it.

- Bomb-sniffing dogs are not perfect and cause the occasional false-positive, but they are still better than any machine that has been created to replace them.

- New high-tech bomb-detecting devices have trouble distinguishing between cheese and bombs.

- Until we win the War on Terrorism—which probably won't be anytime soon—airport security around the world will remain annoyingly stringent.

Chapter 18

Tightening Our Borders

In This Chapter

- ◆ Immigration
- ◆ Plugging holes
- ◆ North vs. South
- ◆ Coastal security

The most difficult task regarding keeping our nation secure is protecting our borders and coastlines, making sure that people and things we don't want in our country do not enter.

In this chapter we will look at the ways that the BCIS (Bureau of Citizenship and Immigration Services—known until 2003 as the Immigration and Naturalization Service or INS), the U.S. Customs Service, and the U.S. Coast Guard are (and in some cases aren't) keeping our borders an coast lines safe from unwanted intruders and cargo.

Tourism and Immigration

Each year, more than 500 million people cross the borders into the United States, some 330 million of whom are noncitizens. There are 350 official ports of entry that connect our homeland to the rest of the world.

Keeping track of those who enter the country and making sure that those who have entered the country temporarily leave when they are supposed to is the massive task of the BCIS.

There was a time when your average illegal immigrant wanted to enter the United States as a part of their pursuit of happiness. They were looking for work and perhaps a better life for their country. Today, that has drastically changed. The BCIS must now make sure that …

- People suspected of being terrorists are not allowed to enter the country.

- Documents presented by those entering the country are real.

- People attempting entry into the country are who they say they are.

The INS employs 4,775 inspectors to handle this job at all of the country's points of entry. This is not nearly enough. In these dangerous times that number needs to be greatly expanded.

Immigration Rules Today

The new Department of Homeland Security now includes the BCIS. This separates immigration services from immigration law enforcement. The department has an immigration services organization that administers our immigration law in an efficient, fair, and humane manner. The Department of Homeland Security has assumed the legal authority to issue visas to foreign nationals and admit them into the country. The State Department, working through the United States embassies and consulates abroad, administers the visa application and issuance process.

One post-9/11 crackdown by the BCIS was a new requirement for men and women from 13 mostly Islamic countries to register periodically with immigration authorities.

Author's Corner
McLean: Our BCIS policy and practice has put us in jeopardy and it will take years to sort that out. We have many enemies right here that we cannot account for. That may be the biggest problem that we face.

Around 3,000 visitors from Iraq, Iran, Libya, Sudan, and Syria were required to register by December 2002. Another 7,200 men from Afghanistan, Algeria, Bahrain, Eritrea, Lebanon, Morocco, North Korea, Oman, Qatar, Somalia, Tunisia, the United Arab Emirates, and Yemen had to register by January 2003. An estimated 14,000 visitors from Saudi Arabia and Pakistan were given until February 2003 to register.

At the first deadline for registration, in December 2002, more than 400 men were arrested or detained, many of them in Southern California. These men had violated immigration law or were wanted by law enforcement officials. Some feared that this sweep of illegals was too severe and would discourage those who needed to register from doing so by future deadlines.

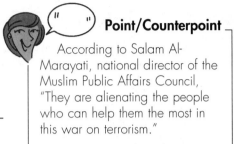

Point/Counterpoint

According to Salam Al-Marayati, national director of the Muslim Public Affairs Council, "They are alienating the people who can help them the most in this war on terrorism."

The second deadline, however, which took place in January of 2003, did not feature nearly as many arrests. According to the Justice Department, 124 foreigners with suspected visa violations were arrested across the country during the second registration period. This is out of an estimated 7,200 men and boys 16 and older who were photographed, fingerprinted, and interviewed at Immigration and Naturalization Service offices nationwide.

"R" Visas

It is possible, under current immigration rules, for terrorists to enter the United States under the guise of "religious leaders." Minimal scrutiny is given to Middle Easterners who enter the country with an "R" Visa, claiming to be an imam or other mosque employee. An imam is a Moslim religious leader. He can be anything from a prayer leader to someone claiming to be a descendant of Muhammad.

The R Visa program was created by Congress in 1990, with the purpose of encouraging the entrance of religious figures into our country to fill alleged domestic shortages among ministries, nunneries, and other religious groups. In 1998, eleven thousand foreigners entered the United States using R Visas.

By 1999, federal investigators had uncovered fraud rings involving religious institutions supposedly based in Fiji, Colombia, and Russia. Sheikh Omar Abdel Rahman, the mastermind behind the 1993 World Trade Center bombing, had an R Visa.

According to *New York Post* columnist Michelle Malkin, "The R visa program is a notorious law enforcement evasion scheme under which a number of religious facilities have been established as fronts to enable foreign nationals to enter the U.S. using false identities and evade criminal and terrorist watch lists."

Point/Counterpoint

In 1999, the General Accounting Office said, "Neither Immigration and Naturalization services nor the State department knows the overall extent of fraud in the religious worker visa program."

Better Scrutiny of International Travel

Under an antiterrorism rule that the Immigration and Naturalization Service proposed at the start of 2003, Americans traveling abroad would have to give the government detailed personal information before leaving or returning. According to the proposal, airlines and shipping companies would be forced to submit to the government the name, birth date, sex, passport number, home country, and address of every passenger and crew member. The rule would apply to U.S. citizens and noncitizens alike. Through 2002, air and shipping lines were not required to provide such information to the government about Americans. The information would be gathered while the aircraft or ship was en route to the United States and electronically transmitted to immigration officials on the ground at the port of entry.

Author's Corner

McLean: The Chinese seem to have quiet ways to do their sneak-and-peak in our American Open Society. Here's one example, according to a news report in 2000 that Wilson McLean noted in the *Washington Times*: "China's state-run news service Xinhua recently purchased a seven-story apartment building overlooking the Pentagon and plans to evict the residents to turn the 32-unit building into its Washington news bureau. Several specialists in Chinese intelligence expressed surprise that the U.S. government would allow this because Xinhua is described by Western intelligence as a front for the Ministry of State Security (MSS), China's version of the Soviet KGB … Although the Pentagon said it didn't matter, that this type of threat had been present and been dealt with for fifty years, as criticism increased the State Department stated that it will block the deal."

Carriers would have to provide information about people who are leaving the United States within 48 hours of their departure. Tickets from one country to another could no longer be purchased on a last-minute basis. The rule would take effect after a 30-day comment period. It would apply to passengers and crew members on airlines, cargo flights, cruise ships, and other vessels. The information would then be checked against watch lists and databases of suspected terrorists and criminals. The changes are part of a border security bill passed overwhelmingly by Congress and signed into law by President Bush on May 14, 2001.

The law also increased the number of immigration inspectors and investigators. One manifestation of the law is the heightened scrutiny of visa applications from countries listed as sponsors of terrorism. The FBI and CIA would have to increase information sharing with those who issue the visas, namely, the State Department. Without proper information sharing, visas could be issued to individuals the FBI and CIA are interested in keeping out of the country. This problem must be stopped and authorities are working to do so.

U.S. Customs

The Customs Service is in charge of finding and stopping illicit cargo from entering the United States—whether that contraband be coming in on a ship, a truck or automobile, or in an aircraft. The service employs approximately 20,000 who monitor 300 points of entry. Most of these points of entry are on our borders or coastlines, but not all. An airport inland can be a point of entry as well.

The service collects tariffs and prevents prohibited products (illegal drugs, certain foods, weapons, etc.) from entering the country. Traditionally, the Customs Service inspected about 2 percent of the containers entering the country by ship, and about 5 percent of the containers arriving by truck from Mexico. Since 9/11, these numbers have increased. About 10 percent of containers are now inspected, but this—for obvious reasons—still is not nearly enough. Inspections are done mostly on a random basis and, of course, always if there is something suspicious.

> **Ounce of Prevention**
>
> A proposal by former Coast Guard officer and scholar at the Council of Foreign Relations, Stephen Flynn, says that the most efficient way to keep unwanted cargo out of the country is to complete much of the inspecting before the packages reach American shores or borders. This would need to be done with the cooperation of shipping and trucking companies, as well as overseas port authorities.

It has been recommended that the Coast Guard and the U.S. Customs Service coordinate their efforts better and that technology such as that offered by global positioning satellites be used to help the cargo-tracking process.

Just as is the case with the U.S. intelligence community, the U.S. Customs Service needs to share information better, in this case with the BCIS, the Coast Guard, and private shipping companies.

The Container Security Initiative

Three months after 9/11, U.S. Customs began a program called the Container Security Initiative (CSI). This was designed to prevent terrorists from sneaking unwanted items and materials into the United States inside containers. It will hopefully enhance security of the sea cargo container—a vital link in global trade. Some 200 million sea cargo containers move annually among the world's top seaports, and nearly 50 percent of the value of all U.S. imports arrive via sea containers.

The CSI places U.S. Customs inspectors at major foreign seaports to pre-screen cargo containers before they are shipped to America. U.S. Customs officials, working with their foreign counterparts, will then be in a position to detect potential terrorist materials in U.S.-bound containers at these foreign ports. Since nearly 70 percent of all U.S.-bound sea containers pass through 20 major seaports around the globe, Customs focuses on those 20 ports.

Custom's Gizmos

Gizmos used by U.S. Customs inspectors at the Mexican border include those that peer down gas tanks and spot drug stashes inside tires. They can also scan the payloads of big trucks with deep-penetrating gamma rays and search all types of vehicles for drugs with hand-held sniffing machines.

Under development are high-tech ways to disable cars whose drivers elude border inspections. The BCIS uses electronic fingerprinting and computer-stored photographs to track more than one million immigrants who have previously been caught entering without documents.

There is also a camera that scans the license plates of cars lined up to cross the border. The license number is "read" by the camera which then automatically runs a computer check on it so that when the car arrives at the border patrol booth, the operator's computer screen tells him about the car, if and how often the vehicle has ever crossed the border before, and so on, all without any human intervention.

Porous Security

The job of patrolling the U.S. land borders belongs to the U.S. Border Patrol, an organization that, a year and a half after the 9/11 attacks, remains grossly understaffed.

Like the Immigration and Naturalization Service, the U.S. Border Patrol is overwhelmed by its responsibilities. Their efforts are futile. Anyone who seriously wants to sneak across a land border into the United States would have no trouble doing so.

Even though 15 of the 19 terrorists who committed the 9/11 attacks were in the country illegally, our attitudes toward illegal aliens remains lax.

Because the terrorist attacks of 9/11 have put an expensive strain on border security, some streamlining of former redundancies in the system have been made. For example, Customs and Immigration Services often performed the same duties with the same people attempting to enter the country. Therefore, in January 2003, Homeland Security Secretary Tom Ridge announced that plans were underway to combine border security and inspection agencies so that people entering the United States would only have to deal with one Homeland Security official, instead of as many as four.

According to newspaper columnist Bill O'Reilly, "The feds have looked the other way for a couple of reasons. Cheap immigrant labor fuels profits, and immigrant-rights groups can hurt a politician who is considered unfriendly. In New York, Chicago, Los Angeles, Houston, San Francisco, and many other cities, local authorities simply ignore federal law. It is illegal for anyone to enter the U.S. without a valid passport or visa. Yet in New York, Executive Order 124, signed by then-Mayor Ed Koch in 1989, discourages and in some cases prohibits city workers, including police, from reporting known illegal aliens to the BCIS, even after they have been arrested."

Security Factoid

The United States has 37,000 troops patrolling the border between North and South Korea? That is 37,000 more than they have patrolling the U.S. borders between Mexico and Canada.

As Martin Peretz of *The New Republic* wrote, "We can no longer assume that every immigrant is here looking for education or for freedom. Some are here in the interest of chaos, and we should never be so naive as to forget that."

Security Factoid

Because, historically, the problem of illegal immigrants entering the country was far more severe along our southern border with Mexico than it was along our northern border with Canada, the security in place was greatest in the south. Unfortunately, with the increased risk of terrorism inside the United States, it has become clear that terrorists do not care which border they cross, yet—despite the fact that the United States has 5,525 miles of border with Canada and 1,989 miles with Mexico—the Canadian border still lacks the attention given the Mexican border. Our maritime border includes 95,000 miles of shoreline, and a 3.4 million-square-mile exclusive economic zone. The protection of our maritime borders is the responsibility of the U.S. Coast Guard.

Fake IDs

According to U.S. government investigators, U.S. border guards do not scrutinize identification as they should and it is possible—even easy—to get into the country using false identification.

The investigators, testifying before a Senate committee in January 2003, said that undercover agents using false identification had no trouble crossing the border with Canada or Mexico. The fake IDs, it was said, were made using common computer equipment.

Border guards, they testified, failed to realize that the holograms on the false identification were fake or that birth certificates supplied by the undercover agents did not have watermarks. "Bouncers at college bars could spot the kind of fake ID's that were used by investigators," said Senate Committee Chairman Chuck Grassley (R-Iowa).

Security Factoid

A common problem in past years has been illegal aliens being allowed to stay in the country because they had purchased counterfeit green cards. These cards were nearly identical to the real thing, close enough to avoid detection upon casual inspection. Efforts are now being made to make counterfeiting of green cards next to impossible. A sophisticated new green card for resident aliens employs holograms and laser-etched data to deter fakes.

St. Regis Mohawk Reservation

The problems with stopping terrorists from entering the United States though Canada are the same as those of stopping smugglers, a problem that has existed for many years. The most common items to be smuggled from Canada to the United States are cigarettes, drugs, guns, and illegal aliens.

One especially soft spot in U.S. security may be the 16,000-acre St. Regis Mohawk Reservation. The reservation straddles the Canada/U.S. border on the northern edge of New York State and two Canadian provinces. Eight miles of border are covered by the reservation.

The reservation is not far from Cornwell Island in St. Lawrence. It is a sparsely populated area, made up of rivers, lakes, and a whole lot of wilderness. Because of this it has long been a favorite spot for smugglers to bring their goods into the United States from Canada. Now, of course, it is feared that terrorists will have the same idea.

The problem is that U.S. authorities, in this case the U.S. Border Patrol, have no authority on Native American reservations. The same is true on the other side of the river, where the Royal Canadian Mounted Police have no authority inside the reservation.

Interestingly, although the smuggling of illegal goods in the area remains about the same as it was before 9/11, the smuggling of illegal aliens has greatly decreased. The reason is that the Native Americans' own security systems have cracked down on this practice.

The St. Regis tribe is not only made up of war veterans who consider themselves patriotic Americans, but many members of the tribe were among the "skywalkers" who helped construct the World Trade Center towers.

Being a steelworker when you are more than one hundred stories up is something that takes a special type of person, a rare form of courage. Who in their right mind would want to do such a thing? A disproportionate number of the men who worked building the World Trade Center towers were Mohawk Indians.

> **Point/Counterpoint**
>
> According to Can Broeker, an undercover agent who has worked both for the Royal Canadian Mounted Police and the U.S. Secret Service, Native American reservations remain a soft spot in border security. "Anybody who wanted to move products or people over the other side went through the rez. [among these were] Iranians and Iraqis with rugs and drugs. ... It's nothing, a half mile, like crossing [New York City's] East River."

The Mohawks had apartments across the East River in Brooklyn where they went after each day's work, but on weekends they commuted back home—to the St. Regis reservation. After 9/11, many members of the tribe also helped with the cleanup at Ground Zero.

The police chief for the tribe on the U.S. side is Andrew Thomas, who says that, when it came to those sneaking illegal aliens through the reservation, "We put them on notice after 9/11. It was going to stop. Enough is enough." One can only hope that the St. Regis police will have the same effect on terrorists who might choose this route into the United States.

The U.S. Border Patrol in the region of the St. Regis Mohawk Reservation added 20 new positions during 2002—but that is not nearly enough.

The Least You Need to Know

- One post-9/11 crackdown by the Immigration and Naturalization Service was a new requirement for men and women from 13 mostly Islamic countries to register periodically with immigration authorities.

- Under an antiterrorism rule that the Immigration and Naturalization Service proposed at the start of 2003, Americans traveling abroad would have to give the government detailed personal information before leaving or returning.

◆ Like the Immigration and Naturalization Service, the U.S. Border Patrol is overwhelmed by its responsibilities.

◆ The problems with stopping terrorists from entering the United States through Canada are the same as those of stopping smugglers, a problem that has existed for many years.

Chapter 19

Understanding Chemical Warfare

In This Chapter

- ◆ Death underground
- ◆ The Iraqi menace
- ◆ IDing the substances
- ◆ Contaminating the well

In this chapter we will examine the potential use of chemical weapons against the United States. By this we mean poisons, which can be either liquid or gaseous, and are fatally toxic. Poison gases were used during World War I. Chemical attacks were used by Iraq in 1980 and 1984 during the Iraq-Iran War, and by Saddam Hussein against his own people in 1988. The deadliest use of a chemical weapon by a terrorist group came only a few years back, in Japan.

What Are Chemical Weapons?

Chemical weapons or warfare agents are poisonous vapors, sprays, aerosols, liquids, or solids that have toxic effects on people, animals, or plants. These materials can be released by bombs, sprayed from aircraft such as crop chemical applicator planes, boats, or other vehicles. They also can be used as a liquid to create a hazardous situation, much as crop dusting or crop spraying airplanes apply pesticides to farm crops to kill and control harmful insects.

Chemical weapons are potentially lethal but are difficult to deliver in lethal concentrations. Outdoors they often dissipate quickly. Also, they are more difficult to produce than biological materials. However, nations with chemical and biological warfare laboratories could produce and make such material available to other terrorists. These are considerations the U. S. government must keep in mind when dealing with rogue nations and groups as well as terrorist cells.

Japanese Subway Attack: Lessons Learned

In March 1995, the Aum Shinrikyo sect (which means Supreme Truth)—a small group of religious fanatics—killed 12 people and injured more than 5,000 by releasing sarin nerve gas in the Tokyo subway system. Details about sarin will be discussed later in this chapter in the section called "Sarin." Discussions of other chemical agents will follow.

The leaders of the group preached doomsday messages and their followers tried to make the prophecies self-fulfilling. The cult also unsuccessfully tried to use biological weapons such as anthrax and botulism to kill people.

The perpetrators of the attack were arrested and convicted of murder. At their trial they claimed they were innocent because they were only obeying orders from God. At least partially because of this attack, Japan has been an active ally in the War on Terrorism. They have helped by …

- ◆ Freezing terrorist assets.

- ◆ Sharing intelligence.

- ◆ Maintaining a watch list of 300 groups and individuals.

Now let's look at some of the chemical weapons that the United States has to protect itself against.

Mustard Gas Ain't for Your Hot Dog

Mustard is a blister agent that affects the eyes, lungs, and skin. There is no known antidote. The process of cellular destruction is irreversible. It was first synthesized as a weapon in the 1800s and first used in warfare by the Germans in 1917 during World War I.

Security Factoid

As of January 2003, Iraq was thought to have 550 artillery shells filled with mustard gas.

In liquid form, the weapon called mustard is colorless when pure, but also effective in less than pure form. In that state it is a brown oily substance—which is why it has become known as mustard. The U.S. Army does not consider mustard a lethal substance, but complications from mustard exposure have been known to cause death.

Exposure to mustard may cause very little pain at first and victims may not notice symptoms right away. The longer the exposure, however, the worse the eventual symptoms will be. The organs most apt to be affected are the eyes. The effect on the skin can range from redness to severe blisters. Inhalation will cause the following:

♦ Irritation of throat

♦ Tightness of chest

♦ Hoarseness

♦ Coughing

Unless medical treatment is received right away, the victim may develop severe pneumonia and high fever.

Ounce of Prevention

Biological agents can be dispersed by an aerosol spray that must be inhaled. However, these agents can also be used to contaminate food, water, and other products. Attention to basic food hygiene when traveling abroad is very important.

To keep damage to a minimum, the victim must have the mustard removed as quickly as possible. Wash with soap and water after applying an absorber of mustard, such as flour. Or, wash skin and clothes with 5 percent solution of sodium hypochlorite or liquid household bleach. If affected, flush the eyes with water. If the mustard has been ingested, do not induce vomiting. The victim should drink lots of milk.

Sarin

Sarin was developed in 1938 in Germany as a pesticide. Its name is derived from the

Security Factoid

A Scud warhead filled with the nerve agent sarin, the nerve agent that was used in the Japan subway attacks, could contaminate 140 square miles.

names of the chemists involved in its creation: Schrader, Ambros, Rudriger, and van der Linde. It is a colorless nonpersistent liquid—nonpersistent meaning that it does not last long. Symptoms of overexposure may occur within minutes or hours, depending upon the dose.

Symptoms include the following:

◆ Miosis (constriction of pupils) and visual effects

◆ Headaches and pressure sensation

◆ Runny nose and nasal congestion

◆ Salivation

◆ Tightness in the chest

◆ Nausea

◆ Vomiting

◆ Giddiness

◆ Anxiety

◆ Difficulty in thinking

◆ Difficulty sleeping

◆ Nightmares

◆ Muscle twitches

◆ Tremors

◆ Weakness

◆ Abdominal cramps

◆ Diarrhea

◆ Involuntary urination and defecation

◆ Convulsions

◆ Respiratory failure

If exposed to sarin, hold your breath or put on a gas mask. If sarin has already been inhaled, a nerve agent antidote kit will need to be administered to prevent the life-threatening effects.

Ricin

Another chemical agent that could be used by terrorists is ricin (pronounced *RICE-in*). The poison dates back to the Cold War when it was developed from the castor oil bean plant by the Soviet Union for use by the KGB.

Early symptoms of ricin poisoning are flulike, including nausea, vomiting, diarrhea, and high fever. Death can follow within three days of exposure.

In 1978, Bulgarian agents used ricin to kill the exiled dissident Georgi Markov in Britain. The assassin used a specially equipped umbrella to push a ricin capsule into the victim's leg while he was crossing the Waterloo Bridge in London. (Not until the autopsy did doctors know what had actually killed Markov.)

> **Ounce of Prevention**
>
> Some chemical agents may be volatile. They may evaporate rapidly to form clouds of the agent. Others may be persistent. These agents may act directly on the skin, lungs, eyes, and respiratory tract, or be absorbed through your skin and lungs, causing injury.

In January 2003, traces of the highly toxic poison ricin were found in a North London apartment in the Wood Green section after British antiterrorism police arrested six men, all of North African origin. A seventh, also North African, was arrested two days later. A week after that, six more people, five men and a woman, were also arrested, this time in Bournemouth on England's south coast. During one subsequent arrest involving this group, a British agent was killed.

Back in Washington, a representative of the Bush Administration said that there were "indications" that the gang with the ricin in London were connected with Ansar al-Islam, a Kurdish group with ties to Al Qaeda.

Ricin, if either inhaled or ingested, is one of the world's most lethal poisons. It is twice as potent as cobra venom. One gram can kill as many as 36,000 people. The poison can exist in a liquid, crystal, or dry powder form. In extremely low doses, it could be used as a laxative.

Ricin, when in a terrorist's possession, could cause the most damage if converted into an aerosol and sprayed into the air in a crowded area. However, experts say this is hard to do. It is more likely that ricin would be used by terrorists in liquid form, which could be spread on a subway turnstile, for example.

The ricin found in England was the second discovery of the substance since the 9/11 attacks. Traces of ricin were also found in Afghanistan in 2002 in a house known to be occupied by Al Qaeda operatives. Intelligence sources have also reported that ricin is part of Iraq's chemical and biological weapons program.

Security Factoid

According to Magnus Ranstorp, a terrorism expert at St. Andrews University in Scotland: "I would call it a weapon of mass disruption. It goes to the very essence of terrorism—the fear that it creates. In all likelihood a suicide bombing would kill more people. But ricin doesn't have to kill a lot of people or even succeed to produce a wave of panic."

In response to the discovery of ricin in Great Britain, the FBI warned local police throughout the United States that there might be plans in the works for a ricin attack in the United States. A bulletin distributed nationwide to 17,000 law enforcement officials familiarized police with the toxin's hazards, the symptoms that the poison causes, and how to treat potential victims.

Part of the bulletin read, "Ricin could be used in a terrorist operation to contaminate closed ventilation systems such as heaters or air conditioners, drinking water, lakes, rivers, and food supplies."

VX Nerve Gas

British chemists inadvertently discovered VX more than 50 years ago while searching for new insecticides. Because the compound was found to be extremely toxic to humans, the discovery was shared with the U.S. Army in 1953. The army's team of scientists refined the compound to make it even more toxic. The "V" in VX stands for "venomous." VX, as a liquid, can either be clear, odorless and tasteless, or amber in color, similar in appearance to motor oil.

If VX is inhaled or ingested, only those in possession of nerve agent antidote kits will be treatable. If VX comes in contact with the eyes, 15 minutes of flushing with water is recommended. Severe exposure could lead to convulsions and respiratory failure.

If exposed to VX, symptoms will become apparent in minutes or hours—depending on the extent of the exposure. Symptoms include:

- Constriction of pupils
- Headaches
- Runny nose and nasal congestion
- Uncontrollable drooling
- Breathing difficulties
- Nausea and vomiting
- Shakiness
- Confusion

If skin contact is made, put on a gas mask and remove your clothes. Wash with a combination of plenty of soap and water, 10 percent sodium carbonate solution, or 5 percent liquid household bleach. Rinse well with water to remove excess decontaminant.

Security Factoid

VX is so deadly that one warhead, loaded with 140 liters of the stuff, could kill up to one million people.

Soman-GD

Soman-GD, a nerve agent, has the chemical name Pinacolyl methyl phosphonofluoridate. Discovered in Germany in 1944, it is a colorless liquid with a fruity odor when pure, but the industrial version is yellow-brown with a camphor-like odor. Doses that are potentially life-threatening may be only slightly larger than those producing lesser effects. Symptoms may occur within minutes or hours, depending upon the dose. Those symptoms include:

- Constriction of pupils and visual effects
- Headaches and pressure sensation
- Runny nose and nasal congestion
- Salivation
- Tightness in the chest
- Nausea
- Vomiting
- Giddiness
- Anxiety
- Difficulty in thinking and sleeping
- Nightmares
- Muscle twitches
- Tremors
- Weakness
- Abdominal cramps
- Diarrhea, involuntary urination, and defecation

Severe exposure symptoms progress to convulsions and respiratory failure. The only way to prevent inhalation is by holding one's breath or donning a protective mask. A nerve-agent antidote kit would be necessary to prevent death if the victim has already been exposed.

Taban-GA

Tabun-GA is a nerve agent that has the chemical name Dimethylphosphoramido-cyanidate. It was the first nerve agent ever discovered, and was first developed as an insecticide in Germany in 1936. It is a colorless and tasteless liquid with a slightly fruity odor.

The symptoms of Tabun-GA exposure are:

♦ Runny nose

♦ Tightness of the chest

♦ Dimness of vision and pinpointing of the eye pupils

♦ Difficulty in breathing

♦ Drooling and excessive sweating

♦ Nausea

♦ Vomiting, cramps, and involuntary defecation and urination

♦ Twitching, jerking, and staggering

♦ Headache, confusion, drowsiness, coma, and convulsions

Security Factoid _____

Dr. Gerhard Schrader first noticed the effects of nerve agents on humans when he and his lab assistant began to experience shortness of breath and contraction of the pupils.

If exposure is to the skin, a victim may live up to two hours. A nerve-agent antidote kit would be necessary to prevent death if the victim has already been exposed. The only way to prevent inhalation is by holding one's breath or donning a protective mask.

If left untreated, the symptoms will worsen, breathing will stop, and death will soon follow. The symptoms are much worse if the substance is inhaled than if the exposure is to the skin. If inhaled, Tabun will kill you in one to ten minutes.

Cyanide

As anyone who has ever read a hard-boiled detective novel knows, you can tell if something is cyanide because it smells like burned almonds.

During the Orange Alert of February 2003, New York City hospitals were told to be on high alert for a terrorist attack involving cyanide gas. The city's health department told hospitals to increase the levels of sodium thiosulfate they had on hand, as this is the antidote for cyanide poisoning.

The alert warned local hospitals to be on the lookout for a "cluster" of patients complaining of respiratory, neurological, and skin conditions—as these could be the first indications that a cyanide gas attack had taken place.

If you are exposed to cyanide gas in the air, you will suffer:

◆ Breathing difficulties

◆ Chest pains

◆ Vomiting

◆ Severe headaches

A prolonged exposure to cyanide could lead to coma and death. If cyanide is eaten, add convulsions to the list of symptoms. If you find yourself in an area contaminated with cyanide, get away from the area as quickly as possible. If a vctim is exhibiting symptoms of cyanide exposure, call an ambulance or summon medical help.

> **Ounce of Prevention**
>
> Do not give mouth-to-mouth resuscitation to a victim of cyanide poisoning as you may be contaminated as well in the process. Instead, resuscitate victim by applying an oxygen mask.

If cyanide has been ingested, induce vomiting immediately.

How Chemical Weapons Can Be Used

Chemical weapons can be used against an enemy in several forms. They could be placed in the warhead of a missile. They could be dropped from an aircraft onto a populated area. On the battlefield, canisters of chemicals could be propelled upon an enemy using artillery.

If the chemicals are in the hands of terrorists and are intended for use against a civilian population, as we have seen, crowded areas such as subways may be the target, as was the case in Japan. Or, as in the following case in Israel, plans may be made for the liquid chemicals to be dumped into water supplies and waterways.

> **Ounce of Prevention**
>
> If there is an imminent threat of a chemical attack, it is a good idea to seal your house's windows and doors with plastic sheeting and duct tape.

Poison Plot in Israel

One chemical attack, apparently the idea of Iraqi leader Saddam Hussein, involved the use of poison in water supplies and waterways. Luckily for the civilized world, it was foiled by Israeli intelligence and law enforcement.

In January of 2003, a Palestinian terrorist—Mohammed Farouq Abu Roub—arrested in Israel said that Hussein had given him money and ordered him to carry out attacks using poison in Israel.

"I was told to be ready to spread poison in the major Israeli pipelines, the River Jordan, or the Lake of Galilee," said the 29-year-old terrorist, who was a former junior officer in Palestinian intelligence.

Security Factoid

Abu Roub quoted Saddam Hussein as saying, "I want a mega-attack with a lot of casualties that will paralyze the life of Israel."

"I got these instructions in Iraq," Abu Roub continued, "where I was given thousands of dollars to carry out mega-attacks. I made a strong commitment to Saddam, just as he made a commitment to the Palestinian people. Our destinies are linked. [In Iraq] there was no problem getting weapons, ammunition, poisonous powders. Everything was in big quantities. There were no limits."

Baghdad's Deadly Trap

According to Hussain al-Shahristani, who was the ex-chief adviser to the Iraqi Atomic Energy Commission, Saddam Hussein planned to use chemical weapons to create a "ring of death" around Baghdad in case of an American invasion.

The former adviser said, "There had been discussion within Saddam Hussein's circle to set up a 'chemical belt' around Baghdad using his chemical weapons to entrap the residents inside … Saddam has mastered his concealment tactics. These materials are hidden deep underground or in a tunnel system."

Other sources have said that Saddam planned to fire artillery shells filled with VX and sarin from inside Baghdad on approaching U.S. forces. As we now know, the capture of Baghdad by U.S. forces was accomplished without a major battle and no "ring of death" materialized.

Author's Corner

McLean: When we were first trained about CBR (chemical, biological, and radiological warfare), an old sergeant gave us gas masks and told us to put them on when we first smelled tear gas in the test room. Young, cocky, we thought we could tough it out. He gave us a good dose and most of us barely got our masks on. Even then, 90 percent of us had tear-filled eyes. Just proved how fast you can get hit with a gas. You really need a warning system.

The Least You Need to Know

◆ A deadly chemical attack involving the nerve agent sarin took place in a crowded Japanese subway.

◆ The ricin found in England in January 2003 was the second discovery of the substance since the 9/11 attacks.

◆ Saddam Hussein of Iraq has deadly chemical weapons and has used them in the past—even on his own people.

◆ Terrorists have planned to poison large numbers of people by putting toxic substances in water supplies and waterways.

Chapter **20**

Understanding Biological Warfare

In This Chapter

- ◆ Monitoring system
- ◆ Reacting to the bio-alarm
- ◆ Anthrax at home—and elsewhere
- ◆ Germ-free air and food

In this chapter we will take a look at one of the most terrifying forms of terrorist attack: biological weapons. This is a silent but deadly form of attack. Using germs—bacteria and viruses—to kill and terrorize seems almost unimaginably monstrous, but we Americans know from experience that biological weapons are a reality.

Not long after the 9/11 attacks we endured a series of biological attacks that had the entire country nervous, many of us putting on rubber gloves just to pick up the mail. The name of the agent used: anthrax.

What Are Biological Agents?

Basically, biological agents are organisms or toxins that can kill or incapacitate people, livestock, and crops. There are three basic groups of agents: bacteria, viruses, and toxins. Most are difficult to grow and maintain. Others, such as anthrax spores, can live for decades.

Security Factoid _____

During the Korean War, the United States was falsely accused of using bio-warfare. The charges were instigated by Chinese field advisers to the North Koreans in 1952. At the time the North Korean population was suffering from a massive outbreak of cholera and plague. To buttress their claims, the Communists infected North Koreans awaiting execution with plague and cholera, so their bodies could be shown to outside investigators. They also forced 25 captured U.S. pilots to sign "confessions." A huge Communist propaganda campaign, blessed by Joseph Stalin and backed by Mao Tse-tung, was subsequently waged through the press and the "World Peace Council," complete with staged public demonstrations in Western Europe. In 1953, the Soviet Union realized that the stories were false. A Soviet document says, "The Soviet government and Central Committee were misled. The spread of information in the press about the use by the Americans of bacteriological weapons in Korea was based on false information. The accusations against the Americans were fictitious."

Biological agents can be dispersed by spraying them into the air or infecting animals, which carry the disease to humans, as well as through food and water that can be contaminated. There is an incubation period after exposure to biological agents. It is essential that you seek appropriate care for illnesses acquired while traveling abroad to assure prompt diagnosis and treatment.

Some may fear that the recent SARS (Severe Acute Respiratory Syndrome) outbreak may be the result of terrorism, but there is no evidence that this is the case. As doctors say, SARS has "Mother Nature written all over it."

Person-to-person spread of some infectious agents such as smallpox and plague is possible. That is one reason the government is planning smallpox vaccination, especially for first responders and other emergency teams (see the later "Smallpox" section).

Anthrax

Not long after the 9/11 attacks, a second terror campaign began. The U.S. mails were used to distribute a *weaponized* version of anthrax, a deadly spore. At first it was feared that the letters were a plot by the Al Qaeda terror network, but—though the crimes have not been solved—the best theory today is that the plot was of domestic origin.

The following is a list of the different types of anthrax:

Cutaneous or skin anthrax occurs when the bacteria enter a break in the skin. This is the most common naturally occurring type, and most frequently occurs when humans handle contaminated animal products (meat, wool, or hides). The first symptom is a small bump. This progresses into a larger blister in one to two days. That is followed by a black scab called an eschar. Even if left untreated only 5 to 20 percent of all cutaneous anthrax cases would be fatal. Death is extremely rare if the disease is treated with antibiotics.

Security Speak

Biological and chemical agents need to be **weaponized,** that is, they need to be put in the form of a weapon, if they are to be used by an enemy to cause many casualties. They can be transformed into aerosal form, or—as was the case with the anthrax—placed in a powder and distributed through the mail system.

Gastrointestinal (ingested) anthrax is a very rare disease. In fact, there are no documented cases in the United States since the nineteenth century. Symptoms are nausea, loss of appetite, vomiting, and fever. These would be followed by severe abdominal pain, vomiting blood, and severe diarrhea. This form of anthrax is fatal in 25 to 60 percent of all cases.

Inhalational anthrax can occur when inhaling as few as 5,000 to 6,000 anthrax spores. That number could be inhaled in a single breath. Symptoms begin in one to six days and at first resemble those of the flu. But these symptoms rapidly worsen into severe breathing problems and shock. When left untreated, the death rate is very close to 100 percent. Death usually occurs within 48 hours of the initial symptoms.

Ounce of Prevention

The good news is that anthrax responds to antibiotics and there is a vaccine that will immunize you against it. Like all vaccinations, there is a small risk. In a small number of cases, the vaccine causes headaches, muscle aches, and other temporary symptoms. Pregnant women should not be vaccinated against anthrax.

As the United States learned the hard way, anthrax is not only deadly, but is very difficult to protect yourself from and to kill. Here is a list of additional things we know about anthrax:

- Anthrax spores can be spread in the air by missiles, rockets, artillery, aerial bombs, and sprayers.

- Anthrax can travel downwind for hundreds of miles.

◆ Anthrax spores remain dangerous for decades. (We know this is true because, during World War II, the British experimented with anthrax on Gruinard Island in Scotland and 40 years later, the island was still uninhabitable and had to be decontaminated.

◆ Anthrax can be produced in large quantities with relatively basic technology.

Security Factoid

A Japanese cult called Aum Shinrikyo, infamous for releasing sarin in the Tokyo subway system (see Chapter 19), spent millions of dollars on the development of biological weapons and actually attempted to release anthrax in Tokyo.

◆ Naturally occurring anthrax spores remain dormant in the soil for decades. Grazing animals can ingest them and become infected with the disease.

◆ Any country with basic health care or a basic pharmaceutical industry has the expertise to produce anthrax.

◆ Anthrax is treatable if that treatment is initiated promptly after exposure. The post-exposure treatment consists of certain antibiotics administered in combination with the vaccine.

◆ An anthrax vaccine that confers protective immunity does exist, but is not readily available to private parties. Efficacy and safety of use of this vaccine for persons under 18 or over 65 and pregnant women have not been determined.

◆ The anthrax vaccine is produced exclusively by Bioport under contract to the Department of Defense. Virtually all vaccine produced in the United States is under Defense Department contract primarily for military use and a small number of other official government uses.

Anthrax in the United States

In the months following 9/11, Americans in Florida, Virginia, Washington D.C., New Jersey, New York, and Connecticut were intentionally exposed to anthrax, probably through spores placed in the U.S. mail as part of a terrorist campaign.

Victims suffered both cutaneous (skin) and inhalational anthrax. Out of seven confirmed and four probable cases of cutaneous anthrax, all survived. Eleven victims contracted inhalational anthrax, of which five died.

Mail containing anthrax spores was found addressed to elected officials of the U.S. government, as well as to major media outlets. Thousands of letters may have been cross-contaminated after the first anthrax-bearing letters were processed through mail-sorting machinery in Washington D.C., New Jersey, and New York City.

> **Point/Counterpoint**
>
> Soon after the first anthrax infections in the United States in 2002, the director-general of the World Health Organization, Dr. Gro Harlem Brundtland said, "There are three lessons from recent events: first, public health systems have responded promptly to the suspicion of deliberate infections; second, these systems must continue to be vigilant; and third, an informed and responsible public is a critical part of the response."

Thousands of congressional staffers, mail handlers and media personnel needed the protection of antibiotics and vaccination. Many office buildings and post offices were shut down, and the situation was further aggravated by a series of hoaxes that followed.

As we all learned on the nightly news, anthrax bacteria produce spores that can be processed to become easily airborne. Mail-sorting machinery can easily aerosolize anthrax in envelopes sent via regular methods through the U.S. Postal Service.

Anthrax in Iraq

During the early weeks of 2003, as U.N. weapons inspectors searched inside Iraq for evidence that Iraq has not discontinued and dismantled its programs to develop weapons of mass destruction, among the evidence the team was looking for was thousands of pounds of unaccounted-for materials for producing anthrax.

According to White House sources, among the items being searched for by U.N. weapons inspectors are two tons of growth media that could produce 26,000 liters of anthrax. Also in Saddam's arsenal, again according to the White House, are 1,200 liters of botulinum, the organism that causes the deadly food poisoning known as botulism.

 Security Factoid

A Scud warhead filled with botulinum (anywhere between 300 pounds and a ton of the stuff, depending on the warhead) could contaminate an area of 2,300 square miles.

We know that the anthrax exists because, in the aftermath of the Gulf War, defectors forced Iraq to reveal that it had an extensive biological weapons program, including anthrax. UNSCOM, the United Nations Special Commission, found evidence of anthrax-filled weapons in Iraq. Although UNSCOM destroyed the Al Hakam production facility in Iraq, which had been used to produce anthrax, Iraq could have easily rebuilt its anthrax-producing capabilities. UNSCOM also discovered that Iraq conducted extensive aerosol dispersion tests using simulated anthrax.

How soon we forget and how quickly times change. Iraq's bio-weapons program reportedly got its start in the 1980s with U.S. assistance. Strains of all the germs Iraq used to make weapons, including anthrax, the bacteria that make botulinum toxin, and the germs that cause gas gangrene, along with other deadly pathogens such as the West Nile virus, were sent to Iraq. The exports were legal at the time and approved by a program administered by the Commerce Department, under the guise of providing public health support, with the destination of Baghdad University, a rather naive cover. Other sample shipments were sent in 1986 to the Iraqi chemical and biological weapons complex at al-Muthanna. At the time U.S. strategic interests dictated support for Iraq in its war with Iran, including intelligence support, when Iran appeared to be winning the war. The introduction of chemical warfare by the Iraqi army staved off defeat.

Saddam Hussein's chief of bioterror is a one-legged Jordanian man named Abu Mussab al Zarqawi, who also has plotted terror attacks for Osama bin Laden's Al Qaeda.

 Point/Counterpoint

According to former counter-terrorism director for the CIA, Vincent Cannistrano, "There is information that Al Qaeda sees war with Iraq as a new opportunity to exploit tensions in the region for its own purposes."

Al Zarqawi was badly injured during the American bombing of Afghanistan in 2002 and apparently went to Baghdad to have the leg amputated in August 2002. He is suspected of being the mastermind behind the planned ricin attacks in London in January 2003 (as discussed in Chapter 17) and the assassination of American diplomat Laurence Foley in Jordan in October 2002.

Information that al Zarqawi was back in Iraq in 2003—info received through intercepts of phone calls he made to his family in Jordan—was chilling news.

Anthrax in the Soviet Union

During the Cold War, the principle biological testing area in the Soviet Union was Vozrozhdeniye Island, which has been dubbed "Anthrax Island" by the *New York Times*. When the Soviet Union dissolved in 1992, the island was abandoned. It is currently uninhabited, but is reportedly still being scavenged by looters.

During the 1950s, the island was photographed by the CIA's U-2 spy plane, piloted by Buster Edens. Those photographs revealed that the center of activity was a walled compound that contained stables, warehouses, and laboratories. It was the apex of roads and trails that led to the test sites and to the port of Kantubek.

According to the former head of the installation: "To achieve the effect of killing one half of the population in a square kilometer costs $2,000 with conventional weapons, $800 with nuclear weapons, $600 with chemical weapons, and $1 with a biological weapon."

In 1989 a Soviet defector, Vladimir Pasechnik, revealed the existence of a Soviet "Biopreparat" complex for chemical and germ warfare weapons development. The complex, during the 1980s, employed at least 25,000 people in military and civilian laboratories. The defector claimed that the Soviets had plans for producing more than just anthrax bacteria. There were plans to develop smallpox and plague viruses as weapons as well. (More about smallpox later in the chapter.)

The former Soviet Union had reportedly weaponized anthrax employed on missiles, bombs, and artillery. In case of a war in Europe, the anthrax weapons were to be used against U.S. forces.

In 1992 Boris Yeltsin renounced the biological warfare program, which dwarfed Iraq's, and ratified a Biological and Toxic Weapons Convention. In 1992, Russia tried to arrange to have the complex inspected by the United States and Great Britain, but the plans faltered two years later when the inspectors insisted upon access to military installations.

Aflatoxin

Another germ that Saddam Hussein had reportedly weaponized is aflatoxin. If exposed to aflatoxin, symptoms include:

◆ Headache

◆ Jaundice

◆ Gastrointestinal distress

Effects if untreated: Liver disease, internal bleeding, possible death.

Cholera

Cholera could also be weaponized. Symptoms of exposure include:

◆ Vomiting

◆ Abdominal distension

◆ Pain

◆ Diarrhea

Effects if untreated: Severe dehydration, shock, and death.

Security Factoid _____

In 1763, Captain Simeon Ecuyer ended a siege by Chief Pontiac's troops surrounding Fort Pitt in Pennsylvania by sending the Native American warriors smallpox-infected blankets, thus starting an epidemic.

Smallpox

Throughout most of mankind's history, smallpox was one of the deadliest and most-feared viruses, killing one out of three of its victims and leaving those who survived blinded or horribly scarred. Through vaccination, the disease was eradicated. Indeed, there has not been a case reported since 1977.

Unfortunately, the virus still exists in laboratories, and could be used as a weapon by fiendish terrorists.

Are You Immunized? Are You Sure?

If you are a middle-aged American who was given a smallpox vaccination as a child—and no doubt you have the round scar on your upper arm to prove it—you may think that you are immune to smallpox for life.

> **Ounce of Prevention**
>
> To relieve a frightened American public about the safety of the new smallpox vaccination, President George W. Bush was himself vaccinated at Walter Reed Hospital in December 2002. The vaccination of the commander in chief officially began a program in which a half a million military personnel were to be vaccinated. The president was also hoping that 10 million emergency workers, like police officers and firefighters, as well as health care workers, would be given the vaccine on a voluntary basis. As this is written, the vaccine is not expected to be available to the general public until 2004.

Unfortunately, this is not necessarily the case. The immunization begins to wear off, apparently, after about ten years. So if it has been that long or longer since your vaccination, you probably will need a new vaccination to guarantee complete immunity.

Smallpox facts:

- There is no treatment for those infected.
- The live vaccinia virus that protects against smallpox is the most dangerous vaccine in use, but in the past it has caused only about 15 life-threatening illnesses per million vaccinations, and one or two deaths.

♦ A vaccine given in the first two or three days after exposure—before symptoms appear—can still stop someone from becoming sick.

♦ There is more than enough smallpox vaccine to vaccinate every American.

Not everyone thinks that a mass vaccination program in the United States against smallpox is a good idea. There are many doctors who believe that there shouldn't be mass vaccinations unless a smallpox attack seems "very likely." *The New England Journal of Medicine*, for example, says that any vaccination program should be undertaken with great caution because of the risks of the vaccine.

Another criticism of the president's proposed vaccination program was that the time it would take health care professionals to administer those millions of vaccination would take away services that those professionals were already providing.

Point/Counterpoint

According to Harvard professor of health policy and political analysis, Dr. Robert J. Blendon: "It has been a long time since Americans have had experience with smallpox and we have a shocking lack of basic understanding of it."

"We understand the need to be prepared, but the load for doing this is falling principally on local health departments, and we're not getting additional funding," said Dr. Lloyd F. Novick, president of the New York State Association of County Health Officials and the commissioner of health for Onondaga County, which includes Syracuse. "We have to transfer staff from other functions to do this. It just cannot be absorbed as business as usual. We need more resources."

New Drugs Being Developed

There is good news. A safer smallpox vaccination is under development. VaxGen, a California biotechnology company, said it hoped to begin clinical trials on the new vaccine—which was first created in Japan—in early 2004 and to win approval from the Food and Drug Administration to begin sales later that year.

The Japanese vaccine was tested on 50,000 small children in the 1970s and was approved there in 1980. It caused no serious side effects and fewer cases of fevers and redness on the arm than conventional vaccines.

Security Factoid

The Japanese vaccine—like the conventional vaccine—produces the characteristic scab at the vaccination site (usually the upper arm), which is a sign of effectiveness.

Like the conventional vaccine, the Japanese vaccine consists of a live vaccinia virus, a cousin of the smallpox virus. But the Japanese virus is attenuated, chosen to be weak and to produce fewer signs of brain inflammation than the conventional vaccines in animal tests.

The only down note regarding the new vaccine is that, because it was developed after smallpox was eradicated, there is no historical evidence that it works.

Early Detection

The best way to combat biological terrorism is to detect the substance early in the attack and pinpoint its source before it can become too widely spread. Steps have already been taken to help accomplish this difficult feat.

If a bio-weapon attack took place, the front line of defense would be the Global Outbreak Alert and Response Network. This network links more than 70 separate information and diagnostic networks around the world. Formal and informal sources of information are combined to create the best and most up-to-date information on disease outbreaks around the world. Formal sources of information include the 191 World Health Organization member countries.

Security Factoid

The new environmental monitoring system designed to provide early detection of a biological attack was first tested during the 2002 Winter Olympics in Salt Lake City.

Here in the United States, the federal government—in hopes of detecting anthrax, smallpox, or another deadly agent early in an attack—has deployed environmental monitors all around the country. The system, called Bio-Watch, retrofitted the existing environmental monitoring stations in the United States with new filters designed specifically to detect deadly biological agents. The existing system was in place to detect levels of air pollution.

With the new system in place, experts feel that a biological attack—such as anthrax released over a populated area from an airplane—could be determined and confirmed in a laboratory within 24 hours, thus enabling officials to quickly get large quantities of antibiotics (or vaccines, depending on the agent) into the affected area.

The system does have its weak points. The system will not detect releases in such places as shopping malls, subways, and other covered areas. But the system is calibrated to detect relatively small amounts of some of the agents of greatest concern such as smallpox and anthrax.

The new system uses monitoring technology and methods developed in part by the Department of Energy's national laboratories. Samples of DNA are analyzed using something called "polymerase chain reaction techniques." These examine the genetic signatures of the organisms in a sample, and make rapid and accurate evaluations of that organism.

Security Factoid

Biological weapons are hundreds to thousands of times more lethal than chemical weapons. A few pounds of biological agents can be as devastating as thousands of tons of chemical agents.

The government is still working to develop cheap and reliable instant hand-held detectors; the technology has yet to be perfected. The imperfect detectors have been distributed in some cities, but provide too many false positives.

Bioterror Drills

Some cities—such as Tucson, Arizona—have been holding practices to improve their reaction time and efficiency in the face of an anthrax attack. The exercises have helped cities prepare for a real disaster by forcing coordination among police, fire, public health, pharmacists, and others.

Some have criticized the practice exercises, however, because they don't adequately simulate a real disaster in the sense that those in charge knew even before the test began exactly how the disaster was to unfold and just how they would handle it.

Security Factoid

In January 2003 a bioterrorism drill was held at the White House, playing out their response to a hypothetical international smallpox attack.

The practice sessions are mandatory. The federal government has distributed $1 billion to help states plan for bioterrorism, and states are required to show they are making progress.

While some communities feel they have a grip on how to respond in case of a bio-attack, others are still in the dark. According to one 2003 report, only one state (Florida) is ready to receive the federal stockpile of drugs and medical supplies needed in a disaster. Many communities have little clue how they would handle a surge of injured patients or produce enough isolation beds to keep a crush of infectious people away from others.

Security Factoid

The mastermind behind Saddam Hussein's Iraqi bioweapons program is a diminutive woman named Rihab Taha, who has been dubbed "Dr. Germ" by the American press. She says that Iraq was justified in producing biological weapons to defend itself.

Protecting Our Food Supply

If terrorists attacked the United States by poisoning our food supply, our first line of defense would be the Emerging Infections Program Foodborne Diseases Active Surveillance Network, which, thankfully, is better known as FoodNet.

FoodNet's active surveillance system, which is headquartered at the federally operated Centers for Disease Control, coordinates information from the U.S. Department of Agriculture and the Food and Drug Administration, plus doctors and more than 300 clinical laboratories.

The idea is that, if there is an outbreak of food-related illness, the source of that contamination can be pinpointed as quickly as possible, and warnings can be issued to keep the number of casualties to a minimum. Quick identification of the problem's source will also maximize the chances of catching the culprits responsible.

The Least You Need to Know

♦ Bioterrorism is the spreading of fear, illness, and death, with bacteria and viruses being the weapon.

♦ The anthrax attacks in the United States in 2002 demonstrated the fear and horror such an attack can cause. Some communities are preparing for an another biological attack.

♦ There is enough smallpox vaccine for all Americans, but some doctors feel that a mass vaccination program should not be undertaken unless a bioterror attack is very likely.

♦ If there is an outbreak of food-related illness, the source of that contamination can be pinpointed as quickly as possible, and warnings can be issued to keep the number of casualties to a minimum.

Chapter 21

Understanding Radiological and Nuclear Warfare

In This Chapter

- ◆ No nukes
- ◆ Korean crisis
- ◆ Unclean bombs
- ◆ Risky reactors

In this chapter, we'll look at radioactivity as a weapon. Terrorists could attack the Free World by obtaining a nuclear bomb and exploding it in a populated area, by building or obtaining a radiological bomb and contaminating a populated area, or by attacking a currently functioning nuclear power plant.

Preventing Nuclear Proliferation

Combating nuclear proliferation is one of the major tasks of the U.S. national security effort. We want to make sure that the people who have nuclear weapons don't use them and that the people who don't have nuclear weapons do not get them. Especially those unstable governments and individuals with terrorist connections.

There have been concerns that terrorists will obtain a nuclear device from a nation that already possesses nukes. The Russians, once our arch-enemies, are now every bit as interested as we are in preventing nuclear proliferation.

Security Factoid

The 1997 Intelligence Authorization Act established a "Commission to Assess the Organization of the Federal Government to Combat the Proliferation of Weapons of Mass Destruction."

Elizabeth Rindskopf, formerly the General Counsel for the CIA and also for the NSA, recently addressed the human dimension of Russian nuclear nonproliferation. She wrote that although a number of U.S.-sponsored programs are now in place, ultimately the real reason why Russian weapons-grade nuclear material has not fallen into the hands of terrorists, criminals, or rogue nations, is because of the dedication of Russian nuclear scientists and engineers.

Security Factoid

The nuclear and military threat presented by Russia gets smaller every year. Analysts have predicted that Russia's nuclear arsenal—currently estimated to be in the neighborhood of 6,000 warheads—could shrink to 600 to 800 by the year 2010. The quality of Russia's war machine is also suffering. Dozens of submarines have been decommissioned. Others are inactive in harbors, and only three subs are believed to be on patrol at any one time. Bombers are obsolete and pilots are allowed too few flying hours per year to maintain combat readiness. Russia's early warning defense is deteriorating, raising the specter of an inadequate capability to evaluate threats and disastrous emergency decisions. U.S. delegations are helping Russia address the problems of controls on nuclear materials and warning adequacy. Severe economic problems in Russia aggravate the problem, and increase the likelihood that they might sell missile and nuclear arms technology to states that are not considered in U.S. national security interests. The role for U.S. intelligence in monitoring this process is vital.

Visiting the Kurchatov Institute, she was concerned by the dilapidated buildings with their stockpiles of nuclear weapons-grade highly enriched uranium—and the lack of guards——the Institute cannot afford to pay them. She wrote that with all the money the United States is spending on programs to prevent proliferation of Russian fissile materials, more thought needs to be given to the human dimension of nonproliferation.

Many of the employees in Russian nuclear labs and storage facilities have been paid only a fraction of their normal salaries, or not paid at all for months at a time.

In early October employees from various Russian nuclear facilities marched to the Ministry of Atomic Energy in Moscow to demand unpaid wages. A hunger strike recently took place at a nuclear power plant in Primorsky. With the current wave of inflation the problem is becoming acute. Ms. Rindskopf's message is that we need to pay attention.

North Korea Crisis

The latest crisis over the North Korean nuclear program erupted last year, when U.S. intelligence obtained strong evidence that North Korea had secretly developed a uranium enrichment program, which would represent a second track toward the development and production of nuclear weapons. Now American officials fear that North Korea may be poised to break out with full-scale nuclear weapons production. The Yongbyon Nuclear Research Center (2,224 acres, 390 buildings) closed for eight years because of an international treaty, has been re-opened for business.

The Center is located in a mountainous region 55 miles north of Pyongyang. It was designed from the git-go to produce weapons rather than power, and was constructed during the 1980s with financial assistance from the Soviet Union.

Once a bright and shiny facility, the complex was closed down in 1994 when North Korea agreed to discontinue its nuclear program. The population of the town, once as high as 50,000, dropped to 10,000, and the nuclear facility itself fell into disrepair.

We know that the facility was built to produce weapons rather than power because its five-megawatt reactor lacks the size to produce meaningful quantities of power and, even if it did, the complex is not connected to the North Korean power grid.

Producing Plutonium

Intelligence sources theorize that the reactor was designed to produce plutonium 239, which can be used to build nuclear bombs. Plutonium is a man-made element created by mutating uranium and is the most suitable isotope for making nuclear bombs. The reactor uses fuel rods of natural uranium, which the North has in abundant supply. These can be used to create a controlled nuclear reaction.

The spent fuel rods later could be removed and plutonium extracted from them. In fact, the North Koreans appear to have a reprocessing facility at Yongbyon designed for just that. The reprocessing building is six stories high and 240 yards long. North Korea says it is a radiochemical laboratory.

> ### Author's Corner
>
> Wilson: I have observed on more than one occasion that intelligence often graphically and compellingly tells us important things we need to know and those in the intel community pass facts along to our national leaders. Unfortunately we can't make leaders make what we may think are the right decisions. Without taking logical steps, national leaders can make mistakes that can prove costly later. In the War on Terrorism, we can't afford to miss key points or overlook threats anymore.

Closed on Three Occasions

Satellite photographs suggest that the North Koreans closed down the reactor on at least three occasions during the 1990s, each time long enough to remove some fuel rods to extract plutonium. International inspectors concluded from studies of plutonium samples that the North produced as much as 30 pounds of weapons-grade plutonium. That is a quantity sufficient to build two nuclear bombs.

> ### Author's Corner
>
> McLean: Wanna buy a bomb? Or maybe a missile? Get your own mail order catalog and shop today. Russia's Defense Ministry and military industry have produced the first public encyclopedia on its strategic nuclear arsenal, providing unprecedented details about Moscow's weapons systems. The book was produced in cooperation with arms exporters and is a comprehensive collection of photographs and diagrams on most Soviet, and now Russian, strategic weapons systems, including intercontinental ballistic missiles, missile-launching submarines, bombers, and testing and support facilities and equipment. The book appears to be a "sales brochure" for Moscow's weapons exporters. For obvious reasons U.S. national security officials are worried that Moscow is preparing to put its nuclear warhead and missile know-how up for sale.

It is doubtful that the North Koreans can get the complex up and running at its former level of efficiency any time soon. In the intelligence and diplomatic communities there is some debate about North Korea's technical capabilities, given the overall state of decrepitude in which the impoverished country finds itself.

"Everything Was Broken"

Sean Tyson, a former U.S. Energy Department employee said Yongbyon was in terrible shape in 1998 when he last visited. "Everything was broken, everything was just disintegrating. The barbed wire was covered in rust and falling down in places. It was pathetic."

He recalled that the North Koreans were unable to make simple infrastructure repairs because their cement was substandard. Even the pool for storing fuel rods was leaking.

But Yongbyon is not the only North Korean facility worth watching for nuclear activity. In recent years, suspicion has focused on underground activity at more remote sites. About 25 miles north of Yongbyon, a suspiciously large underground complex of tunnels and pipelines at Kumchangri was inspected in 1999 by U.S. officials, but they found nothing. According to Barbara Demmick in the Los Angeles Times (January 13, 2003), another facility, buried under Mt. Chonma near the Chinese border, is suspected of being used to enrich uranium.

North Korean Missile Program

U.S. intelligence has been watching for indications that North Korea will test a ballistic missile capable of delivering a nuclear warhead to American soil.

We know that the North Koreans have such a weapon under development and that it is called the Taepo Dong 2; the specifications are as follows:

Range: 3,700 miles from launch point to target

Stages: Two or three of fuel to propel missile. (Empty stage ejects so remainder is lighter, and therefore, easier to propel.)

Payload: 1,450–2,000 pounds of explosives.

Development Began: 1987

There is no current evidence that preparations are being made for such a test. A test of a Taepo Dong 2 missile could increase the pressure from Pyongyang, intelligence officials said. In 1998 the North Koreans unsuccessfully attempted to put their own satellite in orbit using a Taepo Dong 1 missile.

Iran's Shahab-3 missile program, one watched closely by U.S. intelligence agencies, is believed to be based on North Korean No Dong missile technology. The missile, which is still in testing, gives the Iranians the capability to strike Israel and U.S. troops in Saudi Arabia and parts of Turkey.

According to General Barry R. McCaffrey, the Olin Professor of National Security Studies at West Point who led the 24th Mechanized Infantry Division in the 1991 Gulf War, "We are facing a gigantic North Korean missile development program which has acted in secret collusion with Pakistan, Syria, Libya, Iran, and Yemen.

Their next customers could include terrorist organizations. They have produced and deployed more than 500 Scud missiles, all of which are capable of carrying chemical and biological weapons. Their 500 kilometer basic Scud C can target most of South Korea. They are now mass-producing liquid fuel No Dong missiles on mobile launchers with a range of 1,300 km. These missiles can effectively target Japan and U.S. regional military forces."

Point/Counterpoint

Lt. Gen. Ronald Kadish, head of the Pentagon's Missile Defense Agency, said, "Along the way, if we get threatened by North Korea, I think the American people understand we would not just sit by with five missiles in the hole and do nothing. Iran continues to test, continues to make progress. They're moving from the capability of having very good systems in the short range to intermediate and long-range missiles. The Libyans have been pretty active in trying to get missile capability, and not just short-range. They have enough money to buy it. Their indigenous capability is not as good as they thought it was."

Security Factoid

At the beginning of February 2003, U.S. intelligence satellites observed covered trucks taking on cargo at the nuclear storage facility at Yongbyon. About 8,000 spent nuclear fuel rods were believed to be stored there, and the activity was considered a sign that the government in Pyongyang was preparing to reprocess the rods into weapons-grade plutonium.

Tensions regarding North Korean missiles increased in February 2003 with the revelations that, in addition to the Taepo Dong 2 missiles, North Korea was developing Taepo Dong 3 missiles that would, in theory, be capable of reaching the West Coast of the mainland United States. The Taepo Dong 3 specifications are as follows:

Range: 9,300+ miles

Stages: Three

Payload: Unknown

Development Began: 2002

Thank You, Russia

We can thank Russia for much of what we know about North Korea's nuclear facilities. Russian intelligence officers working for the SVR reportedly placed CIA nuclear detection devices inside locations in Pyongyang during the 1990s.

Locating facilities that enrich uranium is made easier by the fact that this process requires a great deal of water and electricity, and such activities can usually be seen in satellite photographs.

The reprocessing of plutonium is trickier to detect. It requires less power and water, but does emit an isotope of krypton in gaseous form that can be tracked and measured, even in very small amounts.

Author's Corner

Wilson: It may seem ironic at times the way the political world changes. Not long ago America was helping the Taliban to drive the Russians out of Afghanistan. Now Russia is helping us in the War on Terrorism and otherwise. Fortunately, the Russians had and have a wide-ranging, effective intelligence system that has been very helpful in the past few years.

Risks of a Preemptive Strike

The North Korean nuclear weapons program, of course, could be set back for years with a precision strike on the plant. Plans for a strike against the complex were first developed during the Clinton Administration in case diplomacy failed in the 1994 nuclear crisis. But such a strike is a big risk.

North Korea could retaliate against South Korea or Tokyo. Also, a preemptive strike might not be decisive. North Korea has admitted to a hidden second nuclear program, involving enriched uranium.

"Dirty Bombs"

Another potential type of terrorist attack that fits into this category is what has become known as a "dirty bomb" attack. A dirty bomb, also known as a radiological weapon, is a bomb that, though it would not necessarily cause a large explosion, would release enough radioactive material into the atmosphere to case many casualties and/or contaminate a large area.

Security Factoid

Although the United States and Great Britain could not be closer allies, their intelligence services do not always agree. In January 2003, British intelligence reported that Osama bin Laden's Al Qaeda terrorist network had built a dirty bomb. The information reportedly came from British intelligence agents who had infiltrated Al Qaeda and had discovered documents that stated such a device had been built near the town of Heart in western Afghanistan. U.S. officials disagreed with the report, however, stating that they "had no evidence" that Al Qaeda had built a dirty bomb.

These bombs could be conventional dynamite attached to radiological material. A dirty bomb could come in any size, from a miniature device to a truck bomb.

One of the most frightening things about dirty bombs is that, unlike a nuclear bomb, they do not need a great deal of expertise to build. The hard part would be in acquiring the radioactive material to attach to the bomb.

> ### Ounce of Prevention
>
> If a radiological "dirty" bomb explodes near your home, here are some suggestions: (1) Listen to your radio or TV news. Instructions may be broadcast. (2) Try to stay upwind of the bomb. (3) If exposed to the radiation, go directly to the hospital.

> ### Security Factoid
>
> There are several conditions that would determine the amount of damage a dirty bomb could cause. These are: (a) the sophistication of the bomb, (b) wind conditions, and (c) speed of evacuation.

Of course, the more expertise the bomb-builder had, the more dangerous the weapon could be. This would tend to be true no matter what type of bomb was being built, but particularly so in the case of dirty bombs. It would be extremely difficult, for example, for a bomb maker to handle high-grade radiological materials without giving themselves a fatal exposure to the substance.

More Terror Than Destruction ... Probably

Although dirty bombs are technically considered weapons of mass destruction, the biggest danger of such a bomb would be in its ability to cause mass terror and to disrupt normal activities, rather than its ability to cause mass destruction.

Fears about dirty bombs increased exponentially during May 2002, when a plot to use such a bomb against the United States was discovered and foiled.

> ### Point/Counterpoint
>
> On February 9, 2003, Secretary of State Colin Powell said, "It would be easy for Al Qaeda to produce a radioactive dirty bomb. That is not a difficult thing to do if one can get the source of the contamination, the radiological material. How likely it is, I can't say—but I think it is wise for us to at least let the American people know of the possibility."

The suspect in the case, born Jose Padilla (also known as Abdullah Al Muhajir), a native of Chicago, was charged as an enemy combatant, and was therefore denied many of the rights that he would have been granted had he been designated a peacetime criminal.

The Foiled Plan

Padilla, 31 years old, was arrested at O'Hare International Airport in Chicago, arriving from Pakistan, on May 8, 2002. Since his arrest, Padilla has been held in Consolidated Naval Brig in Charleston, South Carolina, where he has undergone regular interrogation by military personnel.

Padilla had suspected ties to Al Qaeda. U.S. officials have said Washington was the probable target of the plot. According to FBI Director Robert Mueller, the plot was in the "discussion stage" when the suspect was arrested.

In the weeks before he flew to Chicago, Padilla was tracked flying between Pakistan, Egypt, and Switzerland. An associate of Padilla's, in Pakistan, was already under arrest when Padilla arrived in Chicago.

At the time of Padilla's arrest, officials said that they suspected his visit to Chicago was a reconnaissance mission and that he was looking for potential sites for the dirty bomb attack.

Security Factoid

There has never been a dirty bomb attack anywhere in the world. According to a U.N. report, Iraq tested a one-ton radiological bomb in 1987 but discontinued the program when it was determined that the generated levels of radiation were not deadly enough.

Security Factoid

Only two detainees since 9/11 were categorized as enemy combatants. The other is Yasser Esam Hamdi, who was designated as an enemy combatant after being captured on the battlefield in Afghanistan. Hamdi was born in Louisiana and is therefore a U.S. citizen.

Point/Counterpoint

In January 2003, Michael B. Mukasey of the Federal District Court in Manhattan ruled that Padilla could have access to a lawyer to help him change his designation as an enemy combatant. The Bush administration, however, quickly asked the judge to change his ruling. According to a Bush administration representative: "Allowing a lawyer into the process would threaten permanently to undermine the military's efforts to develop a relationship of trust and dependency that is essential to effective interrogation. That could set back his interrogations by months, if not derail the process permanently." The representative also noted that the Padilla interrogations had "helped to thwart an estimated 100 or more attacks against the United States and its interests since Sept. 11, 2001." Judge Mukasey, it should be noted, affirmed even with his original decision President Bush's power to detain enemy combatants and said the government needed to make only a minimal showing to justify such action.

According to the U.S. Justice Department, Padilla served time in prison in the United States during the early 1990s. After his release, he traveled to Afghanistan and Pakistan and met with senior Al Qaeda officials.

Padilla studied how to wire explosive devices and researched radiological dispersion devices. Al Qaeda officials knew that, as a U.S. citizen with a valid passport, he would be able to travel freely in the United States without drawing attention to himself.

Information regarding Padilla's activities came from Abu Zubaydah, the most senior al Qaeda figure captured by U.S. authorities.

False Alarm

According to the *Journal of the American Medical Association*, a New York man with Graves' disease, a thyroid disorder, set off radiation alarms in Manhattan subway stations in December 2002 after he was treated with radioactive iodine.

The man was strip-searched by police who were on the alert for nuclear-armed terrorists. This patient's experience indicates that radiation detection devices are installed in public places in New York City and perhaps elsewhere.

Patients who have been treated with radioactive iodine or other isotopes may be identified and interrogated by the police because of the radiation they emit.

Protecting Nuclear Power Plants

The Nuclear Regulatory Commission is a body created by the Federal Atomic Energy Act. It is solely up to the federal government, in other words, to decide whether nuclear reactors are sufficiently safe and should remain in operation.

The commission does not consider the threat of terrorism as an excuse to close nuclear power plants. That is understandable, as it would be buckling under to the threat of terrorism. The troubling part is that the commission, as of early 2003, did not see the threat of terrorism as a reason to improve emergency plans either.

Indian Point Criticized ... Maybe Closed

New York governor George Pataki criticized the Indian Point nuclear power plant in New York State because it had not adapted its emergency plans sufficiently for the possibility of a terrorist attack. The power plant, which is operated by a firm called Entergy, is located in the town of Buchanan in New York's Westchester County.

According to the most recent census, 20 million people live within 50 miles of Indian Point. It is located only 35 miles from downtown Manhattan.

As of January 2003, according to representatives of the Federal Emergency Management Agency, Indian Point's evacuation plans remained based on regulatory compliance rather than "a strategy to protect from radiation exposure."

The report stated that the plant has other problems as well, including:

◆ Outmoded or nonexistent technology

◆ Inadequate drills

◆ Insufficient public education regarding evacuation procedures

In response to the report, Entergy would only say that future changes "may" be necessary. The response to the report of inadequate emergency planning was much more strident from the public.

On January 13, 2003, Dennis McNerney, the executive of Bergen County, New Jersey, said, "I promise that I will use every means at my disposal, including legal action, if necessary, to shut down the reactors if it is not done voluntarily."

McNerney said that he would agree to the plant reopening if the emergency plans were improved. There may be no way for the public outcry to lose the plant, however, since Nuclear Regulatory Commission rules do not require county and state approval of emergency procedures for a plant to continue operating.

Eight days after McNerney's comments, Westchester County's legislature voted 16–1 for an immediate shutdown of Indian Point. The cause to shut down the plant was joined by Sen. Hillary Rodham Clinton (D-NY), who said that she had signed a petition asking the Federal Emergency Management Agency to withdraw its approval of the plant's emergency plan.

Keeping Our Nuke Secrets Secret

One problem that has been and must continue to be addressed is the potential for foreign spies to infiltrate the United States' nuclear weapons and power programs. According to Notra Trulock, one-time Director of Intelligence for the Department of Energy, China and other countries have been known to use such spies, with success.

Los Alamos nuclear scientist Wen Ho Lee provided sensitive weapons data to China during unreported meetings with nuclear-weapons scientists. A Justice Department report on the Lee case concluded that electronic surveillance of Mr. Lee should have been carried out based on evidence that he and his wife were spies for China.

Security Factoid _____

Other foreign governments who have attempted to gather intelligence regarding U.S. nuclear programs include Russia, Iran, Iraq, Syria, and Pakistan.

A surveillance application to a secret federal court "established probable cause to believe that Wen Ho Lee was an agent of a foreign power, that is to say, a United States person currently engaged in clandestine intelligence activities for, or on behalf of, the [People's Republic of China] and that his wife, Sylvia Lee, aided, abetted, or conspired in such activities."

The FBI conducted an earlier counterintelligence probe of Lee for providing documents to Taiwan and meeting improperly with Taiwanese intelligence agents. The FBI probe was closed in 1984 and no action was taken against Mr. Lee.

Security officials at Los Alamos National Laboratory recommended in 1984, after the Taiwan investigation, that Mr. Lee be removed from the laboratory's sensitive program to build the W-88 small nuclear warhead, but he was allowed to keep his job.

If the Unthinkable Occurs ...

So what do you do if the unthinkable occurs and there is a massive quantity of radiation released into your environment? During a severe radiation emergency, local authorities (first responders) must be able to:

- Measure radiation levels
- Measure accumulated radiation dose
- Understand radiation shelter/shielding concepts

As individuals, we must learn how to protect our thyroid glands from radioactive iodine. The clear majority of casualties from a nuclear accident or other radiation emergency result from exposure to and/or ingestion of radioactive iodine (radioiodine, 131I, Iodine-131). Like normal iodine from table salt, radioactive iodine is collected, and stored, by the human thyroid gland. Over time, the thyroid is exposed to destructive doses of radiation, resulting in thyroid cancer, among other similarly dreadful ailments.

Children are the greatest risk population, probably because in general they have a lower intake of iodine in their diet, though the threat to the remainder of the population is very real. Potassium iodide, if taken in time, saturates the thyroid with a safe, stable form of iodine, resulting in radioiodine being cleared from the body via the kidneys. Potassium iodide is safe, stable, and FDA-approved for over-the-counter sale. Everyone would benefit from potassium iodide as a daily dietary supplement.

They are taken orally in tablet form. For more information visit the U.S. Food and Drug Administration's discussion of the topic at: www.fda.gov/cder/drugprepare/kiprep65mg.htm.

The Least You Need to Know

◆ We want to make sure that the people who have nuclear weapons don't use them and that the people who don't have nuclear weapons do not get them.

◆ American officials fear that North Korea may be poised to break out with full-scale nuclear weapons production.

◆ A dirty bomb, also known as a radiological weapon, is a bomb that, though it would not necessarily cause a large explosion, would release enough radioactive material into the atmosphere to case many casualties and/or contaminate a large area.

◆ One problem that has been and must continue to be addressed is the potential for foreign spies to infiltrate the U.S.' nuclear weapons and power programs.

Chapter 22

Understanding Cyberterrorism

In This Chapter

- ◆ Viruses
- ◆ Hackers
- ◆ Preventing I.D. theft
- ◆ Cybersecurity

Cyberterrorism is the creation of fear through attacks on our computers, computer networks, and upon the information that our computers contain. There have been cyberterrorist attacks in the past but, like earthquakes in Southern California, there has not been the "big one."

Computers do three things: store information, process information, and communicate. A computer virus is a program designed to disrupt the function of, or completely shut down, a computer or computer network. A hacker is the cyber equivalent of a breaking-and-entering man, who breaks into and disrupts other people's computer systems. A hacker is not necessarily a terrorist, however. He (or she, of course) might just be a thief, or even mischievous. Because of computer viruses, created by hackers, websites have been defaced and some Internet servers have been blocked and stored information permanently lost. Viruses can do even worse damage and are spread by other malicious people as they could be by terrorists.

But, because Americans have become increasingly reliant on their computers, there remains fear that "the big one" could occur, and shut us down—at least temporarily.

"America Depends on Computers"

The Pentagon became concerned with the possibility of cyberterrorism long before 9/11. According to a 1991 statement by the National Research Council, "We are at risk. Increasingly, America depends on computers. They control power delivery, communications, aviation, and financial services. They are used to store vital information, from medical records to business plans to criminal records. Although we trust them, they are vulnerable—to the effects of poor design and insufficient quality control, to accident, and perhaps most alarmingly, to deliberate attack. The modern thief can steal more with a computer than with a gun. Tomorrow's terrorist may be able to do more damage with a keyboard than with a bomb."

Ounce of Prevention

Update your anti-virus software daily. It takes only seconds. Make it a habit to do so before clicking to check for incoming mail. This is far less painful than trying to eliminate a virus once an infection has taken place. Here's another tip: do not download or open attachment files, even from friends—after all, the virus uses their address book and you're in it. Only open files you were expecting or that have been prescreened by your anti-virus software.

Back in 1997, a cyberattack was simulated by the U.S. military. The results were disconcerting. Using everyday computers and commercial software, it was discovered that a clever hacker could disrupt emergency systems, military communications, and the supply of electrical power to portions of the country.

Terrorists Will Turn to Hacking

Fear that terrorists will turn to hacking to do their dirty work stems from the knowledge that such an attack would not need to cost a lot of money, and wouldn't even need to have proximity to their targets. A cyberterrorist, in other words, could attack from the other side of the world with a common home computer. They could attack from any country, even those whose ideals greatly differ from their own, and the attacks could be perpetrated anonymously.

It is also feared that a cyberterrorist could work in conjunction with another terrorist attack. For example, emergency reaction to a terrorist attack could be prevented by a simultaneous cyber attack. It is also possible that a conventional form of terrorist attack could be used to accomplish cyberterrorist goals. For example, a bomb could be used to destroy telephone switching equipment, Internet infrastructure, etc.

A cyberterrorist could:

- ◆ Erase key data
- ◆ Steal classified files
- ◆ Change the content of Internet websites
- ◆ Try to sabotage military operations
- ◆ Clog communications by *spamming*
- ◆ Disrupt some media broadcasting
- ◆ Try to disrupt financial markets

> **Ounce of Prevention**
>
> There are several organizations designed to protect American computer systems from attack. These include the government-funded Computer Emergency Response Team (CERT) Coordination Center, which has other functions, too, and the FBI's National Infrastructure Protection Center, which probably will be moved to the new Department of Homeland Security or reinforced there.

Security Speak

Spamming is the mass-sending of unwanted e-mails. Those e-mails are known as *spam.*

Cyber-Limitations

Although a cyberterrorist could disrupt commercial flights by tinkering with the airlines' computers, we should note that it would be impossible for a cyberterrorist to cause planes to fly into one another. They could make the air traffic controller's job more difficult by taking away his or her computer, but the computers themselves do not control flight paths, and therefore, couldn't alter them.

Control really is the key here. No cyberterrorist can take away the human control factor—and people control computers, not the other way around. No transportation system is computerized to the point that great damage could be caused by a hacker. If a cyberterrorist tried to cause a train accident by automatically turning a switch on the tracks, a human being (there's always a human being) would notice and take the necessary steps to prevent catastophe.

Ounce of Prevention

To keep sensitive information out of the hands of terrorists, federal research dollars are increasingly coming with strings attached. Federal agencies are pressing to review papers on certain topics and ban foreign researchers who have not been specially screened.

Most disruption caused by a cyberterrorist probably would be temporary. If a terrorist, for example, used a computer to alter the balance of ingredients in an automated food manufacturing plant so that the resulting food was toxic, the change would only last until ingredients began to diminish at noticeably different rates or someone tasted the product and went "Bleccchhh." Chances are no one would even get sick. However, as the mass arsenic poisoning at the New Sweden Church proved, even such a seemingly secure place can be subject to action by an unsuspected person, local or terrorist it seems.

In the case of attempted food poisoning at a manufacturing plant the damage would be in the money it would cost that company to throw out the toxic food its plant had created and figure out how to reset the computer back to the way it was, and prevent the system from being hacked into or otherwise changed again.

Cyberattacks Do Exist

In case all of this is striking you as merely theoretical, cyberattacks do exist, and they have been linked to terrorist activities. In January 2003, the National Infrastructure Protection Center at the Federal Bureau of Investigation reported that there had been a recent rise in cyberattacks against "government and military computer networks." The report termed the situation a "potential crisis." The report did not state how many attacks there had been and how successful they were. It did not blame Iraq itself for the attacks but rather those who were "ideologically motivated" and "pro-Iraq."

According to Rep. Robert E. Andrews of New Jersey, a Democrat on the House Armed Service Committee who has been active on cyberwarfare issues: "Iraq is certainly among the places in the world that we think a cyberattack might well be launched from. A cyberattack really fits Saddam Hussein's paradigm for attacking us." Or, we might add, by others who wish to harm America.

According to Gordon Johndroe, a spokesman for the Department of Homeland Security, "I wouldn't tie this in to a state-run operation. Iraq is more interested in obtaining weapons of mass destruction—chemical, biological and nuclear—than in pursuing the sophisticated skills and equipment necessary for a successful cyberattack."

However, there are other terrorists and groups who might focus on cyberterrorism. That's why our country must continue to develop more effective shields in various ways and places.

"The fact is, we are attacked and we defend on a daily basis," said Tim Madden, a spokesman for Maj. Gen. J. David Bryan, commander of the military's Joint Task Force–Computer Network Operations. "Less than 2 percent of those attacks are successful in that the intruders gained root-level access."

Pro-Iraqi hacker groups control hundreds of automated search robot networks that could be used to attack government systems. In 1998 U.S. military computers were penetrated by suspected Iraqi agents and briefly disrupted troop exercises in the Persian Gulf.

> **Author's Corner**
>
> McLean: In the year 2000, several Israeli websites containing the government's perspective on the Mideast conflict crashed after Islamic groups abroad jammed them with fake traffic.

Security Factoid

The military has 3 million computers and 10,000 local area networks in its information infrastructure.

Inslaw's Claims

According to the president of the Inslaw, Inc. software company, the U.S. Intelligence community's versions of the firm's Promis database software were bought by Osama bin Laden and used in computer-based espionage operations against the U.S. Inslaw says that FBI traitor Robert P. Hanssen provided the software to the Russians. Bin Laden then bought it from the Russian mafia on the black market.

Inslaw further claims that members of U.S. law enforcement forces, who prefer to remain anonymous, state that bin Laden was able to monitor U.S. investigations of his network, including electronic banking transactions. Inslaw has asked that their information be investigated by the Commission on Terrorist Attacks.

The U.S. Government is looking at Inslaw's claims with a skeptical eye, however, because the software company has also long claimed that the Justice Department stole the Promis software for its own use, a claim that the government denies.

Code Red: Attack on the White House Website

The most disturbing computer virus—or worm, as they are sometimes called—to ever attack the United States was called "Code Red." It attacked during the summer of 2001,

Security Factoid

The Code Red worm exploited a vulnerability in Microsoft Internet Information Server 4.0 and 5.0 and affected computers running Windows NT 4.0 and Windows 2000.

and was designed to specifically disrupt the White House website. Code Red infected 225,000 Web servers, programming the machines to attack Whitehouse.gov with a flood of data. Note that worms are specific types of viruses and not all viruses are worms.

The White House domain remained operative however, due to quick-thinking administrators who moved the site to an alternate Internet address. The virus was called Code Red because of evidence suggesting it was launched from China. The worm caused an estimated $1.2 billion in damage worldwide.

Attack of the E-Worm

A fast-spreading, virus dramatically slowed Internet traffic on January 25, 2003. It overwhelmed the world's digital pipelines and interfered with Web browsing and e-mail delivery. At least 39,000 computers were infected. Hundreds of thousands of other systems worldwide were disrupted.

Security Factoid

The January 2003 virus sought out vulnerable computers on the Internet to infect using a known flaw in popular database software from Microsoft Corp. called "SQL Server 2000." The attacking software scanned for victim computers at the rate of thousands of probes a second. This probing saturated many Internet data pipelines. It is good to know that Microsoft specialists are ever alert and watching for problems. They periodically provide patches to repair problems that may be found.

Among those most severely affected was the Bank of America Corporation, one of the nation's largest banks. During the virus strike, many Bank of America customers were unable to withdraw money from 13,000 ATM machines. It took the bank 24 hours to return ATM service to normal. Customers of the Canadian Imperial Bank of Commerce in Toronto also were unable to withdraw money using ATM machines. The virus that caused so much trouble came to be known as the "Slammer Worm" or the "Sapphire Worm."

A New Cybersecurity Strategy

On January 31, 2003, President Bush announced his approval of a national cybersecurity strategy. The strategy was designed to protect the nation's most critical information systems from cyberattack. The strategy had been in development since shortly after the 9/11 attacks.

> ### Security Factoid
>
> In the year 2000, it was reported in the British press that Israeli agents had been able to hack into the White House e-mail system and recover information being sent from the president to senior staff in the National Security Council and outside government departments. Agents were successfully able to infiltrate Telrad, a subcontractor of Nortel, the telecommunications company that helped to develop the White House system. According to the report, chips installed during the development process enable data to be shunted to a secret Israeli computer in Washington. The information was then transferred to Tel Aviv several times a week.

The strategy recommended steps that the industry and government could take to improve the nation's cybersecurity. The majority of the document directed the government to lead by example and tighten the security of federal information systems.

Starting in the year 2000, the FBI reinforced its mission to counter cyberattacks with the formation of new investigative teams specializing in computer intrusions and attacks. The teams exist at all 56 of its field offices around the country. The agency also assigns at least one computer forensics examiner to each field office.

Identity Theft Victims' Guide

Identity theft has become a problem in recent years and promises to become a bigger problem in the future. Because of that you'll find some key points included here with important references.

If you suspect that your identity has been stolen, act quickly. The longer you wait the more damage can be done, and the harder it will be to fix the damage that is repairable.

It is important to call authorities as soon as you have discovered a problem. When you do call the authorities and various financial institutions regarding the theft of your identity, keep a written log of the time of each call, the phone number you called, with whom you spoke, and what

Ounce of Prevention

A California man who once made a living using other people's identities offered helpful advice on how to avoid being an identity-theft victim. He said living off of the credit cards of others was easy: "We'd go through the garbage of mortgage companies and department stores because they often would throw away paperwork and receipts with customers' Social Security numbers and other personal information on it."

was said. When possible, confirm conversations in writing. Keep copies of all written communications. Also keep track of any expenses you might incur while trying to fix your problem. If the thief is caught, this might help you with any requested restitution.

If your credit cards, or their numbers, have been stolen, immediately contact the major credit recording companies:

- Experian 1-888-EXPERIAN
- Equifax 1-800-525-6285
- Trans Union 1-800-680-7289

Report the theft and request a free credit report. Your file should be flagged with a fraud alert. Make these contacts both on the phone and in writing. Do not pay any bill for any goods or services that you did not receive.

Author's Corner

McLean: Identity theft is nothing new. Terrorists have been using false ID for decades. They find a baby who died in infancy who would be around their age and get a birth certificate. From there it is easy. Identity theft today is different, since it uses a living person and taps into their real identity and files. Most of these guys have several passports and names anyway. They are more likely to create their ID before they get here. But, identity theft by those who want to use real names and steal money is a growing threat to all of us today.

Your next step would be to analyze your credit report and get in touch with all creditors with whom fraud has been committed. Fill out affidavits. You can get a blank affidavit at www.consumer.gov/idtheft/affidavit.htm.

Next get in touch with your local police or sheriff's department and report the crime. Request a copy of all police reports. You will be asked to show the credit report indicating the fraud, which is why you get in touch with the credit recording companies first.

If you have had checks stolen, call your bank and put stop payments on any outstanding checks. Cancel all of your bank accounts and open new ones. In the same vein, if your ATM card has been stolen, have it canceled immediately and get a new one. Use a new and different password. Do not use a password that could easily be guessed by someone who knows your birthday, Social Security number, etc. The same is true of your phone service. Change your phone accounts and passwords if you are the victim of I.D. theft.

Ounce of Prevention

Civilians are not the only ones who are at risk of ID theft. Thousands of military personnel overseas or awaiting deployment are at risk as well. In January 2003, it was reported that the names, addresses, telephone numbers, birth dates and Social Security numbers of about 562,000 troops, dependents, and retirees were on laptops and computer hard drives stolen from a building in an industrial park at an undisclosed location.

Call your lawyer. If you don't have one, get one. If the identity thief should commit other crimes in your name, you will want to have your legal rights represented.

If your Social Security number has been misused, contact the Social Security Administration (www.ssa.gov). Order a copy of your Personal Earnings and Benefits Statement and make sure it is correct.

Security Factoid

The potential problems that could be caused by a computer-savvy terrorist became all-too-clear during January 2003 when a fast-spreading virus struck the Internet and slowed Web traffic and e-mail all around the world. According to the FBI, the virus resembled blueprints for a computer code that had been published several weeks before on a Chinese computer hacking website. According to Howard Schmidt, a presidential cybersecurity adviser, disruption to the U.S. government was "minimal." The incident did expose the Internet's vulnerability and showed that the strategies that managers of computer networks have adopted for security sometimes are inadequate. Fortunately cyber threats have become well recognized and more safeguards are being built into systems.

If you suspect an identity thief is using your postal address to commit fraud or has submitted false change-of-address forms, immediately contact your local Postal Inspector. If you are uncertain about whom to get in touch with, call (800) 275-8777 for info.

Contact the passport office whether or not you have a passport. You do not want someone else getting a passport using your identity. Log on to www.travel.state.gov/passport_services.html. Next, call the Department of Motor Vehicles or whatever that group is called in your state to make sure no other driver's licenses have been issued in your name.

If the person who stole your identity is caught, be sure to write a letter to the judge of the trial itemizing the impact the theft has had on your life.

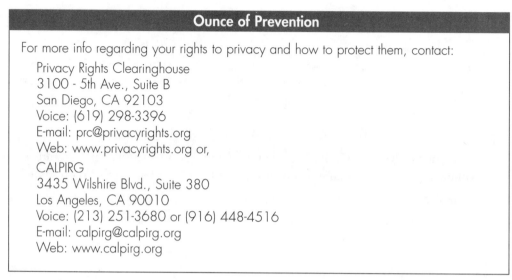

Ounce of Prevention

For more info regarding your rights to privacy and how to protect them, contact:

Privacy Rights Clearinghouse
3100 - 5th Ave., Suite B
San Diego, CA 92103
Voice: (619) 298-3396
E-mail: prc@privacyrights.org
Web: www.privacyrights.org or,

CALPIRG
3435 Wilshire Blvd., Suite 380
Los Angeles, CA 90010
Voice: (213) 251-3680 or (916) 448-4516
E-mail: calpirg@calpirg.org
Web: www.calpirg.org

Thinking Before We Post

Staying on the cyber theme, there has been an effort in recent months to reduce the amount of intelligence that can be gathered by enemies and potential enemies simply by visiting U.S. Defense Department websites.

The fact that information was being gathered in this fashion became obvious when an Al Qaeda training manual included info available on DoD websites.

According to a 2003 statement by Defense Secretary Donald Rumsfeld, "One must conclude our enemies access DoD websites on a regular basis. Thinking about what may be helpful to an adversary prior to posting any information to the Web could eliminate many vulnerabilities. The fact that 'For Official Use Only' (FOUO) and other sensitive unclassified information continues to be found on public websites indicates that too often data posted are insufficiently reviewed for sensitivity and/or inadequately protected. Over 1,500 discrepancies were found during the past year. This continuing trend must be reversed."

Legal Ramifications of Cyber-Warfare

The United States, back in the 1990s, considered for a time using cyber-warfare as an offensive weapon, with Yugoslavia being the target. The full-scale cyber attack would have been aimed not only at military operations but also designed to disrupt basic civilian services.

The attack was not executed, however, because of operational and legal considerations surrounding the emerging field of cyber warfare. Midway through the operation, the top Defense legal office issued general guidelines warning that misuse of cyber attacks could subject U.S. authorities to war crimes charges.

The guidelines, entitled "An Assessment of International Legal Issues in Information Operations," advised commanders to apply the same "law of war" principles to computer attacks that they do to bombs and missiles.

Not Just Terrorists Do It

It has been known for several years that several countries are carrying out electronic reconnaissance today on our civilian infrastructure computer networks for potential use in conflict. One of these countries is our enemy, North Korea. North Korean hackers had left behind a malicious code designed for possible activation as a kind of Trojan horse.

Representatives of the U.S. Intelligence Community have told Congress that China and Russia are also among a number of countries developing "information warfare" capabilities. They are doing this, of course, to offset the lopsided U.S. military superiority.

The Least You Need to Know

- A cyberterrorist, in order to carry out an attack, would need neither a lot of money, nor proximity to his target.

- Hacker groups control hundreds of automated search robot networks that could be used to attack government systems.

- A national cybersecurity strategy was designed to protect the nation's most critical information systems from attack.

- If you suspect that your identity has been stolen, remember, act quickly—the longer you wait, the more damage can be done.

- There has been an increased effort in recent months to reduce the amount of intelligence that can be gathered by enemies and potential enemies that you can find by visiting U.S. Defense Department websites.

Part 4

Feeling Safe vs. Feeling Free

In this section we are going to look at you, the reader, and how you feel about the world situation. National security, of course, is all about the security of Americans. How secure do you feel? Chances are, not as secure as you felt before the 9/11 attacks. Most of you are concerned that terrorists are planning another devastating attack on U.S. soil. We will be discussing in detail some of the things you can do to make you and your family safer if an attack should come.

Chapter 23

The Civil Rights Question

In This Chapter

- Taking freedoms away
- Abusing the law
- The question of profiling
- The Big Brother factor

Many new laws have been passed since the 9/11 attacks designed to make it easier for the U.S. intelligence community and federal, state, and local law enforcement to prevent future terrorists attacks. However, many of these new laws have been criticized by advocates of civil liberties because they compromise time-honored rights to privacy and other freedoms that American's cherish.

In these dangerous times, two uncomfortable truths have come to the fore. They are: No totally free and open country can be totally safe, and, no totally safe country can be totally free and open.

So the idea is to make America as safe as possible while giving up a minimum of civil rights. A happy medium is sought. But where that happy medium lies will be a constant cause of debate between those seeking security and civil libertarians, and thus, the focus of this chapter.

Spying on Us

Here's an example: During February 2003, New York City's police commissioner succeeded in abolishing a 20-year-old court decree governing the limits on police spying and surveillance of its own citizenry. The decree, signed in 1985, prohibited police from photographing and carrying out surveillance of political demonstrations.

To infiltrate lawful political and social organizations, police had to establish a suspicion of criminal activity and gain the permission of a special three-person authority. The city's argument was that they needed more "elbow room" to photograph, tape, and infiltrate groups of citizens in attempts to disrupt potentially terrorist groups. Similar debates have begun in other cities—such as Chicago and San Francisco.

This seemed like an easy enough decision, except for one thing: Domestic spying has an ignoble history.

Point/Counterpoint

"We are seeing a national phenomenon where, in the name of protecting national security against a new and subtle danger, there is a massive effort to eliminate protections for political protest," said Donna Lieberman, executive director of the American Civil Liberties Union, in late 2002. "These safeguards were put in place in the aftermath of a documented history of systematic spying, infiltration and dirty tricks by police agencies and the FBI."

Surveillance Targets?

Years ago, when the New York City Police Department last had these rights, some officers were known to abuse them and use the spying privileges to blackmail political dissidents.

During the 1950s, the New York Police Department's Red Squad compiled large files on political meetings of leftist organizations. The FBI was supplied with lists of names of people who the Red Squad believed were communist sympathizers.

A decade later, the NYPD's Bureau of Strategic Services spied on prominent liberals and others. During the 1970s, Manhattan district attorney Frank Hogan ordered undercover police officers to infiltrate the Black Panthers.

Undercover cops instigated illegal activities that were later carried out. The Black Panthers were a seriously dangerous group, but juries later found it difficult to distinguish between the Panthers' crimes and actions instigated by undercover agents. The same sorts of things happened in other cities. That was why the privileges were taken away to begin with.

Because the great majority of terrorist acts around the world are carried out by Muslims, the fear is that Muslim groups here in the United States will be—sometimes unfairly—targeted for surveillance.

Security Factoid _____

New regulations brought about by post-9/11 fears caused unexpected results. Because Arabs were under greater scrutiny, many required to register regularly with the American Immigration Service, illegal aliens of the Muslim faith were trying to sneak out of the United States. Much had been said about the problem of unwanted aliens sneaking from Canada into the United States across a border that was sparsely protected, but this was the opposite problem. Hoping to take advantage of Canada's political asylum law, they were trying to sneak across the border, heading north.

The Nature of Public Peril

On February 12, 2003, Manhattan's Federal Judge Charles Haight ruled to loosen the 1985 consent decree that limits police surveillance powers. The ruling cleared the way for police to monitor political activity without having to show that the activity is connected with a crime.

Said Federal Judge Charles Haight: "The [U.S.] Constitution's protections are unchanging, but the nature of public peril can change with dramatic speed, as recent events show. We live in a different, more dangerous time than when the consent decree (1985) was approved. This ruling removes restrictions from a bygone era and will allow us to more effectively carry out counterterrorism investigations."

National ID Cards

One idea for tightening National Security, proposed by some members of Congress and endorsed by several business leaders, calls for the creation of a national computerized registration system. This suggestion has caused a major outcry.

By forcing all Americans to carry a card that, in theory, could not be acquired or forged by terrorists, the hopes would be that other security precautions, in particular at airports, could be greatly simplified.

The 9/11 attacks proved that the current system of national identification (the Social Security card) is inadequate. All 19 of the 9/11 terrorists had Social Security cards. Thirteen of them had acquired the cards illegally.

It has been suggested that a national ID card should include individuals' photographs, fingerprints, and even retina scans. Here is what some people think about this:

> According to Jonathan S. Shapiro, assistant professor in the Johns Hopkins University Department of Computer Science, "Airport security guards and other officials think they are relying on the cards when in fact they are relying on the integrity of the human process by which the cards are issued."

> According to Rep. Mary Bono (R-Cal.), "When we consider ourselves to be at war, people are going to have to recognize that some of their freedoms are going to be gone. Whether we are talking about national ID cards I don't know, or fingerprinting everybody, I don't know where we are going to go with security."

> According to former California representative Tom Campbell, later a Stanford University law professor, "If you have an ID card, it is solely for the purpose of allowing the government to compel you to produce it. This would essentially give the government the power to demand that we show our papers. It is a very dangerous thing."

The Patriot Act

The 107th Congress passed the USA Patriot Act (an acronym for Provide Appropriate Tools Required to Intercept and Obstruct Terrorism) less than two months after the 9/11 attacks. The acts are intended to secure the nation's airports, borders, and critical infrastructure against future terrorist attacks.

Because the bill allows more electronic surveillance and wiretapping of private citizens, it was criticized by civil liberties advocates. The law broadened federal phone and electronic surveillance authority, and made it easier for government officials to obtain phone, Internet, and business records. It is considered by most to be a vital tool to help prevent terrorism.

> **Point/Counterpoint**
>
> According to Center for Democracy and Technology Associate Director Alan Davidson, "The Patriot Act is one of the most serious blows ever dealt to American civil liberties."

Some think that the Patriot Act does not go far enough and, in 2003, an 80-page draft of proposed legislation from the Justice Department was leaked to the press. The proposed legislation would:

♦ Invalidate state legal consent decrees that sought to curb police spying.

♦ Eliminate the requirement that the attorney general personally must authorize using certain intelligence evidence in a criminal case.

♦ Allow the collection of DNA samples by "such means as are reasonably necessary."

♦ Bar Freedom of Information Act efforts to gain information about detainees.

♦ Allow citizenship to be revoked from people who support terrorist groups.

The uproar from civil libertarians was immediate.

Author's Corner

Allan: As a card-carrying member of the ACLU, and the Overseas Press Club and Life Member of AFIO, I focus on the importance of stopping terrorism dead in its tracks. If that means we must investigate some people who have not yet done anything, but may indeed be involved in association with others or by themselves be a potential threat, it seems logical and sane to keep such people under observation. I trust our FBI to use good judgment and to protect us all. It is insane to risk another 9/11 by being overly cautious about civil rights of those who would harm our country and kill thousands of people without a second thought, as we have seen.

The Department of Justice for many years mandated that there be a clear separation between intelligence functions and criminal functions even if the two sections of the FBI were investigating the same group or individual. In effect information developed in the two cases could not be shared. This requirement was not mandated by the legislation that created the FISA Court, but rather imposed by Department of Justice lawyers.

This caused huge bureaucratic hurdles that were in effect insurmountable in many cases. A unanimous ruling of the U.S. Foreign Intelligence Court of Review found that the passage of the Patriot Act in 2002 insured that no such wall between officials in the intelligence and criminal arms of the Department of Justice existed. The Court went on to declare that the 20-year requirement to keep the two separated was never required and never intended by

Ounce of Prevention

By 2005, all U.S. Defense Department workers will enter their facilities via fingerprint or iris authentication. The biometric technologies will become part of a redesigned Common Access smart card issued to all active-duty and civilian personnel, and to military reservists and contractors working in secure DoD facilities.

Congress. This Court ruling will allow agents to share information in both criminal and intelligence cases and to better protect the national security.

In May 2003, members of the U.S. Senate, who had been seeking to make the sweeping antiterrorism powers given to the government in the Patriot Act permanent, backed down from that position. The powers given to the government by the Patriot Act are scheduled to expire in 2005.

Homeland Security Act

Another law passed in 2002 caused consternation among civil libertarians. It was the Homeland Security Act. This is the law that created the Department of Homeland Security. It is designed to protect critical national infrastructure, and focus U.S. resources on protecting the safety of U.S. citizens and responding to emergencies. But, when it comes to aspects of the act regarding the Internet, some feel it has gone too far.

The law shielded Internet service providers from customer lawsuits if providers share private subscriber data with law enforcement authorities. In the past, law enforcement agencies could obtain information regarding private Internet subscribers if they had first obtained a search warrant. The search warrant is no longer necessary. Your e-mail can be read and the purchase of airline, train, and bus tickets can be monitored.

The Act also allowed law enforcement to trace the location and identity of an Internet user suspected of posing an "imminent threat to national security interests," or perpetrating attacks on "protected computers"—both government machines and any system used in "interstate commerce or communication."

The law also allowed companies to share information with the government about electronic vulnerabilities—without having to worry that such disclosures will be publicized by the news media.

Total Information Awareness (TIA)

Another controversial proposal was the Pentagon's Total Information Awareness system, or TIA, headed by retired Vice Adm. John Poindexter. TIA was a data-mining program that would have provided access to public and private records, such as travel and bank documents and cell phone usage particulars, to help identify terrorists. The Total Information Awareness (TIA) program is a project of the Information Awareness Office (IAO), which is under the Defense Advanced Research Projects Agency (DARPA), part of the Defense Department.

According to the Information Awareness Office, the TIA is designed to "imagine, develop, apply, integrate, demonstrate and transition information technologies, components and prototype, closed-loop, information systems that will counter asymmetric threats by achieving total information awareness useful for preemption; national security warning; and national security decision making."

Sen. Ron Wyden (D-Oregon), a sponsor of the move to block the program, said, "TIA crosses the line with respect to the balance people want to see struck. In a sense, this is a very powerful message that with a reach like this one, Congress has drawn a line in the sand and said it will not go forward unchecked."

The Least You Need to Know

♦ Some fear that, since the great majority of terrorist acts around the world are carried out by Muslims, that Muslim groups here in the United States will be—sometimes unfairly—targeted for surveillance.

♦ The right to privacy, long cherished by Americans, has been compromised by several new laws passed by congress since the 9/11 attacks.

♦ The Patriot Act grants the government powers designed to secure the nation's airports, borders and critical infrastructure against future terrorist attacks.

♦ The Homeland Security Act—designed to protect critical national infrastructure, and focus U.S. resources on protecting the safety of U.S. citizens and responding to emergencies—has granted the government the right to monitor e-mail and Internet activity without a search warrant.

♦ The controversial Total Information Awareness program would have provided access to public and private records, such as travel and bank documents and cell phone usage particulars, to help identify terrorists.

Chapter 24

Conclusion: Be Vigilant, Not a Vigilante

In This Chapter

- ◆ Up the alert level
- ◆ Tension in the subways
- ◆ Missiles in D.C.
- ◆ Preparation lists

If you are an American civilian and not a member of a law enforcement agency, then it would probably be a bad idea for you to personally try to rout out and destroy any terrorist cells that might still exist in the United States.

Such vigilante behavior would probably cause more harm than good. Either you yourself will be injured or killed, you will attack the wrong people, or you will inadvertently get in the way of a large secret operation.

We are not suggesting that you "go to war" against the terrorists. On the other hand, there are things you can do to help prevent a terrorist attack, and to better prepare yourself and your family in case such an attack comes. That's what this chapter is about.

Being Prepared

In February 2003, the Department of Homeland Security raised the alert level in the nation from yellow to orange. The raised level of alertness was due, they said, to intercepted Al Qaeda communications that indicated that the terror network had plans for a series of attacks either just before or just after the start of a U.S.-led war on Iraq.

> **Ounce of Prevention**
>
> Citizen Corps, a vital component of USA Freedom Corps, was created to help coordinate volunteer activities that will make our communities safer, stronger, and better prepared to respond to any emergency situation. If there is not a Citizen Corps Council in your area, please contact your State Citizen Corps representative and work with your local officials to get one started. For more info, check out their website at www.citizencorps.gov.

The attacks, officials said, were to come between February 9 and 21, which was the time of the yearly Muslim *Hajj*, or pilgrimage to Mecca. An FBI memo written early that month said, "In that situation, Al Qaeda attacks will be described as an effort to defend Iraqi Muslims against the attack of the U.S.-led crusaders."

By mid-February, word was that the government had raised the alert level to orange after American intelligence obtained evidence that agents of Al Qaeda might be positioning themselves to carry out two major attacks, including one inside the United States. Intercepts of telephone conversations, e-mail messages and other intelligence had indicated that terrorists were moving closer to an attack.

According to one Bush administration official, "One of the reasons taken into consideration in moving to orange was the concern that Al Qaeda was moving from the planning stages to going operational. It is why we need to do more, to deploy more assets and physical barriers, because we are more concerned about the potential for attack."

The alerts are necessary. Things are done differently during different levels of alert. When the alert level switches from yellow to orange, things change dramatically with regard to law enforcement. Cars are searched at airports, bridges, and other strategic locations. Most times the basis comes from foreign sources and sometimes they turn out to be unreliable, but still the country must be warned. The government has to guard against a "sky is falling" mind set on the part of the people. Too many alerts will begin to be ignored and Homeland Security will become a joke.

Focus on New York City as the possible site of a terror attack increased on February 10, 2003, when the media announced that an intercepted communication stated that the attack was going to be "underground" and "at the site of our greatest victory."

This was widely interpreted to mean that the attack would be to the New York City subway system, because the "victory" referred to was assumed to mean the destruction of the World Trade Center towers.

Point/Counterpoint

DCI George Tenet stated in testimony delivered to the U.S. Senate Select Committee on Intelligence in 2003 that the move from a yellow to an orange threat warning was based on multiple sources: "The information we have points to plots aimed at targets on two fronts, in the United States and on the Arabian peninsula …. The intelligence is not idle chatter on the part of terrorists …. It is the most specific we have seen." Perhaps the increased warning level scared the terrorists off. Perhaps the "specific" chatter was merely intended to terrorize us. Whichever, no terrorist attack took place.

In response to this information, National Guard weapons specialists and the New York Police Department (NYPD) hazardous materials unit was stationed within the subway system. They took air samples regularly in various locations to test for a chemical or biological attack.

By February 12, the NYPD was on the lookout for terrorists armed with conventional or improvised weapons involving deadly chemicals—such as sarin or cyanide—concealed in an innocent-looking container. Among the containers suspected were plastic bottles, fire extinguishers, aerosol spray cans, light bulbs, glass jars, and briefcases.

Ounce of Prevention

Picture a terrorist. Chances are the image you conjured was of a swarthy man of Middle Eastern descent. Trouble is, the next wave of terrorists may look nothing like that. They might have fair skin, blond hair, and blue eyes. Iran and Al Qaeda began recruiting and training Bosnian Muslims for war against Orthodox Christian Serbs and Catholic Croats long ago, in order to expand the Muslim base in Eastern Europe. There has been some fear that these blond-haired, blue-eyed guys might link up with American neo-Nazis since they have the same goals and the same hatreds. So far, luckily, they just don't like each other.

An NYPD bulletin warned NYPD personnel to be prepared for the "release of toxic substances in populated and contained environments." Environments suggested in the bulletin included sports venues and the subway.

New York City was prepared. The MTA, the organization in charge of New York's subway system, installed sensors in the subways tunnels and stations that were capable of sniffing out a biological or chemical agent.

The devices are the size of shoeboxes and work like fire alarms. They would sound a warning the instant they detected a toxic substance in the air, and reaction to the emergency could be immediate. Similar devices were also installed during February 2003 in the Washington, D.C. subway system.

To better cover the entire system, the devices are also being attached to the subway's garbage collecting trains, which pass through stations late at night when the stations are least populated.

Security Factoid _____

In reaction to the heightened levels of security during the orange alert, in the nation's capital humvees equipped with missile launchers guarded key sites while F-16s cruised overhead. Police in Washington, D.C. were carrying gas masks and several Avenger surface-to-air missile launchers were deployed to protect the White House, Congress, and the Pentagon. These batteries were capable of firing eight Stinger missiles from a launcher atop a radar-equipped Humvee. There were also troops with shoulder-held Stinger launchers deployed in the city.

If You Find a Suspicious Package ...

One thing that all U.S. citizens can do to help the fight against another terrorist attack is to be on the lookout for suspicious packages. Anytime someone sets a package down in a public area and walks away from it, that is highly suspicious. Any package that has been left unattended should be considered suspicious.

Here is an FBI checklist of what to do if you should discover a suspicious package. Some of these rules, as you'll notice, are particularly geared toward postal workers:

- Handle with care. Don't shake or bump.

- Isolate and look for "indicators." Common indicators are, but not limited to, the following:

  - No return address

  - Restrictive markings, i.e., "Personal"

  - Possibly mailed from a foreign country

  - Excessive postage

  - Misspelled words

  - Addressed to title only or incorrect title

  - Wrong title with name

- Badly typed or written

- Protruding wires

- Lopsided or uneven

- Rigid or bulky

- Strange odor

- Oily stains, discoloration, or crystallization on the wrapper

- Excessive tape or string

- Don't open, smell, or taste.

- Treat as suspicious! Call 911!

If the package is open and/or a threat is identified, evacuate the area immediately. Call 911 (Police) or the FBI.

How You Can Be Safer

Here are some ways we can take action now to help protect our families, help reduce the impact an emergency has on our lives, and help deal with the chaos if an incident does occur.

- Prepare a Family Disaster Supplies Kit to last for at least three days, including drinkable water, nonperishable food (including pet food), first aid supplies, other emergency supplies like flashlights and batteries, clothes and bedding, and specialty items. Disaster Supply Kits should also be prepared for your car and workplace.

> **Ounce of Prevention**
>
> Don't limit your preparations for emergencies to your immediate family. Help others be safer as well. When you help your neighbor, you help your nation. Share what you learn with others.

- Check and change the batteries in your smoke alarms and replace all alarms that are more than ten years old.

- Make sure you know where your local fire department, police station, and hospital are and post a list of emergency phone numbers near all the telephones in your home.

- Organize and practice a family fire drill. Make sure your children know what your smoke detector sounds like and what to do if it goes off when they are sleeping.

- Locate the utility mains for your home and be sure you know how to turn them off manually: gas, electricity, and water.

- Create an emergency plan for your household, including your pets.

- Decide where your family will meet if a disaster does happen: (a) outside your home in case of a sudden emergency, like a fire; and (b) outside your neighborhood in case you can't return home. Ask an out-of-town friend to be your "family contact" to relay messages.

- Prepare a three-day disaster supply kit, complete with flashlights, batteries, blankets, and an emergency supply of water and food.

An organization that could help you join or form a crime and neighborhood watch group is the National Crime Prevention Council, a private, nonprofit educational organization. For more info, contact: National Crime Prevention Council, 1000 Connecticut Avenue, NW, 13th Floor, Washington, D.C. 20036.

Learning from Natural Disasters

Preparing for a terrorist attack is a lot like preparing for a natural disaster. Here are some federal and private agency websites that offer information on how to prepare for disasters. Follow the links from each home page:

- Department of Homeland Security: www.dhs.gov

- Federal Emergency Management Agency: www.fema.gov

- American Red Cross: www.redcross.org

- U.S. Centers for Disease Control: www.cdc.gov

- Washington Post Preparedness Guide: www.washingtonpost.com/preparedness

Survival Tips

September 11, 2001, forever changed the way we as Americans live our lives. Muslim Fundamentalists declared war on us long before that date, but the United States government's response was very limited and by most estimates very weak.

Al Qaeda and other organizations with the same religious goal have as their mission the destruction of Western Civilization. They believe they are on a mission from God to war against the infidels and implement a radical form of Muslim Fundamentalism in this and other countries around the world.

They consider the United States of America and Israel their most dangerous enemies and will continue their religious Jihad against us as long as there is a breath of life in their bodies. It would be foolish for Americans not to take routine precautions against another terrorist attack against our country. We have set out some suggestions that are very simple in their operation and inexpensive in their implementation.

Danny's List

Former FBI Agent Danny Coulson has put together a useful list of survival tips that can serve as a checklist for every family as they stock up on things they may need.

For example, assume that your cell phone will not be operational if there is a crisis in or near your community. The cell phone systems may not be damaged, but the tremendous volume of phone traffic generated by emergency responders, law enforcement, and most or all the media will likely overload the system, making it unavailable. Keep your cell phone with you with a car charger, but don't expect it to work.

Keep at least a half tank of gas in all of your cars, and insure that your family members do the same. In the event of an emergency you may be away from your residence and unable to even approach it. It may be necessary for you to go to an alternate location. Be sure you have plenty of gas.

In your car you should keep …

♦ A couple flats of bottled water.

♦ A first aid kit.

♦ Flashlights with extra batteries.

♦ A blanket.

♦ Energy bars that can sustain you for two to three days. They won't be very tasty, but they will keep you alive.

♦ Extra warm clothes, including boots for the winter.

♦ A shovel to dig you out of snow.

♦ Copies of your most important documents (birth certificate, Social Security card, driver's license, etc.).

♦ Consider two very inexpensive two-way radios. They come in two-mile and five-mile versions. Remember your cell phone probably won't work and you may need to link up with family members or friends. Agree on a common channel to operate on and advise family members.

- Prescription drugs that are necessary for health maintenance.

- A rubber poncho to protect you from the rain also gives some protection from chemical or biological fall out.

- Place these items in a backpack or a similar bag that is easy to carry. Remember the heaviest thing on the list is the water.

In your home you should keep …

- Three days' supply of food and water. Preferably canned food that will not spoil.

- Insure that prescriptions are filled and up-to-date. You don't want to find yourself confined to your residence and out of a badly needed prescription.

- The government has recommended duct tape and plastic to cover windows and doors in the event of nuclear, chemical, or biological fall out.

- FM radio and extra batteries.

- Flashlight and extra batteries.

- Arrange for a meeting place for family members. Consider some place other than a heavily congested area in the middle of the city. Family members should be informed of a rendezvous point, which may be the family home, and also an alternate location.

In case of an emergency, bring your brain and listen to the radio for news updates and instructions from the government. It is highly unlikely that you will be affected by an attack, but it is best to be prepared. Preparation will give you peace of mind, and greatly assist you in keeping you and your family safe.

Allan's List

The key question in everyone's mind about what to do in case of an attack or sudden emergency is "what kind of emergency supplies should I have?"

Here in Maine, we had set up our own system to cover periodic electric outages or other problems from Nor'easter storms, ice storms, and other natural disasters including the few but sometimes pounding hurricanes that hit. Here's our checklist:

- Have a three-day supply of water and food. We have a shelf of canned, dried, and packaged foods along with water sealed in glass and plastic gallon jugs. Rule of thumb is a gallon of water per day per person for drinking and cooking. Wash water is separate and we have 4 old 5-gallon pickle buckets full of water for toilets, washing, clothes, etc., but not drinking.

- Clothing—a change of clothing for each person, underwear to outerwear plus sweaters or jackets. In cold weather we keep heavy jackets handy to grab if needed.

- Paper plates, paper towels, and plastic utensils.

- Plastic bags for storage and also waste disposal.

- Extra bedding, i.e., sheets and blankets.

- Battery-operated radios upstairs and downstairs for weather and emergency information.

- One-week supply of medicines in seven-day holders, which we replace monthly to keep it fresh.

- Set of tools—hammer, pliers, screwdriver, small saw.

- Multipurpose pocketknife for each person.

- Emergency set of keys with small pocketknife and identification.

- Toiletries including soap, toothbrushes, toilet paper, and cleaning supplies.

- Duct tape for multiple purposes.

- Pet food for pets and carrying case handy.

- Extra diapers, baby formula if young children (even for breast-fed babies, in case something should happen to the mother), plus toys.

- Games, books, maps, entertainment, tape recorder.

- First aid kit—portable that includes adhesive bandages, gauze pads, adhesive tape, tweezers, scissors, needle, thermometer, moistened towelettes, antiseptic ointment, Vaseline, soap, rubber or vinyl gloves, safety pins, aspirin or pain reliever you prefer, antacids, other needs for your family.

- Individual or double-burner camp stove and fuel.

- Maps, compass, and small pocket flashlight.

> **Author's Corner**
>
> Allan: Key items from first aid to maps, radios, medicines, toiletries are in backpacks so we can pick them off the wall of the closet and evacuate if required. We keep a large Coleman cooler handy to load extra foods, but it serves as our emergency food storage chest with a three-day supply in it plus water and water purification pills for camping out.

We all can add to our lists. For example, mine also includes a holster, 22 cal. automatic, gun license, 30 cal. hunting rifle, plus ammunition for both.

A Comprehensive Guide

For a comprehensive guide to preparing yourself for a terrorist attack, we suggest *Are You Ready? A Guide to Citizen Preparedness* (published by the United States Government Printing Office, 2003), which brings together facts on disaster survival techniques, disaster-specific information, and how to prepare for and respond to both natural and man-made disasters.

It is published by the Federal Emergency Management Agency (FEMA) and provides a step-by-step outline on how to prepare a disaster supply kit, emergency planning for people with disabilities, how to locate and evacuate to a shelter, and even contingency planning for family pets. Man-made threats from hazardous materials and terrorism are also treated in detail.

The guide details opportunities for every citizen to become involved in safeguarding their neighbors and communities through FEMA's Citizen Corps (www.citizencorps. gov) initiative and Community Emergency Response Team training program. Copies of *Are You Ready? A Guide to Citizen Preparedness* are available through the FEMA Publications warehouse (1-800-480-2520), FEMA publication H-34.

The Least You Need to Know

- In February 2003, the alert level in the nation was raised from yellow to orange due to intercepted Al Qaeda communications indicating plans for a series of attacks.

- New York City installed sensors in its subways tunnels and stations capable of sniffing out a biological or chemical agent.

- Moslem Fundamentalists recognize the United States of America and Israel as their most dangerous enemies.

- You should memorize our lists of preparations, which will help keep you safe in case of an emergency.

Glossary

Abwehr   German Intelligence Service during World War II. Organization pre-dated the Nazi party and was often at odds with them—until 1944 when the Nazis absorbed Abwehr. Organization discontinued at the end of World War II.

affirmative mode   A term borrowed from sales management specialists, this refers to setting a mood or stage that is affirmative or positive to elicit a good feeling to gain positive responses and cooperation. For example, by simply observing that it is a beautiful warm day and nodding during conversation one sets the scene for a nodding agreement of "Yes, it is," which is designed to lead to better rapport and cooperation.

agent   An agent also may be known as an asset. This word agent is often confused with officer. Intelligence officers are the trained and dedicated staff employees who are patriots in the United States. Agents are the people recruited by intelligence officers to provide information and intelligence needed by the United States and if necessary to betray their own countries.

analysis   Determining the significance of collected information. Putting information together with other known facts to gauge its intelligence value. To make conclusions based on collected information.

ANSIR   Awareness of National Security Issues and Response (FBI). ANSIR keeps organizations and corporations briefed on the best ways to protect themselves against terrorist threats.

asset *See* agent.

backstopping Taking steps and arranging information to back up information given out about a person which can include placing records and documents at colleges, businesses, public offices, and elsewhere so that anyone checking will find the "facts" that they had been given.

bigot list A term used by some to identify a select group of key people who have access to intelligence reports from or about a particularly sensitive operation or project.

blot out A rather old term that describes using radio to "blot out" or otherwise interfere with recordings of conversations which makes understanding the recording difficult without use of special electronic equipment.

blowback Bad publicity. Also known as flap.

bug Small electronic listening or recording device. Such a device may be placed in an area where valuable information may be recorded and used to obtain information of conversations at meetings, individual phone calls or other situations. A bug is usually considered an electronic device. Many types have been invented and perfected by the technical experts at the CIA. The FBI also has experts in bugging for investigations of crimes.

Camp Perry The legendary training base outside Williamsburg, Virginia, where career intelligence officer trainees are given courses in many aspects of intelligence work. These include detecting explosives, surveillance and countersurveillance, and training in a wide variety of conventional and sometimes unconventional weapons. Officer trainees also are taught how to run counterterrorism, paramilitary operations, recruit and run agents, and otherwise gain basic training for their careers. Also used for refresher course training. Often called "the Farm," a nickname for this facility.

case officer A member of an intelligence organization who is responsible for recruiting and handling agents or assets. Sometimes called an Operations Officer.

Center for the Study of Intelligence Division of the CIA that maintains the agency's historical materials and promotes the study of intelligence as a legitimate and serious discipline. The current director is Lloyd Salvetti.

chatter Increased volume of intercepted communications indicating that the enemy is up to something.

CIA The Central Intelligence Agency was created in 1947 with the signing of the National Security Act by President Harry Truman. The National Security Act charged the Director of Central Intelligence (DCI), with coordinating the nation's intelligence activities and correlating, evaluating and disseminating intelligence that affects national security. The DCI serves as the head of the U.S. intelligence community and principal advisor to the president for intelligence matters related to national security, and also is head of the CIA. The CIA is an independent agency responsible to the president through the DCI and accountable to the American people through the intelligence oversight committees of the U.S. Congress, including both the House of Representatives and the Senate.

clandestine   Secret, secretly.

clandestine operations   These are operations carried out in secret, or without general public knowledge. Sometimes referred to as undercover operations.

classification   A division of sensitive intelligence, military or policy information that usually includes three levels. *See* confidential, secret, and top secret.

classified documents   Documents, maps, and information that have been classified by a government primarily for its importance to that government. This is the type of secret information that often has value to U.S. leaders and is the target of intelligence activities in many parts of the world, especially in foreign countries viewed as adversaries or potential threats to America.

collect   Acquire information.

commercial cover   A protective device whereby a person is given a job and title with a business or other organization and uses that position to hide his or her real work as an intelligence operative. In such cases the person does not have the benefit of diplomatic immunity as is possible when the cover is from a U.S. governmental agency.

The Company   Nickname for the CIA.

confidential   A security classification, the lowest, defined as information, the unauthorized disclosure of which reasonably could be expected to cause damage to the national security.

consumer   Client who obtains information from the intelligence-gathering service. Basically this is the person or organization that receives intelligence and uses it.

contract employee   Most members of the CIA are staff employees, but some specialists from the military or with expertise in needed fields may be hired under contract. Often military officers are assigned to the CIA for specific projects and tours of duty.

counterintelligence   These are activities undertaken by an agency or organization to thwart or foil efforts by hostile intelligence services or individuals to penetrate a country's or organization's intelligence service, files, and operations. This includes the penetration of a foreign service with a "mole" or agent who reports to U.S. intelligence on the work of or activities of the hostile government service.

cover　This is a protective guise or facade given or assumed by an individual or activity to conceal the true nature of the person or organization. For example, an intelligence operative may have credentials and identification as a teacher, student, worker for another government agency, a business or other activity than his/her true intelligence work.

covert action　This is clandestine activity designed to influence events in foreign countries without the role of U.S. intelligence being known. Such actions can range from placement of propaganda in media to attempts to overthrow a government that is deemed unfriendly to this country.

covert intelligence　Information a spy has to find out by snooping around.

cowboy　An unflattering term that denotes an intelligence person who defies rules, regulations and conventions and conducts himself in an unprofessional, flamboyant way. Otherwise called a "loose cannon."

cryptonyms　Code names. Sometimes called crypts for short.

current intelligence　Looks at day-to-day events.

dead drop　Basically, a place where a case officer and agent agree to leave or deposit messages, film, or other material that is to be picked up by the other. It may include directives, payments, and necessary communications. The objective is to leave and retrieve information somewhere that is accessible and without having to meet in person with the risk of being observed.

debriefing　The word used to cover questioning of people with possible worthwhile intelligence information that can range from asking questions of business people who have traveled to foreign countries to interrogating defectors or captured spies.

debug　A term that describes the finding and eliminating of secret recording devices.

defector　A person who has repudiated his own country and citizenship and provides information of intelligence value to another country. There may be defectors who leave their country to be given new names, identification, and even a job in the country whose intelligence service has recruited them to become agents, assets and traitors to their homeland.

Defense Intelligence Agency　The coordinating agency in the Defense Department that reports to the secretary of defense with intelligence collected from all military services, but also is subject to the coordinating authority of the DCI.

Deputy Director for Intelligence The head of the CIA's analytic directorate that evaluates and summarizes raw intelligence reports.

Deputy Director of Central Intelligence Person who assists the Director in his duties as head of the CIA and the intelligence community and exercises the powers of the Director when the Director's position is vacant or in the Director's absence or disability.

Deputy Director of Operations The head of the CIA's clandestine branch, known as the Directorate of Operations. This person manages the CIA stations abroad and also covert operations and assists in other sensitive intelligence collecting abroad.

diplomatic immunity The immunity granted to diplomats and key employees of government agencies and respected by other governments.

direction finder Device that locates the source of electronic emissions using triangulation.

Director of Central Intelligence The top person who oversees and coordinates all U.S. intelligence agencies and also heads the Central Intelligence Agency and is usually considered the president's chief intelligence advisor.

Directorate of Intelligence The analytical branch of the CIA, responsible for the production and dissemination of all-source intelligence analysis on key foreign issues.

Directorate of Operations Branch of the CIA that is responsible for the clandestine collection of foreign intelligence.

Directorate of Science and Technology Branch of the CIA that creates and applies innovative technology in support of the intelligence collection mission.

disinformation False information purposefully disseminated to mislead.

dissem A document that may be disseminated to consumers.

dissemination Distribution of intelligence to consumers via oral, written, or electronic methods.

dumping A term used to describe sending information or messages in short electronic bursts.

ESP Extra sensory perception, the seeming ability of some people, called psychics, to know and be able to sense situations and information beyond ability of other more normal people. One aspect of this has been "remote reading," the seeming ability of some psychics to read letters and documents in other rooms. Research has been conducted by military and CIA on this unusual phenomena, which some scientists believe is actually possible. Others dispute the value of psychics while acknowledging that they do have unique abilities that are not fully understood.

espionage Most commonly, clandestine intelligence collection. Also can be taken to mean destruction activities against an organization or country. In today's world, spying and some forms of espionage are being used by commercial companies against their competition, especially in foreign business situations.

estimate An intelligence product that analyzes and assesses future potential developments and courses of action for review by an intelligence consumer.

estimative intelligence Looks at what might be or what might happen.

evaluation The determination of probable validity and utility of intelligence information, which is subjective and some believe is merely a "best bet" guesstimate.

Executive Director of the Central Intelligence Agency The person who, assisted by an executive board that counts among its membership five mission centers, has duties that enable the agency to carry out its mission, including the chief financial officer, chief information officer, security, human resources and global support. The EXDIR manages the CIA on a day-to-day basis.

finding A written determination by the president of the United States that is required before covert action may be undertaken. This is usually a brief written directive in which the president states that he "finds" a certain "covert action" is important for national security.

flap Bad publicity. Also known as blowback.

foreign intelligence Intelligence concerning or involving areas and activities outside the United States.

front An organization that serves to provide a legend or disguised identification for an operation or project.

G-2 At the Army General Staff level this is the term for intelligence—i.e. the Assistant Chief of Staff for Intelligence. It is the common term for intelligence at Division and higher levels. At lower levels the term is S-2.

G-Agent The name given to a variety of nerve gases that include GA–Tabun and GB–Sarin, which attack through the respiratory system. These nerve gases are "neurotoxic" (poisonous to the nervous system) and usually lethal within minutes.

GRU Stands for *Glavnoye Razedyatel'noye Upraveleniye*. It is the Russian term for military intelligence, their Chief Intelligence Directorate.

honey pot or **honey trap** Terms used by the FBI and CIA for an operation involving sexual entrapment of an agent or person. It was frequently attempted by the Soviets.

human source intelligence Also called HUMINT, this is intelligence collected by means of agents or informers. There has been an ongoing debate about the loss of HUMINT because of a focus on using satellite and high tech intelligence and not investing in the use of human sources on the ground. In a way this compares to the air force focus on bombing and the army focus on forces on the ground in a war situation to combat and win over an enemy force or country.

imagery Representations of objects produced on film, optical displays, radar, or other electronic means for viewing, interpretation and analysis.

information Unevaluated raw data that is not processed to produce intelligence, i.e., which has not been subjected to analysis and evaluation of sources and content.

intelligence The finished product of collection, evaluation and analysis of information that is useable by the recipient. *See* difference between intelligence and information, above.

intelligence community IC, generally used as a term referring to all the U.S. intelligence agencies and employees of which the Director of Central Intelligence is the senior member.

intelligence finding Order by the president of the United States to the CIA to perform a covert action.

Interpol Stands for the International Criminal Police Commission that is based in Lyons, France. It was originally intended for the interchange of data leading to identification, location, and apprehension of criminals. This organization coordinates its efforts with national, state, and local police organizations in member countries.

Ivy League A group of highly respected, top colleges, called the Ivy League, which include Brown, Columbia, Cornell, Dartmouth, Harvard, Princeton, and Yale. Many OSS and CIA officers were recruited from these schools during the early years.

Langley Supposed location of CIA headquarters in Virginia (suburban Washington, D.C.).

laundering A process of hiding sources, transmittal and persons involved in financial matters and transfers of money for intelligence, and today more commonly for criminal purposes, primarily associated with terrorist activity and narcotics trafficking.

legend Term that refers to a cover story made up to provide provable background about an intelligence officer, which can include college attended, home town, family connections, all of which may be fabricated and memorized to become a different person, i.e., "a legend in one's own time," so to speak.

light disguise A simple disguise of wigs and glasses, change of clothing, superficial cover, and appearance changes.

light legend Another basic phrase that refers to a superficial cover story of identify and background.

Lord Haw-Haw Term dating back to World War II describing a British traitor who broadcast German propaganda in the English Language. Obviously from the name, his efforts were largely laughable to the Allied troops.

L pill Old term for a suicide pill, the L standing for lethal. These were actually developed and issued for use by Allied Forces spies or agents during World War II. Originally said to contain a fatal dose of chloral hydrate. Supposedly Soviets used the powerful ricin poison.

Magnum U.S. spy satellite that can eavesdrop on sound signals from Earth.

marginalia Method by which one studies the history of a document, by examining the notes, initials, etc. that have been jotted in the margins.

mole A person inside a government agency, usually an intelligence agency, who is obtaining information about that organization's secrets and activities.

molehunting *See* counterintelligence.

Mossad Israel's major external intelligence organization, similar to our CIA. For reference the organization has a fancy name: Hamossad Mamerkazi Lemodi'in-Vetafkidim Meyu Hadum, which translates to The Central Institute for Intelligence and Special Tasks. That "Special Tasks" phrase stands closer scrutiny because it encompasses some of the toughest assignments given to that group.

Mukhabarat Jordanian intelligence agency.

naked Condition of an agent who is working entirely on his or her own without any direct control by an Intelligence officer.

National Foreign Intelligence Board (NFIB) Made up of the heads of all U.S. intelligence agencies. In effect, this acts as a "Board of Directors" for U.S. Intelligence, is chaired by the DCI and members include representatives from CIA, NSA, DIA, NRO and the intelligence services of the Navy, Army, Air Force, Marines, FBI, and Departments of State, Energy, and Treasury.

National Imagery and Mapping Agency (NIMA) Provides maps of the world from satellite collection, both government and commercial sources.

National Intelligence Daily (NID) A top-secret summary of the main intelligence items from the previous days, with a very limited distribution.

National Intelligence Estimate (NIE) A formal written forecast of future potential events in countries, by leaders or of various intelligence, military, or economical problems. It presents the best collective judgment of all the U.S. intelligence agencies, headed by the DCI.

National Reconnaissance Office (NRO) A lower profile agency responsible for satellite and aerial overhead intelligence gathering that reports to the secretary of defense with coordination by the DCI.

National Security Council (NSC) Includes the president and his senior foreign policy makers with the DCI and chairman of the Joint Chiefs of Staff as advisors.

Noforn Document that is not to be seen by foreign eyes.

non-official cover Intelligence officers who pose as entrepreneurs or employees of private companies to hide their real activities. Also called commercial cover, this is riskier than when using a cover of another U.S. government agency, because it provides no diplomatic immunity.

officer A member of an intelligence organization who is responsible for recruiting and handling agents or assets. Sometimes called an operations officer.

open sources Refers to news, books, and public information of all kinds that is available to intelligence officers as well as the public.

operations officer *See* case officer.

overt intelligence Strategically valuable information that is publicly known, such as that which has been published in newspapers.

paramilitary operations Operations undertaken by military forces separate from the regular armed forces of a nation. Often used in an effort to hide source of control.

plausible denial A nice term that basically means if you get caught, we can disown you and deny that you work for the CIA, or other intelligence agency.

president's daily brief Includes the most exclusive and sensitive items, which are summarized succinctly and sent to the president and a highly select list of leaders and White House aides.

processing Development of collected raw information of possible intelligence value to make it useable for analysis and into a finished intelligence product.

product The finished intelligence which is disseminated to consumers, those who need it for decision-making.

Psywar   A term for psychological warfare, usually putting out black or gray propaganda to influence the action of an enemy armed force, civilians or others to achieve goals for the Psywar activists. An early Psywar Center was set up at Fort Bragg in the 1950s and many military personnel were trained in how to conduct this phase of communications in support of armed forces in hot or cold wartime.

Q clearance   Clearance granted by the Department of Energy for access to restricted data involving atomic energy. That could include research as well as uses of atomic weaponry, delivery systems, or intelligence about both U.S. and foreign atomic capabilities.

ranger   Word that originally applied to those very special individuals who were selected to undergo rigorous Ranger Training at the Ranger School in Fort Benning, Georgia. Today the word ranger has been expanded to include various units that are designed for scouting, reconn, special operations, sabotage, and other assignments beyond what military units do.

reconnaissance   Observation or patrol missions undertaken to acquire by various means useful information about a target of intelligence interest. (The Watergate break-in was *not* one.)

renegade   A person who operates outside of conventional and approved procedures. Also defined by some as a person who has turned on this country in any of a variety of ways.

research intelligence   An in-depth study of a specific issue.

safehouse   Location, usually kept secret, where defectors or agents can be taken for debriefing or hidden during processing. Says author Allan Swenson, "When I was engaged in Special Projects, Wilson and I would rendezvous at a safehouse in lower Manhattan. It was a place we could talk without being seen or heard and a place I could use when pressed during any projects in New York City that required me to disappear for short periods."

scientific and technical intelligence   Information on foreign technologies.

Scotland Yard   Name long associated with Sherlock Holmes. The truth is that it was originally the site of a thirteenth-century palace in London that was used by Scottish monarchs on state visits to England. In 1829 the first headquarters of the newly formed London Metropolitan Police was located nearby and one of the entrances was in the Scotland Yard, which is one of those curious historic facts.

secret   A security classification, second from the lowest, defined as information, the unauthorized disclosure of which reasonably could be expected to cause serious damage to the national security. Secret info is more sensitive than Confidential info, but not as sensitive as top secret info.

secrets   Generally, anything that a person or organization considers of enough importance that they do not want others to know about them. Various governments and agencies have different levels of secret classifications. These may include classified, usually the lowest level for keeping control to selected individuals, secret, top secret, eyes-only, and other special names for specific areas, including nuclear.

security   Measures taken to protect sensitive activities, data, and personnel against compromise by foreign intelligence organizations or anyone including business competitors.

signals intelligence   Called SIGINT, this is intelligence gained or derived from the interception, processing, and analysis of various communications including electronic emissions or telemetry.

sitrep   A situation report.

Special National Intelligence Estimates   (SNIE) Shorter formal evaluations which are completed in days or weeks on key topics of urgent national security interest.

spook   A nickname for an intelligence officer, operative, or person.

spookspeak   Offshoot of the word spook, and refers to the special words, terms and phrases used by spooks in their intelligence duties. Like all professional specialties words take on a meaning of their own that insiders get to know and use as jargon.

strategic intelligence   Intelligence supporting national and international level formulation of policy, plans, and strategy by top government leaders.

sweep   A search for bugs, i.e., concealed electronic listening devices in a building, vehicle or location that are used to transmit conversation or other information to an enemy. Embassies and intelligence offices overseas must be swept regularly to prevent bugging.

target   A person, place, or thing against which intelligence operations are organized and directed.

telemetry   Electronic signals given off by missiles, rockets, vehicles, or machinery during operational testing or use.

top secret   Classified information that includes such material of which the disclosure could be expected to cause exceptionally grave damage to national security. Top secret information is more sensitive than either confidential info or secret info.

tradecraft   The methods used by intelligence officers, gained from training and experience, to do their special intelligence work.

undercover operations   *See* clandestine operations.

virus   A computer program designed to disrupt the function of, or completely shut down, a computer or computer network.

Voice of America   Official U.S. propaganda broadcasting organization used to present good news and favorable focus on America by listeners.

Vortex   Spy satellite that can listen in to communications on Earth from 22,000 miles up.

warning intelligence   Gives notice to our policy makers that something urgent might happen that may require their immediate attention.

wet affairs   Intel jargon for Soviet murders or assassinations, which were coded XPD by the British.

Zulu   Refers to an agent team during World War II that operated in Vichy, France for the Office of Strategic Services, predecessor of the CIA.

Bibliography

Books

Benson, Michael, *Encyclopedia of the JFK Assassination*, New York: Checkmark Books, 2002.

Cilluffo, Frank J., et al, *Combating Chemical, Biological, Radiological, and Nuclear Terrorism: A Report of the Center for Strategic and International Studies Homeland Defense Project*, Washington, D.C.: The CSIS Press, 2001.

Davidson, James West, Pedro Castillo, and Michael B. Stoff, *The American Nation*, Upper Saddle River: New Jersey: Prentice-Hall, Inc., 2002.

O'Hanlon, Michael E. et al, *Protecting the American Homeland: A Preliminary Analysis*, Washington D.C.: Brookings Institution Press, 2002.

Simeone, John, and David Jacobs, *The Complete Idiot's Guide to the FBI*, Indianapolis, Indiana: Alpha Books, 2003.

Swenson, Allan A. and Michael Benson, *The Complete Idiot's Guide to the CIA*, Indianapolis, Indiana: Alpha Books, 2002.

Magazines and Newspapers

"An air space scare in D.C.," *Daily News*, December 30, 2002, p. 8.

"Baghdad bans U-2 'tour,'" *New York Post*, January 21, 2003, p. 4.

Bazinet, Kenneth R., and Bill Hutchinson, "5 in manhunt were invented by informant," *Daily News*, January 7, 2003, p. 6.

Benson, Barbara, "Smallpox pill-push: N.Y. firm creating trailblazing drug," *New York Post*, December 22, 2002, p. 6.

Blomquist, Brian, "Feds Tracking U.S. Hezbollah," *New York Post*, February 28, 2003, p. 9.

———, "Secret Service on Alien Hot Seat," *New York Post*, January 4, 2003, p. 11.

Bode, Nicole, "Curb on flights over city: FAA bars planes from getting too close on New Year's Eve," *Daily News*, December 26, 2002, p.14. (The "city" in the title is New York.)

"Brit big in terror cross hairs," *New York Post*, February 2, 2003, p. 15.

Brugioni, Dino, "Anthrax Island," *The New York Times Magazine*, January 12, 2003, pp. 36-39.

"Buffalo man: I aided Osama," *Daily News*, January 11, 2003, p. 10.

"Bush gives it a shot with vaccine," *New York Post*, December 22, 2002, p. 6. (The vaccine was for smallpox.)

Casimir, Leslie, "Arabs line up to sign up: Deadline to register with feds," *Daily News*, January 11, 2003, p. 10.

Celona, Larry, and Clemente Lisi, "Cops Eye Evil Chem Plot: On guard for deadly gas in common items," *New York Post*, February 11, 2003, p. 5.

Celona, Larry, and John Lehmann, "Oops, wrong 'terrorist': FBI 'border sneak' has never been to U.S.," *New York Post*, January 2, 2003, p. 6.

Celona, Larry, Kate Sheehy, and Kenneth Lovett, "JFK Airport bomb plot: Gas station, Queens office also targets," *New York Post*, January 14, 2003.

"Cheeze whizzes," *New York Post*, December 22, 2002, p. 3.

Chesnoff, Richard, "Beware of unholy terror alliance," *Daily News*, February 11, 2003, p. 33.

Daly, Emma, "Spain Arrests 16 Suspected of Ties to Al Qaeda," *The New York Times*, January 25, 2003, p. A3.

Dan, Uri, "Iraq's thug bares evil poison plot," *New York Post*, February 2, 2003, p. 22.

Donohue, Pete, "Fliers face bag lag: Airport screening may bring delays," *Daily News*, December 31, 2002, p. 25.

Eggen, Dan, and John Mintz, "Homeland Security Won't Have Diet of Raw Intelligence: Rules Being Drafted to Preclude Interagency Conflict," *Washington Post*, December 6, 2002, p. A43.

"FBI alert for terror prisoners," *New York Post*, January 11, 2003, p. 4.

"FBI bioterror bulletin for U.S. cops," *Daily News*, January 11, 2003, p. 9.

"FBI hunts 5 border crossers," *Daily News*, December 30, 2002, p. 8.

"Feds racing to thwart 19-man 'terror team,'" *New York Post*, December 30, 2002, p. 4.

"Feds zap alien-smuggling ring," *New York Post*, January 8, 2003, p. 8

Feiden, Douglas, "U.S. disaster plans include cloned icons: Experts work feverishly to map Liberty, Capitol, Rushmore," *Daily News*, January 5, 2003, pp. 8-9.

"Focus on Indian Point," *Daily News*, January 11, 2003, p. 14.

Frankel, Glenn, "Britain Finds Poison, Holds 6 Suspects: Traces of Highly Toxic Ricin Detected in London Apartment," *Washington Post*, January 8, 2003, p. A13.

Geller, Andy, "Secret Shuttle Hunt: Feds desperate to keep code device out of wrong hands," *New York Post*, February 7, 2003.

Hays, Elizabeth, and Dave Goldiner, "Air safety rules take off: Travelers get with the program," *Daily News*, January 2, 2003, p. 10.

Haberman, Maggie, "Missile shield for jetliners: Project takes off after El Al attack," *Daily News*, December 26, 2002, p. 8.

Hsu, Spencer S., "D.C. Disputes Insurance Study Raising Rates For Terrorism," *Washington Post*, January 7, 2003, p. A1.

"Jets no threat to nuke plants?" *Daily News*, December 23, 2002, p. 5.

Johnston, David, "U.S. to Make Airlines Give Data on Americans Going Overseas," *The New York Times*, January 4, 2003, p. A3.

Kessler, "U.S. Believes N. Korea Rapidly Seeking Stockpile," *Washington Post*, February 1, 2003, p. A1.

Lathem, Niles, "Al Qaeda eyed in new slay," *New York Post*, January 22, 2003, p. 8.

———, "Chilling poison plot suspected," *New York Post*, January 10, 2003, p. 4.

———, "Chilling ricin twist: London poison cell tied to millenium bomb plot," *New York Post*, January 20, 2003, p. 4.

———, "Saddam's Chem Plot Revealed," *New York Post*, February 19, 2003, p. 5.

Lee, Christopher, "Dirty bombs, anthrax and smallpox: An informative guide for to understanding the threat and protecting you and your family." *Washington Post*, December 9, 2002, p. A21.

Lewis, Neil A., "F.B.I. Issues Alert for 5 Illegal Immigrants Uncovered in Terror Investigation," *The New York Times*, December 30, 2002, p. A1.

Lichtblau, Eric, "Computer Security: Warning on Iraqi Hackers and U.S. Safety," *The New York Times*, January 17, 2003, p. A5.

Lisi, Clemente, and Kati Cornell Smith, "Terror hoaxer charged as forger," *New York Post*, January 10, 2003, p. 25.

McQuillan, Alice, and Dave Goldiner, "Orange crush in city: Terror alert expected to clog streets, subways," *Daily News*, February 10, 2003, p. 3.

"Mad hacker: I'll wreck U.S. with 'war' virus," *New York Post*, December 29, 2002, p. 6.

Mahoney, Joe, and Corky Siemaszko, "Mohawk path for FBI 5," *Daily News*, January 2, 2003, p. 7.

Mahoney, Joe, "Indian Point slammed for no terror planning," *Daily News*, January 11, 2003, p. 16.

Malkin, Michelle, "'Religious' Visas: Scam For Terror," *New York Post*, February 12, 2003, p. 25.

Meek, James Gordon, "A daily dose of terrors: Bush gets a flood of chilling reports—most unconfirmed," *Daily News*, February 23, 2003, p. 9.

———, "Colin: Al Qaeda will fight dirty," *Daily News*, February 10, 2003, p. 3.

Mintz, John, "Homeland Agency Launched: Bush Signs Bill to Combine Federal Security Functions," *Washington Post*, November 26, 2002, p. A1.

National Research Council, "Computers at Risk" *National Academy Press*, 1991.

"9/11 heroes faced toxic danger: EPA," *New York Post*, December 28, 2002, p. 6.

O'Brien, Timothy L., With Stream of Intelligence, Powell Makes Case to U.N., *The New York Times*, February 6, 2003, p. A1.

"Osama's nuke bid revealed," *New York Post*, December 30, 2002, p. 4.

"Phony I.D.'s got 'em into U.S.," *Daily News*, January 31, 2003, p. 15.

Pienciak, Richard T., "Mystery Man in 9/11 Terror Case," *Daily News*, January 12, 2003, pp. 8-9.

Pipes, Daniel, "What is Jihad?" *New York Post*, December 31, 2002, p. 21.

Powell, Michael, "Domestic Spying Pressed: Big-City Police Seek to Ease Limits Imposed After Abuses Decades Ago," *Washington Post*, November 29, 2002, p. A1.

Power, Richard, "Current and Future Danger," *Computer Security Institute*, San Francisco, 1995.

"Probe link of vet ills, nerve gas," *Daily News*, December 23, 2002, p. 9.

Recchia, Philip, "The toxic 'terror' in your back yard," *New York Post*, January 12, 2003, p. 12. (Story about how easy it is to make the poison ricin.)

"Ricin-bust cops storm mosque in London sweep," *New York Post*, January 21, 2003, p. 4.

Risen, James, "U.S. Increased Alert on Evidence Qaeda Was Planning 2 Attacks," *The New York Times*, February 14, 2003, p. A1.

Rose, Derek, "Robot eyes in our sky: Unmanned drones will guard U.S. coastlines," *Daily News*, December 26, 2002, p. 33.

Sanger, David E., and Eric Schmitt, "Satellites Said to See Activity at North Korean Nuclear Site," *The New York Times*, January 31, 2003, p. A1.

Schmidt, Susan, and Allan Lengel, "Help Still Wanted: Arabic Linguists: Agencies Rushed to Fill Void, but Found Screening New Hires Takes Time," *Washington Post*, December 27, 2002, p. A23.

Seifman, David, "Times Sq. will have 'war zone' security," December 31, 2002, p. 14.

Shanker, Thom, "Officials Reveal Threat to Troops Deploying to Gulf," *The New York Times*, January 13, 2003, p. A5.

Slevin, Peter, "U.S. Aims to Prove Iraq Has Secret Cache," *Washington Post*, February 1, 2003, p. A16.

Smith, Sam, "Open Door to Drugs and Terror: Border reservation's tangled-up turf lines," *New York Post*, January 12, 2003, pp. 20-21.

Soltis, Andy, "Spy Hunt: Feds quiz 50,000 Iraqis living in U.S.," *New York Post*, January 25, 2003.

"Terror bust at Paris Airport," *Daily News*, December 30, 2002, p. 20.

"Terror-cell link probed in shootings," *Daily News*, January 2, 2003, p. 6.

United States Dept. of State, "Patterns of Global Terrorism," Washington, D.C., 1996.

"U.S. 'ally' Khadafy: We'll help nail al Qaeda," *New York Post*, January 12, 2003, p. 3.

"U.S., Canada terror cells are in touch," *Daily News*, December 26, 2002, p. 10.

Wald, Matthew L., "Demands Grow for Improving Indian Point Emergency Plan," *The New York Times*, January 14, 2003, p. A3.

Weiser, Benjamin, "U.S. Asks Judge to Deny Terror Suspect Access to Lawyer, Saying It Could Harm Interrogation," *The New York Times*, January 10, 2003, p. A9.

Weisman, Jonathan, "A Homeland Security Whodunit: In Massive Bill, Someone Buried a Clause to Benefit Drug Maker Eli Lilly," *Washington Post*, November 28, 2002, p. A45.

Websites

Central Intelligence Agency—Factbook
www.odci.gov/cia/publications/factbook/index.html

Collin, Barry C., "The Future of CyberTerrorism," Proceedings of 11th Annual International Symposium on Criminal Justice Issues, The University of Illinois at Chicago, 1996 www.acsp.uic.edu/OICJ/CONFS/terror02.htm

Federal Bureau of Investigation official website
www.fbi.gov

Intelligence Carreers
www.IntelligenceCareers.com

Jane's Sentinel Global Risk Center
www.janes.com

Jonkers, Roy, ed., *Weekly Intelligence News*. Weekly newsletter of the Association of Former Intelligence Officers
www.afio.com

Journal of Military and Strategic Studies, Centre for Military and Strategic Studies, University of Calgary
www.stratnet.ucalgary.ca/journal

Maritime Security Council
www.maritimesecurity.org

"U.S. authorities capture 'dirty bomb' suspect: His associate captured in Pakistan, U.S. officials say." Posted: June 10, 2002; 11:47 PM EDT
www.CNN.com

U.S. State Department. Travel Warnings and Consular Information
http://travel.state.gov/travel_warnings.html

Appendix C

Abbreviations and Acronyms

A-2   Air Force Intelligence

AEC   Atomic Energy Commission

AFIO   Association of Former Intelligence Officers

AFMIC   Armed Forces Medical Intelligence Center

AFSA   Armed Forces Security Agency

AFTAC   Air Force Technical Applications Center

AIA   Air Intelligence Agency

ASA   Army Security Agency

ASSA   Armed Services Security Services

BI   Background Investigation

CARG   Covert Action Review Group

CEA   Council of Economic Advisers (to the president)

CEP   Circular error probability (when judging probable accuracy of a warhead strike.

CERT   Computer Emergency Response Team

CIA   Central Intelligence Agency, often called internally, "The Company"

CIC   The U.S. Army's Counterintelligence Corps

CIO   Central Imagery Office

COCOM   Coordinating Committee on Multilateral Export Controls

COMINT   Communications Intelligence

Commo   CIA communications apparatus

COMSEC   Communications Security

COS   Chief of Station, CIA

CS   Clandestine Services

DA   Directorate of Administration

D-Branch   Counterespionage Branch of MI 5, Great Britain, U.K.

DCI   Director of Central Intelligence

DCID   Director of Central Intelligence Directive

DDA   Deputy Director of Administration

DDI   Deputy Director of Intelligence

DDO   Deputy Director for Operations

DDPO   Defense Dissemination Program Office

DDS&T   Deputy Director for Science and Technology

DI   Directorate of Intelligence

DIA   Defense Intelligence Agency

DIAC   Defense Intelligence Analysis Center

DIS   Defense Investigative Service

DMA   Defense Mapping Agency

DS&T   Directorate of Science and Technology

DST   French Counterespionage Service, similar to MI 5 of the United Kingdom

ELINT   Electronic Intelligence

EPQ   Embarrassing Personal Question

ERIR   Economic Research Intelligence Report

FBI   Federal Bureau of Investigation, also called "the bureau"

FBIS Foreign Broadcast Information Service

FCC Federal Communications Commission

FSO Foreign Service Officer

G-2 Army Intelligence

GAO General Accounting Office

GPS Global Positioning System

GPU See OGPU, Forerunner of KGB

GRU Soviet Military Intelligence

HUMINT Human Intelligence

IAM Intelligence Analytical Memorandum

IC Intelligence Community

ICBM Intercontinental ballistic missile

INR Bureau of Intelligence and Research (the State Department intelligence agency)

INS Immigration and Naturalization Service

JCS Joint Chiefs of Staff

JJ James Jesus Angleton, the legendary CIA searcher for "moles" and penetration of the CIA by foreign intelligence operatives.

KGB Komitet Gosunderstvennoy Bezopasnosti, the Committee of State Security Of USSR (Russia)

LASP Low Altitude Surveillance Platform

LDC Less developed country

MBO Management by objective

MCIA Marine Corps Intelligence Activity

MI 5 British Security service, formerly Section 5 of Military Intelligence, which gave the service its name. It is still used today.

MI 6 British Secret Intelligence Service, formerly Section 6 of Military Intelligence, which today is a civilian organization with functions similar to the CIA.

MSIC Missile and Space Intelligence Center

NAIC   National Air Intelligence Center

NFAC   National Foreign Assessment Center

NFIB   National Foreign Intelligence Board

NHB   CIA headquarters office building, compared to the OHB, the Old or Original CIA headquarters building.

NIAM   National Intelligence Analytical Memorandum

NIC   National Intelligence Council

NID   *National Intelligence Daily*

NIE   National Intelligence Estimate

NIMA   National Imagery and Mapping Agency

NKVD   Another forerunner name of KGB of USSR

NPIC   National Photographic Interpretation Center

NRO   National Reconnaissance Office

NSA   National Security Agency, primarily a global Hi-Tech Intel Listening organization. Based at Fort Meade, Maryland.

NSC   National Security Council

NSCID   National Security Council Intelligence Directive

OCI   Office of Current Intelligence

OGPU   Another forerunner of the KGB of USSR

OGSR   Office of Geographic and Societal Research

OHB   Old CIA headquarters building

OIS   Office of Intelligence Support (Department of the Treasury)

ONI   Office of Naval Intelligence

ONNI   Office of National Narcotics Intelligence

ONS   Office of National Security (Department of the Treasury)

OPC   Office of Policy Coordination

ORR   Office of Research and Reports

OSI   Office of Scientific Intelligence

OSR   Office of Strategic Research

OSS   Office of Strategic Services, the World War II forerunner of the CIA.

OTR   Office of Training

PDB   President's Daily Brief

PFIAB   President's Foreign Intelligence Advisory Board

PIC   Photographic Interpretation Center, now known as the NPIC

PLO   Palestine Liberation Organization

PSYWAR   Psychological warfare

RADINT   Radar Intelligence

SALT   Strategic Arms Limitation Treaty

SDECE   French secret Intelligence Service, similar to British MI 6.

SDO   Support of Diplomatic Operations

SIGINT   Signals Intelligence

SIOC   Strategic Information Operations Center

SNIE   Special National Intelligence Estimate

TDY   Temporary duty assignment

TELINT   Telemetry Intelligence

TSEC   Telecommunications Security

UNSCOM   United Nations Special Commission

Association of Former Intelligence Officers (AFIO)

Thousands of dedicated Americans served their country in the field of intelligence. They served in the CIA, military services or other government departments, the FBI, or law enforcement. Many now belong to AFIO, a nationwide organization that is dedicated to providing the American public with a better knowledge and understanding of intelligence and the need for it to serve our country and national leaders. For those who didn't serve in the intelligence field but have a strong interest in it, membership is available today with sponsorship by an active member. In addition, serving government professionals may join as Associate Members.

Here are details about AFIO, much directly from their informative website (www.afio.com) for accuracy.

AFIO is a nonprofit, nonpolitical, educational association of former intelligence professionals and supporters, incorporated in Virginia in 1975. AFIO's mission is to build a public constituency for a sound and healthy U.S. intelligence system and capability. The organization's educational focus is on fostering understanding of the vital importance and role of U.S. intelligence for U.S. national security in historic, contemporary and future contexts. This includes the role of intelligence supporting U.S.

policy, diplomacy, strategy, security, and defense. In addition, AFIO focuses on understanding the critical need for effective counterintelligence and security against foreign, political, technological or economic espionage, as well as lawfully authorized covert, clandestine and overt counterterrorist or criminal operations threatening U.S. security, the national infrastructure, or corporate and individual safety. That goal has special significance today.

Since foreign intelligence, counterintelligence and covert activities are necessarily conducted in secrecy, an ever-present "silent war," education on the vital need for effective institutions conducting U.S. intelligence and counterintelligence operations is a challenging, necessary and important mission. As Richard Deacon noted in his *History of British Intelligence*, "A great Power without an efficient intelligence service is doomed; that has been the lesson from the heyday of Troy to the present."

Today, AFIO is an association of people with active intellectual lives, many of whom have participated, or are participating, in events of historic significance and who have played roles of leadership and distinction, dedicated to worthy principles and objectives. AFIO members include primarily individuals from U.S. government departments, but also state and local government, corporate or private professionals and supporters. Aside from a small professional staff and central office, the AFIO organization, and its chapters throughout the country, is run by volunteers who donate their time and talents to the cause of furthering AFIO's objectives and enjoy the fellowship of professional colleagues and supporters.

Honorary Board Of Directors:

Co-Chairmen: The Honorable George H. W. Bush and The Honorable Gerald R. Ford.

Honorary Board members include: Mr. John Barron, The Hon. Shirley Temple Black, The Hon. Frank C. Carlucci, Dr. Ruth M. Davis, Adm. Bobby R. Inman, USN (Ret), Professor Ernest R. May, Mr. John Anson Smith, The Hon. William H. Webster, and The Hon. R. James Woolsey,

The chairman of the AFIO Board of Directors is Lt. Gen. (ret) Lincoln D. Faurer;

The vice chairman is E. Peter Earnest, CIA/SIS (ret).

The AFIO president is S. Eugene Poteat (CIA/SIS ret).

The sr. vice president is Lt. Gen. (ret) Edward J. Heinz.

The AFIO executive director is Col. (ret) Roy K. Jonkers.

The Asst. exec. director is Elizabeth Bancroft.

AFIO's Principles and Objectives

It is helpful to understand AFIO's principles and objectives. AFIO members subscribe to the values of patriotism, excellence, integrity, dedication, and loyalty represented by the active intelligence establishment of the United States engaged in the execution of national policies and the advancement and defense of the vital interests and security of the country, its citizens, and its allies.

In their mission statement, AFIO's principal objective is to foster understanding, by intellectual, political and business community leaders and the general public, of the continuing need for a strong and responsible national intelligence/counterintelligence establishment to deal with a variety of short and long-term threats and issues in the current world environment and the new Information Age. Within this context AFIO stresses education on the need for effective long-term intelligence strategies and capabilities to support national decision makers and to guard against surprise.

To achieve its goals, AFIO seeks to implement its objectives by conducting programs to:

- Contribute balance and expert insight into the public and media discourses on intelligence-related issues.

- Support educational courses, seminars, symposia and research on intelligence and counterintelligence topics.

- Promote public understanding of intelligence and counterintelligence roles, needs and functions.

- Encourage the exchange of information among intelligence professionals.

- Promote the study of the history and current and future role of U.S. intelligence.

There are some very informative publications that support the organizations goals:

- The AFIO Weekly Intelligence Notes (WINs), a weekly email that has commentaries on intelligence issues.

- The monthly electronic Bulletin Board Notes (eBBN), with announcements of member interest.

- The periodic AFIO Periscope newsletter that includes articles on intelligence, the membership and the organization.

- The AFIO "Intelligencer," a major journal of intelligence studies.

♦ The AFIO Homepage—including organizational material and updates, references to AFIO publications, and a data base resource.

Here are some other things the AFIO provides:

♦ A national convention, symposia and seminars plus mini-symposia and chapter meetings provide members with ongoing updates in the field of intelligence and geopolitical impact.

♦ Scholarships are awarded to students interested in studying intelligence and other awards of recognition are made every year for students and instructors.

♦ The academic exchange program supports some 180 professors in their teaching of intelligence or related courses at universities throughout the nation.

♦ A speakers bureau is available where local organizations can obtain qualified speakers for their meetings.

AFIO Chapters

AFIO chapters are semi-autonomous extensions of AFIO, consisting of members who have banded together to form a chapter chartered by AFIO National to conduct activities as authorized by, and in consonance with, its bylaws, principles and educational objectives. These chapters are located throughout the United States. AFIO membership or associate membership at the national level is a prerequisite for chapter membership but may be done at the time one joins a local chapter.

Local chapter programs are both collegial and promote the AFIO mission. Chapters generally conduct two kinds of activity:

♦ Chapters conduct informative educational programs such as meetings, newsletters, etc. for their members. This helps to enable members to be effective "ambassadors of intelligence," promoting public understanding of the role and importance of U.S. intelligence to the security and well-being of the nation. These meetings and publications also serve to maintain and strengthen professional and collegial bonds among those chapter members who are former members of the Intelligence community and other members who support the AFIO mission as associate members.

According to Executive Director Roy Jonkers, "Currently-serving intelligence personnel and U.S. citizens who support AFIO principles and objectives may become Associate Members. Both of these categories of individuals are eligible for AFIO membership, and consequently, for AFIO chapter membership."

◆ Chapters conduct civic outreach programs to support AFIO educational objectives, to accomplish the AFIO mission of building a public constituency for a sound and healthy U.S. intelligence system and capability. This is done by such means as speaking to regional civic associations, guest lectures at local colleges, scholarship awards to high school or college students, or a variety of similar endeavors. Chapter members also serve as mentors for young people interested in an intelligence career.

AFIO is a nonprofit professional educational association recognized as tax-exempt under IRS Code section 501 (c)(3). AFIO also invites corporations or professional and entrepreneurial offices and organizations to partner with AFIO in support of the educational programs and outreach publications the association issues.

For more details about AFIO you can contact the AFIO National Office by sending e-mail to afio@afio.com, or check out their website: www.afio.com.

Index